D0871119

# Northeastern Trees in Winter

ALBERT FRANCIS BLAKESLEE
CHESTER DEACON JARVIS

With a new Table of Changes in Nomenclature by
E. S. HARRAR
*James B. Duke Professor of Wood Science*
*Duke University*

DOVER PUBLICATIONS, INC.
NEW YORK

Published in Canada by General Publishing Company, Ltd., 30 Lesmill Road, Don Mills, Toronto, Ontario.
Published in the United Kingdom by Constable and Company, Ltd., 10 Orange Street, London WC 2.

This Dover edition, first published in 1972, is an unabridged republication of the work originally published in Bulletin No. 69 of the Storrs (Connecticut) Agricultural Experiment Station in June, 1911, under the title *New England Trees in Winter*.
This edition also contains a new Table of Changes in Nomenclature prepared by Dr. E. S. Harrar.

*International Standard Book Number: 0-486-22693-X*
*Library of Congress Catalog Card Number: 77-142875*

Manufactured in the United States of America
Dover Publications, Inc.
180 Varick Street
New York, N.Y. 10014

# TABLE OF CONTENTS

                                                             PAGE

PREFACE .......................................  V
    LITERATURE, ACKNOWLEDGEMENTS

INTRODUCTION ................................  1
    NAMES, HABIT, BARK, TWIGS, LEAF-SCARS, BUDS,
    FRUIT, COMPARISONS, DISTRIBUTION, WOOD.

ANALYTICAL KEY ..............................  25
    METHOD OF USE, KEY TO GENERA AND SPECIES.

DESCRIPTION OF SPECIES ......................  32

    The Pines (p. 344-355); the Larch (p. 356); the
    Spruces (p. 358-367); the Douglas Fir (p. 368);
    the Balsam Fir (p. 370); the Hemlock (p. 372);
    the Coast White Cedar (p. 374); the Arbor
    Vitae (p. 376); the Junipers and Red Cedar
    (p. 378-381); the Ginkgo (p. 382); the Willows
    (p. 384); the Poplars (p. 386-397); the Walnuts
    and Hickories (p. 398-409); the Hornbeams
    (p. 410-413); the Birches (p. 414-425); the
    Alders (p. 426); the Beech (p. 428); the Chest-
    nut (p. 430); the Oaks (p. 432-455); the Elms
    (p. 456-463); the Hackberry (p. 464); the Mul-
    berries (p. 466-469); the Magnolias (p. 470-
    473); the Tulip Tree (p. 474); the Sassafras
    (p. 476); the Witch Hazel (p. 478); the Sweet
    Gum (p. 480); the Sycamore (p. 482); the Pear
    p. 484); the Apple (p. 486); the Mountain Ash
    (p. 488); the Quince (p. 490); the Shadbush
    (p. 492); the Hawthorns (p. 494); the Cherries
    (p. 496-505); the Plums (p. 506-511); the
    Peach (p. 512); the Kentucky Coffee Tree
    (p. 514); the Honey Locust (p. 516); the Red-
    bud (p. 518); the Yellow Wood (p. 520); the
    Locusts (p. 522); the Ailanthus (p. 524); the
    Sumachs (p. 526-529); the Holly (p. 530); the
    Maples (p. 532-547); the Horse-chestnut (p.
    548); the Linden (p. 550); the Dogwoods
    (p. 552); the Tupelo (p. 554); the Ashes
    (p. 556-561); the Catalpas (p. 562).

GLOSSARY .......................................  252

INDEX ..........................................  257

# PREFACE

So much has been written popularly and in a scientific way on trees that no book on the subject would be warranted unless it was designed to meet a decided need. At present there is no general work upon American trees which combines illustrations of the individual forms with keys for their identification based upon winter characters. The forester and lumberman, however, are more called upon to distinguish trees in winter when leaves and flowers are fallen than in summer. Trees, as the most conspicuous elements in the winter landscape, must also appeal to the student of out door life. The interest shown by classes of school teachers in the Summer School in identifying specimens of twigs collected the previous winter indicated that the winter study of trees can be taken up with enthusiasm by teachers in their schools. In our experience, the winter identification of trees has proven to students one of the most interesting subjects of their course. It is of decided value for its training in the power of accurate observation. The work comes at a time when material for natural history study seems scanty and might therefore be used to bridge over the period between fall and spring which are unfortunately considered by many the only seasons when study of out door life is possible in the schools. A tree in winter is far from being the characterless object many believe. Freed from its covering of leaves, the skeleton of the tree is revealed and with the method of branching thus clearly discernible, the species may generally be more readily identified at a distance than in its summer garb. There are many forms, moreover, that are difficult to distinguish from summer features alone but which in winter have twig, bud or other characters which make their separation comparatively easy. It is believed that the combination of keys, text, and illustrations from photographs will furnish the assistance which the current texts fail to supply and render the identification of our common trees in winter a relatively simple task.

The text with keys is an outgrowth of outlines that one of the authors has developed and used with various modifications for the last four years in his college classes in Botany and Forestry.

The photographic illustrations are all originals, most of them by the other author. Although one of us is responsible for the text and for the selection of the material photographed and the other for the photographs, we have freely consulted and the bulletin is therefore to be considered a joint publication.

The order of arrangement of the species in the text and the scientific names follow the usage of the seventh edition of Gray's Manual and the latter are in accord with the rules laid down in the Vienna Congress. The figures and descriptions given are of trees for the most part growing wild in New England. A few rarer species which occur in New England only very locally or in isolated instances have been omitted from illustration. In their places, however, some of the more frequently cultivated trees, have been included because of their value for forestry planting in New England or because of their familiarity in city ornamental plantings. The varieties of cultivated forms are so numerous that it is obviously possible to take account of only the most common types. Their inclusion, it is believed, will add to the value of the publication especially for its use in cities. The keys can be absolutely relied upon only for the species just mentioned from New England. New England, including as it does the meeting ground between the northern and southern floras, is extremely rich in the species of trees represented. The bulletin, therefore, especially in its descriptive text and illustrations should prove of service outside of the geographically restricted region described.

The final keys to the genera and to the species as well as the descriptive text in galley were placed in the hands of the present year's classes in Botany and Forestry. A student after finding the species by the keys, read the twig characters in the galley and signed his name opposite the species if the description corresponded with the twigs supplied. All of the trees described and illustrated have thus been checked up by students and some of them by as many as seventy different persons. In this way limitations to the use of certain of the characters employed as means of separating allied species have been discovered and the constancy of other characters has been confirmed in so far as the material available could allow. The greatest assistance rendered by the students, however, has been in disclosing difficulties in the use of the keys, due to unfortunate choice of contrasted characters or of terms used in their description. The keys in consequence have been considerably modified before final paging. Many of the explanatory phrases which may appear to be unnecessary have been inserted at the demand of the students. Where possible the most obvious characters have been employed and though the keys in consequence have become somewhat more cumbersome it is hoped they will prove more usable. Errors and omissions have no doubt crept in despite the efforts to avoid them. We would be grateful for any additions or corrections that may be suggested in the descriptions or keys in view of a possible revision of the text.

The photographs of the twigs and of the fruit of the deciduous trees are very nearly natural size. They have been slightly reduced in production but all of them to the same scale, except the fruits of the Catalpa, the Chestnut, and the Honey Locust as indicated under these species. Line drawings or touched-up photographs would no doubt show important details more clearly by emphasizing certain of the minute markings. Since, however, these details are often obscure, and moreover receive full recognition in the accompanying text, it has been thought that a truer idea of the twigs would be gained if they were left as they appeared in the photographs. Accordingly, they have not been "doctored" in preparation or reproduction. The leafy twigs of the cone-bearing evergreens have been more or less reduced as indicated under the descriptions of the genera in the key. All the twigs of a single genus, however, are on the same scale.

## LITERATURE

The following is a list of books which will be found useful to the student of New England trees. They have been freely consulted, as well as others not listed, and have been of value in determining the ranges and wood characteristics of the individual species, in confirmation of bark and habit characters, and to a less degree of the other winter features. The dimensions of the trees in the heading "Habit" and the information under the heading "Distribution" have been taken with little change from Dame & Brooks' Handbook, except what is given in the subheading "In Connecticut" which was obtained from the catalog of the flowering plants and ferns of Connecticut; Bulletin No. 14,

Conn. Geol. and Nat. Hist. Survey, 1910. The characters under the heading "Wood" were taken chiefly from Sargent's Manual. To obtain information in regard to the dimensions, the distribution and the wood characters of cultivated species, Bailey's Cyclopædia of Horticulture and various European works have been freely consulted.

## GENERAL WORKS ON TREES.

Sargent, C. S.—Manual of the trees of North America, 826 pp. Houghton Mifflin Co., Boston, 1905. The best general book on the subject. The text and illustrative drawings are taken chiefly from summer characters, but winter characters receive some attention. (Dover reprint).

Sargent, C. S.—Silva of North America in 14 quarto volumes. Houghton Mifflin Co., Boston, 1902. The most extensive work of its kind. Except for the more elaborate drawings, of less general value than the Manual, the text of which is practically the same but more conveniently arranged.

Britton, N. L.—North American Trees, 894 pp. Henry Holt & Co., New York, 1908. Of the same general scope as Sargent's Manual. Contains occasional habit photographs.

Hough, R. B.—Handbook of the trees of the northern states and Canada, 470 pp. Lowville, N. Y., 1907. A most valuable publication, without habit illustrations, but with excellent photographs of leaves, fruit and bark and less successful photographs of winter twigs. The keys and the text are based upon summer characters. This is our only book giving bark photographs for each species treated.

Dame, L.L. & Brooks, H.—Handbook of the Trees of New England, 196 pp. Ginn & Co., Boston, 1901. The best manual for the region covered. (Dover reprint).

Emerson, G. B.—Report on the trees and shrubs of Massachusetts, 624 pp. in two volumes. Little, Brown & Co., Boston, 1875. Especially valuable for its habit descriptions.

Collins, J. F. and Preston, H. W.—Key to New England Trees, 42 pp. Preston & Rounds Co., Providence, 1909. A useful little book. Contains keys only, based on summer characters. Includes cultivated forms.

Rogers, Julia E.—The Tree Book, 589 pp. Doubleday, Page & Co., New York, 1908. The best of the popular books on trees.

Contains habit and twig photographs of some of the species treated and occasional photographs of the bark taken chiefly from museum specimens.

### WORKS DEALING WITH THE WINTER CONDITION OF TREES.

Schneider, C. K.—Dendrologische Winterstudien. 290 pp.; 224 fig. Gustav Fischer, Jena 1903. A very extensive work giving descriptions and drawings of twigs of 434 individual species cultivated and native in Europe, together with keys and an introductory text.

Huntington, Miss A. L.—Studies of Trees in Winter, 198 pp. Knight & Millet, Boston, 1902. A popular book excellent as far as it goes. Figures at least the winter twig, the habit, or the bark of 65 species. Has descriptive text with habit notes and poetical quotations.

Wiegand, K. M., and Foxworthy, F. W.—A key to the genera of woody plants in winter, 33 pp. Ithaca, N. Y. 1904. Treats of wild and cultivated plants of New York state, including shrubs as well as trees, contains keys only. Scientific names alone used, a valuable key to genera, has passed through several editions.

Trelease, Wm.—Winter synopsis of North American Maples, Rep't Mo. Bot. Gard., vol. 5, pp. 88-106, 1894. A critical treatment of the Maples based upon winter characters with keys and twig figures.

Trelease, Wm.—Juglandaceae of the United States. Rep't Mo. Bot. Gard., vol. 7, pp. 25-46. A critical treatment of the genera Carya & Juglans with keys, twig figures and bark photographs.

Schaffner, J. H.—Key to the Ohio woody plants in the winter condition. The Ohio Naturalist vol. 5, no. 4, pp. 277-286, 1905. Keys only, limited to genera, shrubs as well as trees treated.

Hitchcock, A. S.—Keys to Kansas Trees in their winter condition, 6 pp. Keys only, leading to species.

## ACKNOWLEDGMENTS

Acknowledgments are due to Prof. C. S. Sargent, Prof. J. G. Jack, Mr. Jackson Dawson, and Mr. R. W. Curtis for courtesies in the museum and grounds of the Arnold Arboretum where many of the photographs were taken; to Prof. B. L. Robinson for assistance in checking up the scientific names; to the Connecticut State Forester S. M. Spring, for suggestions as to what cultivated trees are of sufficient value in New England forestry to be included in this publication; to Mr. T. F. Rady, for supplying the additional galley sheets used by the students; to Mr. Robert Weller for his painstaking care in the reproduction of the photographs; to Mr. A. F. Schulze for compiling the index; to Miss E. M. Whitney for reading the proof; to the Station Director, L. A. Clinton, for the generous way in which the undertaking has been supported; and especially to the students whose interest in trees in winter first suggested this publication and whose co-operation in its production has given it its finished form.

ALBERT FRANCIS BLAKESLEE.
CHESTER DEACON JARVIS.

Storrs, Conn., June, 1911.

## NOTE ON NOMENCLATURE (1972)

The validity of current scientific names is governed by the International Code of Botanical Nomenclature. One of the principal features of this code is the Law of Priority. Simply stated, it declares that all species may have only one valid scientific name, and that the oldest published name of a species shall take precedence. In consequence some of the scientific names used in this book are now obsolete and a few others, which appear in headings as synonyms, are now recognized as valid names (see red spruce and American mountain-ash).

There are no universal rules governing the selection and application of common names. Some species are known by several common names, and to add to the confusion the same name is sometimes applied to two or more different species.

The U.S. Forest Service, in its Agriculture Handbook No. 41, *Check List of Native and Naturalized Trees of the United States,* lists the valid scientific name and preferred common name for each tree indigenous to or naturalized in continental United States. Using this volume, the accompanying table was prepared to bring the nomenclature in this book up to modern concepts.

It will be of interest to the serious user of this book to know that a few genera have been segregated from older and larger groups, and that in a few instances two or more genera have been united. An example of the former is the genus *Toxicodendron* which embraces poison-sumac and the poison-ivies and which was segregated from *Rhus*. The union of *Padus* and *Amygdalus* with *Prunus* exemplifies the latter.

*March, 1972*                                                      E.S. HARRAR

| BLAKESLEE & JARVIS NOMENCLATURE | CURRENT NOMENCLATURE | PAGE |
|---|---|---|
| WHITE PINE; Soft Pine, Weymouth Pine *Pinus Strobus* L. | EASTERN WHITE PINE *Pinus strobus* L. | 344 |
| PITCH PINE; Hard Pine, Yellow Pine *Pinus rigida* Mill. | PITCH PINE *Pinus rigida* Mill. | 346 |
| JACK PINE; Northern Scrub Pine, Gray Pine, Spruce Pine *Pinus Banksiana* Lamb. *(P. divaricata* auth.) | JACK PINE *Pinus banksiana* Lamb. | 348 |
| RED PINE; Norway Pine *Pinus resinosa* Ait. | RED PINE *Pinus resinosa* Ait. | 350 |
| AUSTRIAN PINE; Black Pine *Pinus Laricio,* var. *austriaca* Endl. | AUSTRIAN PINE *Pinus nigra* Arn. | 352 |
| SCOTCH PINE; Scotch "Fir" *Pinus sylvestris* L. | SCOTCH PINE *Pinus sylvestris* L. | 354 |
| AMERICAN LARCH; Tamarack, Hackmatack, Black Larch, "Juniper" *Larix laricina* (Du Roi) Koch *(L. americana* Michx.) | TAMARACK *Larix laricina* (Du Roi) K. Koch | 356 |
| WHITE SPRUCE; Cat, Skunk or Labrador Spruce *Picea canadensis* (Mill.) BSP. *(P. alba* Link) | WHITE SPRUCE *Picea glauca* (Moench) Voss | 358 |
| RED SPRUCE *Picea rubra* (Du Roi) Dietr. *(P. nigra,* var. *rubra* Engelm.; *P. rubens* Sarg.) | RED SPRUCE *Picea rubens* Sarg. | 360 |
| BLACK SPRUCE; Swamp, Bog, Water or Double Spruce *Picea mariana* (Mill.) BSP. *(P. nigra* Link; *P. brevifolia* Peck) | BLACK SPRUCE *Picea mariana* (Mill.) B.S.P. | 362 |

| BLAKESLEE & JARVIS NOMENCLATURE | CURRENT NOMENCLATURE | PAGE |
|---|---|---|
| BLUE SPRUCE; Colorado Blue Spruce, Silver Spruce<br>*Picea Menziesii* Engelm.<br>*(P. Parryana* (Andre) Sarg.;<br>P. pungens Engelm.) | BLUE SPRUCE<br>*Picea pungens* Engelm. | 364 |
| NORWAY SPRUCE<br>*Picea Abies* (L.) Karst.<br>*(P. excelsa* Link) | NORWAY SPRUCE<br>*Picea abies* (L.) Karst. | 366 |
| DOUGLAS FIR; Red Fir, Douglas Spruce<br>Pseudotsuga taxifolia (Lam.) Britton *(P. mucronata* (Raf.) Sudw.; *P. Douglasii* (Lindl.) Carr.) | DOUGLAS-FIR<br>*Pseudotsuga menziesii* (Mirb.) Franco | 368 |
| BALSAM FIR; Balsam, Fir, Balm of Gilead Fir.<br>*Abies balsamea* (L.) Mill. | BALSAM FIR<br>*Abies balsamea* (L.) Mill. | 370 |
| HEMLOCK; Hemlock Spruce<br>*Tsuga canadensis* (L.) Carr. | EASTERN HEMLOCK<br>*Tsuga canadensis* (L.) Carr. | 372 |
| COAST WHITE CEDAR; White Cedar, Cedar<br>*Chamaecyparis thyoides* (L.) BSP. *(C. sphaeroidea* Spach; *Cupressus thyoides* L.) | ATLANTIC WHITE-CEDAR<br>*Chamaecyparis thyoides* (L.) B.S.P. | 374 |
| ARBOR VITAE; White Cedar, Cedar<br>*Thuja occidentalis* L. | NORTHERN WHITE-CEDAR<br>*Thuja occidentalis* L. | 376 |
| COMMON JUNIPER; Dwarf Juniper<br>*Juniperus communis* L. | COMMON JUNIPER<br>*Juniperus communis* L. | 378 |
| RED CEDAR; Savin, Cedar, Red Juniper<br>*Juniperus virginiana* L. | EASTERN REDCEDAR<br>*Juniperus virginiana* L. | 380 |
| GINKGO; Maidenhair Tree<br>*Ginkgo biloba* L. *(Salisburia adiantifolia* Smith) | GINKGO<br>*Ginkgo biloba* L. | 382 |
| YELLOW WILLOW; Golden Osier<br>*Salix alba,* var. *vitellina* (L.) Koch *(S. vitellina* Koch) | YELLOW WILLOW<br>*Salix alba* var. *vitellina* (L.) Koch | 384 |

| BLAKESLEE & JARVIS NOMENCLATURE | CURRENT NOMENCLATURE | PAGE |
|---|---|---|
| SILVER POPLAR; White Poplar, Silver-leaf Poplar, Abele *Populus alba* L. | WHITE POPLAR *Populus alba* L. | 386 |
| SMALL-TOOTHED ASPEN; American or Quaking Aspen, Popple, Poplar, Aspen *Populus tremuloides* Michx. | QUAKING ASPEN *Populus tremuloides* Michx. | 388 |
| LARGE-TOOTHED ASPEN; Popple, Poplar *Populus grandidentata* Michx. | BIGTOOTH ASPEN *Populus grandidentata* Michx. | 390 |
| BALSAM POPLAR; Balsam, Tacamahac, Balm of Gilead *Populus balsamifera* L. | BALSAM POPLAR *Populus balsamifera* L. | 392 |
| CAROLINA POPLAR; Cotton-wood, Necklace Poplar *Populus deltoides* Marsh. *(P. monilifera* Ait.; *P. canadensis* Moench) | EASTERN COTTONWOOD *Populus deltoides* Bartr. | 394 |
| LOMBARDY POPLAR *Populus nigra,* var. *italica* Du Roi *(P. dilatata* Ait.; *P. pyramidalis* Rozier; *P. fastigiata* Desf.) | LOMBARDY POPLAR *Populus nigra* var. *italica* Muenchh. | 396 |
| BUTTERNUT; Oilnut, White Walnut *Juglans cinerea* L. | BUTTERNUT *Juglans cinerea* L. | 398 |
| BLACK WALNUT *Juglans nigra* L. | BLACK WALNUT *Juglans nigra* L. | 400 |
| SHAG-BARK HICKORY; Shell-bark Hickory, Walnut *Carya ovata* (Mill.) K. Koch *(C. alba* Nutt.; *Hickoria ovata* Britton) | SHAGBARK HICKORY *Carya ovata* (Mill.) K. Koch | 402 |
| MOCKERNUT; Big Bud Hickory, White-heart Hickory *Carya alba* (L.) K. Koch *(C. tomentosa* Nutt.; *Hickoria alba* Britton) | MOCKERNUT HICKORY *Carya tomentosa* Nutt. | 404 |
| PIGNUT; Pignut or Broom Hickory *Carya glabra* (Mill.) Spach *(C. porcina* Nutt.; *Hickoria glabra* Britton) | PIGNUT HICKORY *Carya glabra* (Mill.) Spach | 406 |

| BLAKESLEE & JARVIS NOMENCLATURE | CURRENT NOMENCLATURE | PAGE |
|---|---|---|
| BITTERNUT; Swamp Hickory *Carya cordiformis* (Wang.) K. Koch *(C. amara* Nutt.; *Hickoria minima* (Marsh.) Britton) | BITTERNUT HICKORY *Carya cordiformis* (Wang.) K. Koch | 408 |
| HOP HORNBEAM; Ironwood, Leverwood, Deerwood *Ostrya virginiana* (Mill.) K. Koch | EASTERN HOPHORNBEAM *Ostrya virginiana* (Mill.) K. Koch | 410 |
| AMERICAN HORNBEAM; Hornbeam, Blue Beech, Ironwood, Water Beech *Carpinus caroliniana* Walt. | AMERICAN HORNBEAM *Carpinus caroliniana* Walt. | 412 |
| BLACK BIRCH; Cherry Birch, Sweet Birch *Betula lenta* L. | SWEET BIRCH *Betula lenta* L. | 414 |
| YELLOW BIRCH; Silver or Gray Birch *Betula lutea* Michx. f. | YELLOW BIRCH *Betula alleghaniensis* Britton | 416 |
| RED BIRCH; River Birch *Betula nigra* L. | RIVER BIRCH *Betula nigra* L. | 418 |
| GRAY BIRCH; Old-field, White, Poverty, Small White or Poplar Birch *Betula populifolia* Marsh. | GRAY BIRCH *Betula populifolia* Marsh. | 420 |
| PAPER BIRCH; Canoe or White Birch *Betula alba,* var. *papyrifera* (Marsh.) Spach *(B. papyrifera* Marsh.) | PAPER BIRCH *Betula papyrifera* Marsh. | 422 |
| EUROPEAN WHITE BIRCH; European Paper Birch *Betula alba* L. | EUROPEAN WHITE BIRCH *Betula alba* L. | 424 |
| SPECKLED ALDER; Hoary Alder, Alder *Alnus incana* (L.) Moench | SPECKLED ALDER *Alnus rugosa (Du Roi)* Spreng. | 426 |
| BEECH; American Beech *Fagus grandifolia* Ehrh. *(F. ferruginia* Ait.; *F. americana* Sweet; *F. atropunicea* Sudw.) | AMERICAN BEECH *Fagus grandifolia* Ehrh. | 428 |

| BLAKESLEE & JARVIS NOMENCLATURE | CURRENT NOMENCLATURE | PAGE |
|---|---|---|
| CHESTNUT<br>*Castanea dentata* (Marsh.) Borkh.<br>*(C. sativa,* var. *americana* Sarg.;<br>*C. vesca,* var. *americana* Michx.) | AMERICAN CHESTNUT<br>*Castanea dentata* (Marsh.)<br>Borkh. | 430 |
| WHITE OAK<br>*Quercus alba* L. | WHITE OAK<br>*Quercus alba* L. | 432 |
| POST OAK; Box White Oak,<br>Iron Oak<br>*Quercus stellata* Wang. *(Q. minor*<br>Sarg.; *Q. obtusiloba* Michx.) | POST OAK<br>*Quercus stellata* Wang. | 434 |
| BUR OAK; Mossy-cup or<br>Over-cup Oak<br>*Quercus macrocarpa* Michx. | BUR OAK ·<br>*Quercus macrocarpa* Michx. | 436 |
| SWAMP WHITE OAK<br>*Quercus bicolor* Willd.<br>*(Q. platanoides* Sudw.) | SWAMP WHITE OAK<br>*Quercus bicolor* Willd. | 438 |
| CHINQUAPIN OAK; Chestnut<br>Oak, Yellow Oak<br>*Quercus Muhlenbergii* Engelm.<br>*(Q. acuminata* Houba.) | CHINKAPIN OAK<br>*Quercus mühlenbergii*<br>Engelm. | 440 |
| DWARF CHINQUAPIN OAK;<br>Scrub Chestnut Oak,<br>Chinquapin Oak, Scrub Oak<br>*Quercus prinoides* Willd. | DWARF CHINKAPIN OAK<br>*Quercus prinoides* Willd. | 442 |
| CHESTNUT OAK; Rock Chest-<br>nut Oak, Rock Oak<br>*Quercus Prinus* L. | CHESTNUT OAK<br>*Quercus prinus* L. | 444 |
| RED OAK<br>*Quercus rubra* L. | NORTHERN RED OAK<br>*Quercus rubra* L. | 446 |
| PIN OAK; Swamp Oak, Water Oak<br>*Quercus palustris* Muench. | PIN OAK<br>*Quercus palustris*<br>Muenchh. | 448 |
| SCARLET OAK<br>*Quercus coccinea* Muench. | SCARLET OAK<br>*Quercus coccinea* Muenchh. | 450 |
| BLACK OAK; Yellow-barked Oak<br>Quercitron, Yellow Oak<br>*Quercus velutina* Lam.<br>*(Q. coccinea,* var. *tinctoria* A.DC;<br>*Q. tinctoria* Bartr.) | BLACK OAK<br>*Quercus velutina* Lam. | 452 |

| BLAKESLEE & JARVIS NOMENCLATURE | CURRENT NOMENCLATURE | PAGE |
|---|---|---|
| BEAR OAK; Black Scrub Oak<br>*Quercus ilicifolia* Wang.<br>*(Q. nana* Sarg.; *Q. pumila*<br>Sudw.) | BEAR OAK<br>*Quercus ilicifolia*<br>Wangenh. | 454 |
| SLIPPERY ELM; Red Elm,<br>Moose Elm<br>*Ulmus fulva* Michx.<br>*(U. pubescens* Walt.) | *SLIPPERY ELM*<br>*Ulmus rubra* Mühl. | 456 |
| ENGLISH ELM<br>*Ulmus campestris* L.<br>*(U. glabra* Mill.) | ENGLISH ELM<br>*Ulmus campestris* L. | 458 |
| WHITE ELM; American or<br>Water Elm<br>*Ulmus americana* L. | AMERICAN ELM<br>*Ulmus americana* L. | 460 |
| CORK ELM; Rock Elm, Hickory<br>Elm, Northern Cork Elm<br>*Ulmus racemosa* Thomas<br>*(U. Thomasi* Sarg.) | ROCK ELM<br>*Ulmus thomasii* Sarg. | 462 |
| HACKBERRY; Sugar Berry,<br>Nettle Tree, False Elm,<br>Hoop Ash<br>*Celtis occidentalis* L. | HACKBERRY<br>*Celtis occidentalis* L. | 464 |
| RED MULBERRY<br>*Morus rubra* L. | RED MULBERRY<br>*Morus rubra* L. | 466 |
| WHITE MULBERRY; Silkworm<br>Mulberry<br>*Morus alba* L. | WHITE MULBERRY<br>*Morus alba* L. | 468 |
| CUCUMBER TREE; Mountain<br>Magnolia<br>*Magnolia acuminata* L. | CUCUMBERTREE<br>*Magnolia acuminata* L. | 470 |
| UMBRELLA TREE; Elkwood<br>*Magnolia tripetala* L.<br>*(M. umbrella* Lam.) | UMBRELLA MAGNOLIA<br>*Magnolia tripetala* L. | 472 |
| TULIP TREE; Whitewood,<br>Yellow Poplar<br>*Liriodendron Tulipifera* L. | YELLOW-POPLAR<br>*Liriodendron tulipifera* L. | 474 |
| SASSAFRAS<br>*Sassafras variifolium* (Salisb.)<br>Kuntze *(S. officinale* Nees &<br>Eberm.; *S. Sassafras* Karst.) | SASSAFRAS<br>*Sassafras albidum* (Nutt.) Nees | 476 |

| BLAKESLEE & JARVIS NOMENCLATURE | CURRENT NOMENCLATURE | PAGE |
|---|---|---|
| WITCH HAZEL<br>*Hamamelis virginiana* L. | WITCH-HAZEL<br>*Hamamelis virginiana* L. | 478 |
| SWEET GUM; Bilsted, Red Gum, Alligator-wood, Liquidambar<br>*Liquidambar Styraciflua* L. | SWEETGUM<br>*Liquidambar styraciflua* L. | 480 |
| SYCAMORE; Buttonwood, Buttonball, Plane Tree<br>*Platanus occidentalis* L. | AMERICAN SYCAMORE<br>*Platanus occidentalis* L. | 482 |
| PEAR<br>*Pyrus communis* L. | PEAR<br>*Pyrus communis* L. | 484 |
| APPLE<br>*Pyrus Malus* L.<br>*(Malus Malus* (L.) Britton) | APPLE<br>*Malus pumila* Mill. | 486 |
| AMERICAN MOUNTAIN ASH; Rowan or Service Tree<br>*Pyrus americana* (Marsh.) DC.<br>*(Sorbus americana* Marsh.) | AMERICAN MOUNTAIN-ASH<br>*Sorbus americana* Marsh. | 488 |
| QUINCE<br>*Cydonia vulgaris* Pers.<br>*(Pyrus Cydonia* L.) | QUINCE<br>*Cydonia oblonga* Mill. | 490 |
| SHAD BUSH; Service Berry, Shadblow, Juneberry<br>*Amelanchier canadensis* (L.) Medic. | DOWNY SERVICEBERRY<br>*Amelanchier arborea*<br>(Michx. f.) Fern. | 492 |
| THE HAWTHORNS; Thorns, Haws, Thorn Apples, White Thorns<br>*Crataegus* L. | THE HAWTHORNES<br>*Crataegus* spp. | 494 |
| WILD BLACK CHERRY; Rum, Cabinet or Black Cherry<br>*Prunus serotina* Ehrh. *(Padus serotina* (Ehrh.) Agardh.) | BLACK CHERRY<br>*Prunus serotina* Ehrh. | 496 |
| CHOKE CHERRY<br>*Prunus virginiana* L.<br>*(Padus virginiana* (L.) Roemer) | CHOKE CHERRY<br>*Prunus virginiana* L. | 498 |
| WILD RED CHERRY; Bird, Fire, Pin or Pigeon Cherry<br>*Prunus pennsylvanica* L.f. | PIN CHERRY<br>*Prunus pensylvanica* L.f. | 500 |

| BLAKESLEE & JARVIS NOMENCLATURE | CURRENT NOMENCLATURE | PAGE |
|---|---|---|
| SWEET CHERRY; Mazzard Cherry, European Birch Cherry<br>*Prunus avium* L. | MAZZARD<br>*Prunus avium* L. | 502 |
| SOUR CHERRY; Pie or Morello Cherry<br>*Prunus Cerasus* L. | SOUR CHERRY<br>*Prunus cerasus* L. | 504 |
| CANADA PLUM; Red, Horse or Wild Plum<br>*Prunus nigra* Ait.<br>*(P. americana,* var. *nigra* Waugh) | CANADA PLUM<br>*Prunus nigra* Ait. | 506 |
| PEACH<br>*Prunus Persica* (L.) Stokes<br>*(Amygdalus Persica* L.) | PEACH<br>*Prunus persica* Batsch | 512 |
| KENTUCKY COFFEE TREE; Coffee Nut, Coffee Bean, Nicker Tree, Mahogany<br>*Gymnocladus dioica* (L.) Koch<br>*(G. canadensis* Lam.) | KENTUCKY COFFEETREE<br>*Gymnocladus dioicus* (L.) K. Koch | 514 |
| HONEY LOCUST; Three-thorned Acacia, Honey Shucks, Sweet Locust, Thorn Tree<br>*Gleditsia triacanthus* L. (sometimes called *Gleditschia)* | HONEYLOCUST<br>*Gleditsia triacanthos* L. | 516 |
| REDBUD; Judas Tree<br>*Cercis canadensis* L. | REDBUD<br>*Cercis canadensis* L. | 518 |
| YELLOW WOOD; Virgilia, Gopher Wood<br>*Cladrastis lutea* (Mx. f.) Koch | YELLOWOOD<br>*Cladrastis lutea* (Michx. f.) K. Koch | 520 |
| COMMON LOCUST; Black, Yellow or White Locust, Locust, Acacia<br>*Robinia Pseudo-Acacia* L. | BLACK LOCUST<br>*Robinia pseudoacacia* L. | 522 |
| AILANTHUS; Tree of Heaven, Chinese Sumach<br>*Ailanthus glandulosa* Desf. | AILANTHUS<br>*Ailanthus altissima* (Mill.) Swingle | 524 |
| STAGHORN SUMACH<br>*Rhus typhina* L.<br>*(R. hirta* (L.) Sudw.) | STAGHORN SUMAC<br>*Rhus typhina* L. | 526 |

| BLAKELEE AND JARVIS NOMENCLATURE | CURRENT NOMENCLATURE | PAGE |
|---|---|---|
| POISON SUMACH; Poison Dogwood, Poison Elder, Swamp Sumach *Rhus Vernix* L. *(R. venenata* DC.) | POISON-SUMAC *Toxicodendron vernix* (L.) Kuntze | 528 |
| HOLLY; American Holly, White Holly *Ilex opaca* Ait. | AMERICAN HOLLY *Ilex opaca* Ait. | 530 |
| STRIPED MAPLE; Moosewood, Whistlewood *Acer pennsylvanicum* L. | STRIPED MAPLE *Acer pensylvanicum* L. | 532 |
| MOUNTAIN MAPLE *Acer spicatum* Lam. | MOUNTAIN MAPLE *Acer spicatum* Lam. | 534 |
| SUGAR MAPLE; Rock Maple, Hard Maple *Acer saccharum* Marsh. *(A. saccharinum* Wang. not L.; *A. barbatum* Michx.) | SUGAR MAPLE *Acer saccharum* Marsh. | 536 |
| SILVER MAPLE; White, River, or Soft Maple *Acer saccharinum* L. *(A. dasycarpum* Ehrh.) | SILVER MAPLE *Acer saccharinum* L. | 538 |
| RED MAPLE; Swamp, Soft or White Maple *Acer rubrum* L. | RED MAPLE *Acer rubrum* L. | 540 |
| NORWAY MAPLE *Acer platanoides* L. | NORWAY MAPLE *Acer platanoides* L. | 542 |
| SYCAMORE MAPLE *Acer Pseudo-Platanus* L. | SYCAMORE MAPLE *Acer pseudoplatanus* L. | 544 |
| BOX ELDER; Ash-leaved Maple *Acer Negundo* L. *(Negundo aceroides* Moench; *Negundo Negundo* Karst.) | BOXELDER *Acer negundo* L. | 546 |
| HORSE-CHESTNUT *Aesculus Hippocastanum* L. | HORSECHESTNUT *Aesculus hippocastanum* L. | 548 |
| LINDEN; Basswood, Lime, Whitewood, Beetree *Tilia americana* L. | AMERICAN BASSWOOD *Tilia americana* L. | 550 |

| BLAKELEE AND JARVIS NOMENCLATURE | CURRENT NOMENCLATURE | PAGE |
|---|---|---|
| FLOWERING DOGWOOD; Boxwood, Dogwood, Flowering Cornel *Cornus florida* L. | FLOWERING DOGWOOD *Cornus florida* L. | 552 |
| TUPELO; Pepperidge, Sour or Black Gum *Nyssa sylvatica* Marsh. *(N. multiflora* Wang.) | BLACK TUPELO *Nyssa sylvatica* Marsh. | 554 |
| WHITE ASH *Fraxinus americana* L. | WHITE ASH *Fraxinus americana* L. | 556 |
| RED ASH; Brown or River Ash *Fraxinus pennsylvanica* Marsh. *(F. pubescens* Lam.; *F. Darlingtonii* Britton) | GREEN ASH *Fraxinus pennsylvanica* Marsh. | 558 |
| BLACK ASH; Hoop, Swamp, Basket or Brown Ash *Fraxinus nigra* Marsh. *(F. sambucifolia* Lam.) | BLACK ASH *Fraxinus nigra* Marsh. | 560 |
| HARDY CATALPA; Cigar Tree, Indian Bean, Western Catalpa *Catalpa speciosa* Warder | NORTHERN CATALPA *Catalpa speciosa* Warder | 562 |

A NOTE ON THE DOUBLE PAGINATION

This monograph was originally published on pages 307 to 576 of *Bulletin* 69 of the Storrs Agricultural Experiment Station.

In this edition the original page numbers [in square brackets] appear alongside the new running page numbers. All index references and cross references within the text are to the original, bracketed pagination.

## INTRODUCTION

Before considering the individual trees in detail it seems desirable to give a general discussion of the different terms used as headings in the description of the species.

NAME—A common English name heads the description of each tree and this name is used throughout the book as the designation of a particular species. The same form may be known in different localities by several entirely different common names. Thus the Tupelo in some places is called only Pepperidge, in others, Sour Gum or Black Gum. After consultation with the literature the name Tupelo was chosen as being somewhat more desirable for the whole of New England than the other names given in smaller type as synonyms. Often several common names may be in about equally frequent use. There is, however, only one scientific name at present sanctioned by botanical authorities and this is placed first, followed by the Latin synonyms in italics.

HABIT—By the word habit, we denote the general appearance of a tree seen as a whole. A tree strictly speaking is generally considered as a woody growth having an undivided trunk at the base and rising to at least twice the height of a man. A shrub on the other hand is low-growing and may branch from the very base. No hard and fast line, however, can be drawn between a tree and a shrub. Many trees at the limit of their range or under unfavorable conditions are reduced to the form and dimensions of a shrub and some forms growing as shrubs in New England become trees in states outside this group. A young tree sometimes resembles a shrub, but is more rapid in growth and generally does not bear fruit until it has reached a considerable size. Of the forms on the borderline between trees and shrubs only those have been treated that have demanded recognition on account of their commonness or their relationship with other forms.

The information regarding the dimensions of a tree are of minor importance for purposes of identification, but are of considerable value to the woodsman. The diameter of the trunk may be best measured directly by calipers at breast height from the ground or indirectly obtained by dividing the circumference by 3 (more accurately by =3.1416). A number of rough methods of estimating height are given in books on forestry. For example,

from a distance equal to several times the length of the tree, the
height of a 10 ft. pole beside the trunk or a mark on the trunk
of known height may be compared with the height of the whole
tree.   Instruments for more accurate measurement are on the
market under the name of hypsometers.   A home-made instrument may readily be constructed which has been found to compare
favorably in accuracy with the expensive Faustmann hypsometer
of which it is a modification.   A rectangular board about a foot
in length is ruled in squares or more conveniently has squared
coordinate paper pasted on one side (fig. 1).   Care should be

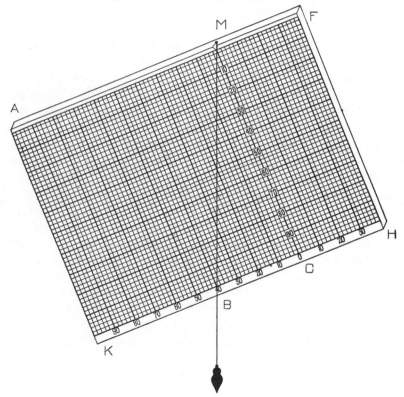

Fig. 1.   Home-made   Height   Measurer.

observed that the top of the board AF is straight and accurately
parallel to the lines running lengthwise of the paper.   The line
MC is numbered from M in any convenient unit, say up to 100,
and using the same unit, the line HK is numbered in both direc-

tions beginning at C.   A thread with a weight is attached at M and hangs free from the zero point of the top of MC.   In use a convenient distance, say 100 ft. from the tree, is first measured off as a base line, and upon this measurement largely depends the accuracy of the height estimation.   At the 100 ft. mark the top of the tree is sighted along the straight edge AF which may more conveniently be fitted with some simple form of sights.   At the point B, where the plumb line crosses the line CK the height of the tree above the eye is indicated in feet.   The height of the eye above the ground is added to this reading if the measurement is on the level, or a second sight may be made to the base of the tree and the reading noted on CH added or subtracted, according to whether the base of the tree is below or above the eye level.   If in the instrument as figured, the base line had been 100 ft. as suggested, the height of the tree above the eye is given as 40 ft.   If, however, the base line had been 50 ft. the height is given as 20 ft., the reading being taken at the intersection of the thread with the line running lengthwise through whatever number on MC has been used to represent the base line.   The two smaller diagrams show the instrument in position for sighting to top and base of tree

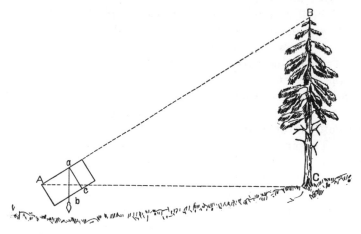

Fig. 2.   Height Measurer in position for sighting to top of tree.

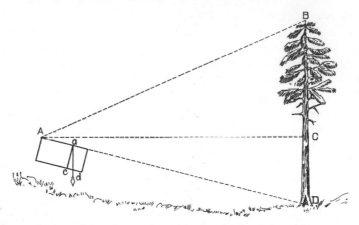

Fig. 3.  Height Measurer in position for sighting to base of tree.

respectively.  In figure 2, the eye is assumed to be on the level with the base of the tree and only a single sight is necessary.  In figure 3, the base of tree is below eye level and the distance CD must be found by a downward sight and added to the reading obtained for BC.  It can be readily seen from inspection of the figures that the method is based upon the similarity of the triangles ABC and ACD with the smaller triangles abc and acd.

Two general habit types are recognized—the spreading and the erect—often termed deliquescent and excurrent respectively.  The former is well represented by the Apple (p. 487) and White Elm (p. 461) and the latter by the Evergreens and those of the Poplars that form narrow conical heads (p. 395-397).  By its more erect habit of growth the Sweet Cherry (p. 503) is readily distinguished from the Sour Cherry (p. 505) and in like manner the Pear (p. 485) from the Apple (p. 487).  It is these habit differences that form the most ready means of separating the contrasted trees just mentioned which may closely resemble each other in twig characters.  The angle which the branches make with the trunk is frequently a diagnostic character of considerable value.  For example, the ascending and gracefully outward  curving limbs of the American White Elm (p. 461) stand in contrast with the sharply divergent limbs of the English Elm (p. 459).  Likewise the horizontal branches of the Tupelo (p. 555) and the strongly pendant lower limbs of the Swamp White Oak (p. 439) are characteristic of these species.  The relative thickness of the branchlets contrasted in the Sweet Cherry (p. 503) and the Black Birch (p. 415) and the arrangement of the branchlets whether opposite or alternate and whether erect or drooping, may further be mentioned as habit characters.

As one becomes more familiar with trees in their winter aspect, the number that cannot be recognized at a distance becomes greatly diminished. We come to know trees by hardly definable traits, much as we recognize our friends at a distance by some peculiarity of form or gait. Watching the trees from a car window is a great help in acquiring this familiarity with the habit characters. The method of branching and other features included in the habit, however, do not furnish such precise marks as do the twigs, and cannot therefore be of much value in a descriptive key. In fact the habit varies considerably among individual trees of the same species, no two trees having exactly the same method of branching. Moreover trees grown in woods in company with other trees are prevented by lateral shading from developing their normal form and produce tall trunks with but little branching. On the other hand trees apart from other trees have usually been planted for ornament or have originally grown in woods but have been left isolated by the cutting down of their neighbors. In the latter case the habit will be more or less that of a forest-grown tree dependent upon the age at which the conditions of light and shade were altered (see lower habit picture p. 463). In the former case the top of the young tree may have been cut in the process of transplanting causing an increased branching at the point of cutting and the lower limbs may have been trimmed off, giving a greater show of trunk. These mutilations, however, have less influence upon the outline of the head or crown than might be imagined since the tree is generally able to accommodate itself to such accidents as those mentioned and express its individuality despite them. The age of the tree is also an important factor in the outline, young specimens being in general narrower and more conical than in later life while those in old age may have lost shape through ice storms, high winds and the attacks of fungi.

So far as possible the photographs have been taken from mature specimens growing in the open and only those have been chosen which have been considered to present an appearance typical of the species. They will help one to form a mental picture of those generalized features of a tree in the landscape which may be recognized at a distance, but which are difficult of analysis.

BARK—Although it is upon the appearance of the bark more than upon any other character that the woodsman depends in his recognition of timber trees, the bark shares with the habit the misfortune of being difficult of precise description. A study of the photographs, however, in connection with the description of the color and texture will enable one to recognize a large proportion of our trees by the appearance of the bark alone. They have been taken from mature trees of moderate size which have developed the characteristic sculpturing of the bark rather than from those of larger size which are less frequently seen. A tape measure surrounding the trunk or in some instances a penknife stuck into the bark may serve to give an idea of the relative size of the markings on the trunk. The heading "Bark" is used throughout the descriptions in reference to the trunk and larger limbs and not to the twigs which are described under another heading.

The color of the outer bark is an important mark of distinction and is the chief means of separating the different species of the Birches (p. 415-425). The color and taste of the inner layers of the bark are in some cases also characteristic. The Black Oak for example is best distinguished from other Oaks by the yellow and intensely bitter inner bark. Similarly, the Black Birch, the Sassafras and the genus Prunus including the Cherries have barks with characteristic flavors. The swamp-loving Poison Sumach (p. 529) is the only poisonous tree in New England so that after this shrubby form is known there need be no fear of tasting bark and twigs of any unknown tree-like species.

The bark varies in character according to the age of the tree. In the young tree the bark is smooth, but, as the trunk expands from the growth of the wood within, the covering of dead bark outside is forced to crack in a variety of ways giving rise to characteristic fissures and ridges which become more prominent as the tree grows older. The bark of few trees such as the Beech (p. 429) and the American Hornbeam (p. 413) remain smooth, their outer layers expanding with the growth of the tree. The barks of others as the Paper and Yellow Birch (p. 417) stretch and peel off in thin papery layers. In the Birches (p. 423) and Cherries (p. 503) the breathing pores (lenticels) become horizontally elongated to form narrow transverse streaks which are characteristic for these forms. When ridges or scales are formed they may be close and firm and with difficulty removed from the trunk as is the case with the bark in the Black Oak group or, on the other hand, they may be easily rubbed off as are the scales of the bark of the White Oak and of most members of the White Oak group. Bark of this latter type is called *flaky* in our descriptions and this distinction between barks that are flaky and those that are not flaky is of considerable importance in classification. To avoid confusion little notice is taken of the minute scales that are likely to occur on the surface of both types of bark. The bark may come off in large sheets as in the Shag-bark Hickory (p. 403) and the Sycamore (p. 483), and the ridges may be long as in the Chestnut (p. 431) or short and run together to form more or less perfect diamond-shaped areas as in the White Ash (p. 557) but these as well as other differences in the sculpturing are shown in the photographs and do not require further discussion in the introduction.

TWIGS—The unqualified word *twig* refers in the descriptions to the growth of the past season only. Older twigs and branchlets are the designations employed for the small growth of several seasons. The Horse-chestnut (fig. 4) may be taken as a convenient form to illustrate the various markings found on the twig. The large triangular patches resembling somewhat closed horse-shoes in shape are the *leaf-scars* showing where the bases of the leaf-stalks were attached to the twig before their fall. The little dots corresponding to the nail holes in a horse-shoe are the *bundle-scars* and mark the location of the so-called fibro-vascular bundles that run up through the leaf-stalks and connect with the veins of the leaf acting thus as the channels for the transference of raw material and manufactured food to and from the leaf. The leaf-scars are located at the *nodes* and the portion between the nodes is called the *internode*. Scattered along the twig are little dots, the *lenticels,* which are openings that function to a certain extent like breathing pores. Above each leaf-scar is normally produced an *axillary bud* so called because located in the *axil* or angle made between the twig and the leaf-stalk when the latter was present. The *lateral*

when they are twisted together into a more or less felt-like mass, but these distinctions cannot be always sharply drawn. A twig if smooth may be dull or shiny in appearance. The lenticels are of most distinctive value in those forms like the Birches (p. 423), in which they become horizontally elongated with age. The color, size and shape of the pith are often characteristic as seen in the wide salmon-colored pith of the Kentucky Coffee Tree (p. 515) and the star-shaped pith of the Oaks and to a less degree in the Poplars (fig. 5). Some few trees have their pith separated by hollow chambers such as the Hackberry and the Butternut (fig. 6) or have solid pith but with woody cross partitions such as the Tupelo.

LEAF-SCARS—The arrangement of the leaf-scars form primary divisions in the classification. They may be *opposite* with two scars at a node as in the Horse-chestnut, or *alternate* with only one scar at the node as in the majority of species. Alternate leaf-scars may be arranged along the twig in two longitudinal rows when they are said to be *2-ranked,* as in the Mulberry (fig. 8), or in several rows when they are *more than 2-ranked* as in the Poplars (fig. 5). Twigs sometimes if rapidly grown have the leaf-scars which are normally opposite pulled apart to appear alternate, but the typical condition will be found on other parts of the tree. A few species like the Chestnut sometimes take the 2-ranked, and sometimes the more than 2-ranked position, and the number of ranks in other forms may be at times somewhat obscured by a twisting of the twig. The distinctions in the main, however, hold good and where a doubt is likely to occur in regard to the arrangement, a place has been made in the key for the species in both the 2-ranked and the more than 2-ranked groups.

The size and shape of leaf-scars are important factors in identification. They may be very narrow as in the Pear and their upper margins may be flat or convex as in the Black Ash (p. 561) or deeply notched as in the White Ash (p. 557) or form a band nearly surrounding the bud as in the Sycamore (p. 483). They may become dingy and inconspicuous or be sharply distinct by color contrast with the rest of the twig. Thus the Elms and the Poplars have their leaf-scars covered with a light-colored cork-like layer which makes them conspicuous irrespective of their size.   Leaf-scars may be level with the twig or more or less raised with their surfaces parallel with the twig or making various angles with it up to a right angle.   Ridges in some cases run down the twig from the base and corners of the leaf-scar.

At the bases of the leaves of some species a pair of small leaflets called stipules are regularly formed and leave, at the fall of the leaf, more or less definite *stipule-scars* at either side of the leaf-scar as shown in the Carolina Poplar (fig. 5).

The number, the size, the relation to the surface of the leaf-scar whether sunken or projecting, and the distribution of the bundle-scars form important points of distinction.   When they are indistinct, as is frequently the case, they may be revealed if a thin slice is taken off the surface of the leaf-scar.   This surface section must be very thin, however, since the number of bundle-scars exposed by a deep cut is often different from that on the surface, and this latter number is the one used in the keys and descriptions.   A distinction is made between a group in which the bundle-scars form a single line and a second group in which they are variously scattered and grouped or in a double line.

BUDS—In regard to their position buds are terminal or lateral.   Buds produced at or near the nodes but not in the axil of a leaf-scar are called *accessory buds.*   Of these there are two kinds: *Superposed buds* located above the axillary buds and *collateral buds* located at either side of the axillary buds.   The former are shown in the Butternut (fig. 6) and the latter in the Red Maple (fig. 7).   Classified according to what they produce there are *flower buds* which contain the rudiments of flowers, *leaf buds* which contain rudiments of leaves, and *mixed buds* which produce both flowers and leaves.   Flower buds are generally stouter than leaf buds.

Fig. 5. Twig of Carolina Poplar.
sx—Stipule Scar.
p--Star-shaped Pith.

Most species by the end of the growing season have formed terminal buds which remain through the winter and are destined to continue the growth the following spring. In some species, however, such as the Mulberry (fig. 8) the terminal bud together with the tip of the twig dies away and drops off before the beginning of winter leaving a small scar at the end of the twig. The presence or absence of the terminal bud is a very valuable point of distinction and is used throughout in the keys. Unfortunately it is not always possible at a cursory glance to say whether the terminal bud is present or absent and a hand-lens must generally be used for an accurate determination of this point. In the Mulberry figured, the self-pruning scar formed by the dropping off of the terminal bud is perched on the tip of the twig with the topmost lateral bud obviously in the axil of the last leaf-scar. Frequently, however, the self-pruning scar may be nearer the lateral bud which bends in and gives the appearance of being terminal. The presence of a leaf-scar below it shows that it is in fact axillary, but since leaf-scars are sometimes present toward the end of twigs without buds in their axils the presence of the self-pruning scar at the twig end must be used as the decisive sign that the terminal bud is really absent.

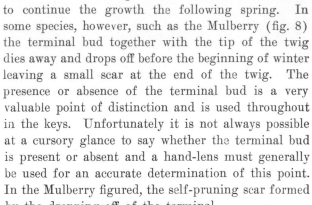

Fig. 6—Twig of Butternut.
tr—terminal bud.
ax—axillary bud.
s p—Superposed accessory bud.
p—chambered pith.

Fig. 7—Twig of Red Maple.
ax—axillary bud.
cl—collateral accessory bud.

Aside from the color, the presence or absence of hairs, stickiness, fragrance and other such surface characters, the position of the buds in relation to the twig may be of importance. Buds that lie close up against the twig as those of the Small-toothed Aspen (p. 389) are called *appressed,* while those that project more or less away from the twig as those of the Carolina Poplar (fig. 5) are called *divergent.* In the Common Locust and a few other forms the buds are sunken below the surface of the twig, and can be found only by cutting the twig lengthwise through the leaf-scar.

The characters of the bud-scales of most importance are the shape, the number visible in the unmutilated bud, their arrangement—whether alternate or opposite—and the number of ranks they form on the bud.

FRUIT—The fruit generally forms a good means of identification when it can be found. Unfortunately there are a number of limitations to its use for this purpose. In the first place many species of trees do not fruit every year, and it may happen that the

Fig. 8—Twig of Mulberry.
ax—last axillary bud often mistaken for a terminal bud.
sc—self-pruning scar left by fall of real terminal bud and tip of twig.

species under examination is not in its fruiting period and consequently all the trees of the region will fail to show fruit. Again, in some species such as the Ash the sexes are separate and consequently only female trees can ever be expected to bear fruit. The fruit generally does not remain on the tree throughout the winter but if the tree is sufficiently isolated from other species, a careful search on the ground will often be rewarded by the finding of specimens of fruit that one can feel sure came from the tree in question. However, some species such as the Poplars and the Red and Silver Maples scatter their fruit early in spring, and fruiting material of such forms in consequence is not to be looked for in winter. The immature fruit of some species may be found on the tree in winter and be of value in identification. Thus the presence of young acorns on an Oak in winter shows that it belongs to the Black Oak group.

The staminate flowering clusters are of similar diagnostic value in certain groups, their presence or absence, for example, separating the American Hornbeam from the Hop Hornbeam.

COMPARISONS—Under this heading are contrasted the different species that are considered likely to be confused. It is believed that the information in this section will prove more valuable to one with some knowledge of trees than the more detailed descriptions first given.

DISTRIBUTION—The habitat first discussed under this heading shows in what kind of locations as to soil, moisture and exposure the species normally grows. The information may be of identificational value by elimination. Thus if one finds a cedar-like tree on a hillside pasture one can be sure it is not a Coast White Cedar since this latter species grows only in swamps. In like manner the geographical limits may assist in identification; a Pine found growing wild in Rhode Island or Connecticut, for example, could not be the Jack Pine since this is a northern form found native only in the northern New England states. Although some cultivated trees have escaped from cultivation, an introduced tree is generally characterized by the places in which it is found growing.

WOOD—Under this heading the information given in regard to the characters of the wood and the economic value of the species is of practically no value for purposes of identification of standing timber, but may prove of general interest to the student of trees.

## ANALYTICAL KEY

### METHOD OF USE

Despite the fact that the appearance of the bark and the method of branching are almost exclusively depended upon by the experienced woodsman in recognition of species, these characters are difficult of precise description and not adapted to use in a key.  The twigs therefore with the scaly buds and leaf-scars are used, as a basis of the following keys.  The word "twig" in the sense here used, it should be remembered, denotes the growth of the past season only, and the word "bark" refers to the bark of the trunk and older limbs and not of the twigs or branchlets.  The student should read the introduction and note the limitation of terms and characters used in the following pages.

Before attempting to identify an unknown tree it is necessary to have good material to work with.  Care should be taken that the twigs selected are normal in appearance, being neither abnormally stunted in growth nor unusually elongated as are twigs on young sprouts.  Frequently the species may be determined by an inspection of the twigs alone but notes on the character of the bark and the habit of growth as well as specimens of the fruit will generally be found useful and sometimes necessary.

In the key a choice is given between two paragraphs preceded by the same number.  This choice leads to a new number or to the name of the species followed by the page where a detailed description of the tree may be found.  The White Ash may be used to show the method of procedure.  Starting with No. 1 we have the choice between trees with "leaves persistent and green throughout winter" and trees with "leaves *not* persistent and green throughout winter."  We choose the latter and this takes us to No. 11 where the decision must be made between "leaf-scars opposite or in 3's" and "leaf-scars alternate."  The leaf-scars on the Ash are opposite and we take the first 11 and are led to No. 12.  At 12 we have the alternative between "leaf-scars, or some of them, 3 at a node" and "leaf-scars always 2 at a node."  The first pair of contrasting characters mentioned are always the most important.  The constant presence in the Ash of two leaf-scars at a node is sufficient to cause us to choose the second 12, and our choice is corroborated by the position of the bundle-scars and by the presence of a terminal bud, so we pass to 13.  The upper lateral buds of

the Ash are not covered by persistent bases of leaf-stalks and there
are 2 or more pairs of scales to the leaf buds, we therefore pass
to 14.  The relatively small size of the buds and their freedom
from stickiness takes us to 15 where the number of the bundle-
scars and the other characters given show us that we have in hand
a twig of one of the Ashes.  We now turn to No. 164 and confirm
our determination of the genus by reading the general description
of the Ashes.  To find out which Ash we are dealing with we
procede with the key of the Ashes and, knowing that the leaf-scars
in our specimens are deeply concave on their upper margins, we
conclude that we have the White Ash *(Fraxinus americana)*.
At page 556 we find a detailed description with photographic
illustrations of this species and may learn the winter characters
of the tree not already given in the key.  If the description and
photographs do not correspond to the tree under investigation, we
know that we have gone astray at some point in the key, and
turning back we repeat the analysis taking if need be the other
alternative of a pair where the choice had been doubtful.

Sometimes a tree is variable in the characters used in the key.
Thus the Chestnut has terminal buds sometimes present on the twigs
though they are generally absent.  In such cases, however, and
where there is a legitimate doubt as to whether the tree should be
placed in the first or the second group, it has generally been placed
in both so that either of the two choices should lead to the correct
name.  The determination of the presence or absence of the terminal bud is perhaps the greatest pitfall likely to be found in the
use of the key, but should give little difficulty if the discussion in
the introduction is understood and the terminal scar is looked for
with the aid of a hand-lens.

## KEY TO GENERA AND SPECIES

1. Leaves persistent and green throughout winter (Evergreens) ....2
1. Leaves not persistent and green throughout winter (dead leaves often persistent in the Oaks and Beeches)..................... 11

2. Leaves broad, prominently spiny-margined. **Holly** *(Ilex opaca)* **p.530**
2. Leaves narrow, often minute and scale-like; Conifers (i.e. cone-bearing trees) ............................................... 3

3. Leaves, except scale-leaves, needle-shaped, in definite, generally sheathed clusters on the sides of the branches. .....**Pine** *(Pinus)* 85
3. Leaves, not in definite clusters ................................ 4

4. Leaves opposite or in 3's, therefore 2 or 3 at a node ........... 5
4. Leaves alternate, scattered, therefore only 1 at a node ........ 8

5. Leaves whorled' in 3's, all alike, whitened above and green below, awl-shaped, sharp-pointed and spreading; fruit bluish, berry-like; a shrub or low tree. (See also juvenile condition of Red Cedar)....... .................... **Common Juniper** *(Juniperus communis)* **p.378**
5. Leaves opposite in 4 ranks, minute, scale-like, closely overlapping 6

6. Young twigs prominently flattened and forming a flat, 2-ranked, fan-shaped spray often mistaken for the true leaves which are minute and of two shapes, those on edges of twig being narrower, those on flat sides being broader and more abruptly pointed with each leaf generally showing a conspicuous raised glandular dot; fruit a thin-scaled, oblong, woody cone. ....................... ........................... **Arbor Vitae** *(Thuja occidentalis)* **p.376**
6. Young twigs not prominently flattened; fruit spherical ........ 7

7. Spray somewhat fan-shaped; young twigs not prominently 4-angled; leaves all alike in shape, some of them with prominent raised glandular dot on back; fruit a spherical woody cone. ............ .................. **Coast White Cedar** *(Chamaecyparis thyoides)* **p.374**
7. Spray not fan-shaped, young twigs with typical leaves and prominently 4-angled; leaves without conspicuous glandular dots, of two kinds; (a) the juvenile form—awl-shaped, spiny-pointed and spreading, in 2's or 3's at a node and resembling leaves of Common Juniper, the usual leaf form on young trees but generally to be found on some parts of older trees; (b) the typical form—smaller, scale-like and closely appressed; fruit bluish, berry-like. ........ ........................... **Red Cedar** *(Juniperus virginiana)* **p.380**

8. Leaves distinctly flattened .................................... 9
8. Leaves not distinctly flattened, needle-shaped, 4-angled, sessile on projections of the bark. ................... **Spruce** *(Picea)* 91

9. Leaf about 1 cm. long with definite leaf-stalk, leaving prominently projecting scar when detached. **Hemlock** *(Tsuga canadensis)* **p.372**
9. Leaf about 2 cm. or more long, without leaf-stalk, leaving a flat or only slightly raised scar when detached ................... 10

10. Buds small, nearly spherical to broadly ovate, their scales covered and glued together by resinous coating; leaf-scars flat. .......... .............................. **Balsam Fir** *(Abies balsamea)* **p.370**
10. Buds larger, narrow conical, without resinous coating; leaf-scars slightly raised .......... **Douglas Fir** *(Pseudotsuga taxifolia)* **p.368**

11. Leaf-scars opposite or in 3's, therefore 2 or 3 at a node ........ 12
11. Leaf-scars alternate, therefore only 1 at a node ................ 16

12. Leaf-scars or some of them 3 at a node; bundle-scars in an ellipse; terminal bud absent ............ **Catalpa** *(Catalpa)* **p.562**
12. Leaf-scars always 2 at a node; bundle-scars not in an ellipse; terminal bud present ........................................ 13

13. Lateral buds, at least the upper ones, covered by persistent bases of leaf-stalks; leaf buds with only a single pair of scales. ........ ..................... **Flowering Dogwood** *(Cornus florida)* **p.552**
13. Lateral buds not covered by persistent bases of leaf-stalks; leaf buds with 2 or more pairs of scales ......................... 14

14.   Terminal buds large, over 1.5 cm. long, sticky or varnished; leaf-scar large, inversely triangular; bundle-scars 3-9, conspicuous. ....
......................**Horse-chestnut** *(Aesculus Hippocastanum)* **p.548**
14.   Terminal buds smaller, under 1.5 cm. long, not sticky-varnished; leaf-scars smaller ......................................... 15

15.   Bundle-scars, minute, numerous in a U-shaped line often more or less confluent; bud-scales scurfy (i.e. rough-downy). .............
.................................................. **Ash** *(Fraxinus)* 164
15.   Bundle-scars definitely 3 in number; bud-scales not scurfy.........
.................................................. **Maple** *(Acer)* 155

16.   Stipule-scars entirely encircling the twig .................... 17
16.   Stipule-scars when present not encircling the twig ........... 19

17.   Terminal bud absent; (the last lateral bud may appear to be terminal but absence of terminal bud is shown by small scar at end of twig); leaf-scar almost completely surrounding the bud. ......
............................ **Sycamore** *(Platanus occidentalis)* **p.482**
17.   Terminal bud present; leaf-scar not surrounding the bud ..... 18

18.   Scar of rudimentary leaf surmounting decurrent ridge on side of bud; buds ovate to conical, hairy at least within. .................
.......................................... **Magnolia** *(Magnolia)* 141
18.   Scar of rudimentary leaf if present at base of bud; buds flattened oblong, smooth without and within. ...........................
........................ **Tulip Tree** *(Liriodendron Tulipifera)* **p.474**

19.   Twigs with thorns, spines, or prickles, or branches ending in thorns ...................................................... 20
19.   Twigs without thorns, spines, or prickles .................... 27

20.   Spines in pairs at the nodes, or twigs covered with weak hair-like prickles ............................................... 21
20.   Spines not in pairs at the nodes, twigs not covered with weak prickles ................................................... 22

21.   Buds rusty-hairy, more or less covered by bark; terminal bud absent................................... **Locust** *(Robinia)* **p.522**
21.   Buds, red, exposed; terminal bud present; a shrub. .............
.... **Prickly Ash** *(Zanthoxylon americanum)* under Comparisons **p.522**

22.   Thorns lateral, regularly placed on the twig at or near the nodes ..................................................... 23
22.   Thorns terminal ........................................... 25

23.   Thorns generally branched, situated above the nodes; buds several in a longitudinal row, the lower ones covered by the bark. ........
.;...................... **Honey Locust** *(Gleditsia triacanthus)* **p.516**
23.   Thorns generally unbranched on twigs, situated at the nodes; sometimes branched thorns on trunk; buds exposed .......... 24

24.   Thorns generally present at all the nodes; bundle-scar single. ....
........ **Osage Orange** *(Maclura pomifera)* under Comparisons **p.494**
24.   Thorns generally absent from many of the nodes; bundle-scars 3.
.................................... **Hawthorn** *(Crataegus)* **p.494**

25.   Terminal bud absent but leaving a terminal scar on twig. ........
............................................... **Plum** *(Prunus)* 150
25.   Terminal bud present, at least on spineless branches .......... 26

26.   Tree with bushy habit of growth; twigs with characteristic licorice-like taste, generally reddish-brown, more or less pale-woolly at least toward apex; lateral buds blunt, flattish, appressed and more or less pale-woolly .......... **Apple** *(Pyrus Malus)* **p.486**
26.   Tree with upright habit of growth; twigs without characteristic taste, generally yellowish green and generally smooth; lateral buds sharp-pointed, smooth or sometimes slightly downy, generally not flattened nor appressed. .......... **Pear** *(Pyrus communis)* **p.484**

27.   Pith in section lengthwise of twig seen to be interrupted by hollow chambers or by woody partitions ........................... 28
27.   Pith continuous; i.e. without hollow chambers or woody partitions ..................................................... 32

28.   Pith chambered but with chambers confined to the nodes. .........
............................................... **Hickory** *(Carya)* 101
28.   Pith when chambered with chambers not confined to the nodes.. 29

29. Pith wide, brown, with hollow chambers; fruit a nut ........... 30
29. Pith narrow, light colored; fruit a small stone-fruit .......... 31

30. Downy patch present above leaf-scar; nut elongated. .............
.................................... **Butternut** *(Juglans cinerea)***p.398**
30. Downy patch absent from leaf-scar; nut round. ..................
.................................... **Black Walnut** *(Juglans nigra)***p.400**

31. Pith with hollow chambers; buds brown, terminal bud absent,
lateral buds appressed. ...... **Hackberry** *(Celtis occidentalis)* **p.464**
31. Pith with woody partitions in the solid ground-mass; buds reddish,
terminal bud present, lateral buds divergent. ....................
................................... **Tupelo** *(Nyssa sylvatica)***p.554**

32. Leaf-scars regularly 2-ranked, i.e. arranged in 2 longitudinal rows
on the twig .................................................. 33
32. Leaf-scars regularly more than 2-ranked, i.e. in more than 2 rows
on the twig ................................................. 49

33. Terminal bud absent (the last lateral bud may appear to be terminal but absence of terminal bud is shown by small scar at
end of twig) .................................................. 39
33. Terminal bud present ....................................... 34

34. Buds stalked .............................................. 35
34. Buds not stalked .......................................... 36

35. Buds, for the most part naked, i.e. with undeveloped leaves serving
the function of scales; woody, 4-parted fruits and the remains of
last season's flowers generally present. .......................
......................... **Witch Hazel** *(Hamamelis virginiana)***p.478**
35. Buds covered with bud-scales; fruit a woody cone-like catkin. ....
.................................................. **Alder** *(Alnus)***p.426**

36. Stipule-scars nearly encircling twig; buds long and narrow,
generally over 5 times as long as wide, divergent; bud-scales in
pairs, 4-ranked, 10 or more scales visible; bundle-scars 5. ........
..................................................... **Beech** *(Fagus)***p.428**
36. Stipule-scars when present relatively short; buds stouter, generally
not over 4 times as long as wide; bud-scales less numerous .... 37

37. Leaf-scars very narrow, V-shaped, swollen at the 3 bundle-scars;
buds long, appressed; bud-scale tipped with dark point; stipule-
scars absent. .......... **Shad Bush** *(Amelanchier canadensis)* **p.492**
37. Leaf-scars relatively broad; buds shorter; bud-scale without conspicuous dark point; stipule-scars present though often inconspicuous ................................................... 38

38. Bundle-scars 3; bark of young stem and branches with horizontally elongated lenticels, often peeling into papery layers; pith
generally elliptical often with irregularly toothed edges; fruit a
catkin, immature catkins generally present on tree in winter. ....
......................................... **Birch** *(Betula)* 104
38. Bundle-scars several; lenticels not horizontally elongated; bark
never peeling in papery layers; pith more or less 5-pointed, star-
shaped; fruit a bur. ............. **Chestnut** *(Castanea dentata)***p.430**

39. Leaf-scar almost entirely surrounding the buds; buds brown,
hairy, several massed together to form a bud-like cone; bundle-
scars raised, generally 5 in a single curved line. ................
............................ **Yellow Wood** *(Cladrastis lutea)***p.520**
39. Leaf-scar not more than half surrounding the bud; buds not massed
together into a hairy cone ................................. 40

40. Bundle-scars 3 or more in a *single* curved line ............... 43
40. Bundle-scars more than 3 in a closed ellipse, double line, variously clustered or irregularly scattered ..................... 41

41. 2-3 scales visible to a bud; bundle-scars not prominently projecting ................................................... 42
41. 4 or more scales visible to a bud; bundle-scars rather prominently
projecting. ............................. **Mulberry** *(Morus)* 140

42. Twigs usually zigzag; pith roundish; buds and twigs mucilaginous
when chewed; fruit spherical, woody, about size of pea, attached to
a leafy bract. ......................... **Linden** *(Tilia)* **p.550**

42. Twigs nearly straight; pith more or less 5-pointed, star-shaped; buds and twigs not mucilaginous when chewed; fruit a large bur. .............................. **Chestnut** *(Castanea dentata)***p.430**

43. Buds superposed, at least at some of the nodes; stipule-scars absent; older pith with reddish streaks. ...............................
.............................. **Redbud** *(Cercis canadensis)* **p.518**
43. Buds never superposed; stipule-scars present; pith without reddish streaks ................................................. 44

44. 2-3 scales visible to a bud ..................................... 45
44. 4 or more scales visible to a bud ............................. 46

45. Buds stout; buds and twigs mucilaginous when chewed; lenticels not horizontally elongated; fruit spherical, woody, about size of pea, attached to leafy bract. ................... **Linden** *(Tilia)* **p.550**
45. Buds narrower, buds and twigs not mucilaginous when chewed; lenticels on stems and branches horizontally elongated; bark often peeling in papery layers; fruit a winged seed-like body borne in catkins. ....................................... **Birch** *(Betula)* 104

46. Bud-scales 2-ranked (i.e. arranged on the bud in 2 longitudinal rows); leaf-scars covered with a smooth corky layer; bundle-scars typically sunken; bark ridged; catkins absent. ............
.................................................. **Elm** *(Ulmus)* 137
46. Bud-scales more than 2-ranked; leaf-scars not covered with smooth corky layer; bundle-scars not sunken; fruit borne in catkins ........................................................ 47

47. Lenticels horizontally elongated with age; bark on young trunks and branches smooth, not becoming fluted, often peeling into papery layers but not flaky; fruit a flat seed-like body borne in catkins; catkins generally present on tree in winter. **Birch** *(Betula)* 104
47. Lenticels not horizontally elongated; bark flaky or fluted; bud-scales 4-ranked; fruit a nutlet attached to a bract .............. 48

48. Bark flaky; twigs 1-2 mm. thick; buds usually 3-7 mm. long; nutlet enclosed by a sac-like bract; staminate catkins generally abundantly present in winter. ........................................
......................... **Hop Hornbeam** *(Ostrya virginiana)***p.410**
48. Bark smooth, close, sinewy-fluted; twigs about 1 mm. or less thick; buds usually 2-4 mm. long; nutlet attached to flattish, toothed bract; staminate catkins enclosed in enlarged scaly buds, therefore no catkins visible on tree in winter. ...................
................... **American Hornbeam** *(Carpinus caroliniana)***p.412**

49. Buds clustered at tips of vigorous shoots; terminal bud not greatly larger than others of the cluster ............................. 50
49. Buds not clustered at tips of vigorous shoots, or if slightly clustered, then terminal bud much larger than others of the cluster 53

50. Bundle-scars numerous, scattered; pith regularly 5-pointed, star-shaped ............................. **Oak** *(Quercus)* 109 and 120
50. Bundle-scars 3; pith not 5-pointed, star-shaped ................ 51

51. Terminal bud absent, but leaving a terminal scar on twig. ........
.............................................. **Plum** *(Prunus)* 150
51. Terminal bud present ........................................ 52

52. Buds woolly at least at tip; collateral buds generally present. ....
............................... **Peach** *(Prunus Persica)***p.512**
52. Buds smooth; collateral buds generally absent....................
..................... **Wild Red Cherry** *(Prunus pennsylvanica)* **p.500**
(See also other cherries 144.)

53. Buds stalked ............................................... 54
53. Buds not stalked ........................................... 56

54. Buds bright yellow dotted, often superposed. ....................
............................... **Bitternut** *(Carya cordiformis)***p.408**
54. Buds not bright yellow dotted, not superposed ............... 55

55. Buds always stalked, blunt; stipule-scars present; catkins present in winter. ................... ............... **Alder** *(Alnus)* **p.426**
55. Buds, except occasionally on rapidly grown twigs, generally not stalked, pointed; corky ridges generally present on branchlets; stipule-scars and catkins absent. .................................
................... **Sweet Gum** *(Liquidambar Styraciflua)***p.480**

56. Buds sunken, partially or completely covered by the bark, for the most part minute and superposed; best seen in a section lengthwise of the twig, through the node at right angles to the surface of the leaf-scar .................................................... 57
56. Buds not sunken and generally not superposed ................. 59

57. Twigs very stout, generally 1 cm. or more thick; pith salmon-colored; buds bronze-silky, exposed but surrounded by an incurved downy rim of the bark; bundle-scars generally more than 3. ...... .................... **Kentucky Coffee Tree** *(Gymnocladus dioica)* **p.514**
57. Twigs rather slender generally less than 5 mm. thick; pith whitish not salmon-colored; bundle-scars 3 ............................ 58

58. Buds smooth, distant, the uppermost breaking through the bark above the leaf-scar, the lower ones submerged, appearing in section of twig as separate green dots. .............................. ......................... **Honey Locust** *(Gleditsia triacanthus)* **p.516**
58. Buds downy, clustered together in cavity below leaf-scar........ ................................................ **Locust** *(Robinia)* **p.522**

59. Bud-scale one, large cap-like, terminal bud absent. ............. .............................................. **Willow** *(Salix)* **p.384**
59. Bud-scales more than one or bud-scales absent; terminal bud present or absent ......................................... 60

60. First scale of lateral bud directly in front (i.e. facing directly out away from twig); leaf-scar covered with a light-corky layer, large inversely triangular; bundle-scars 3, often compound; pith more or less 5-pointed star-shaped. .............. **Poplar** *(Populus)* 96
60. First scale of lateral bud not directly in front ................. 61

61. Twigs branching freely the first season, the branches surpassing the main axis in length ......................................... 62
61. Twigs generally not branching the first season or if branching then branches not surpassing main axis in length .................. 63

62. Bundle-scar one; twigs greenish, spicy, mucilaginous when chewed. .................................. **Sassafras** *(Sassafras variifolium)* **p.476**
62. Bundle-scars 3, twigs not mucilaginous. .................... **Alternate-leaved Dogwood** *(Cornus alternifolia)* under Comparisons **p.552**

63. Bundle-scars 1 or 2; leaf-scars, except on young shoots, mainly densely clustered on short, stout, wart-like branches .......... 64
63. Bundle-scars 3 or more ...................................... 65

64. Bundle-scar single; leaf-scars minute, scattered leaf-scars also present on twigs, very numerous and strongly decurrent; twigs slender; fruit a cone, generally present ........ **Larch** *(Larix)* 90
64. Bundle-scars 2; leaf-scars larger, scattered leaf-scars if present relatively far apart and not decurrent; twigs stouter; fruit a stone-fruit generally absent. .............. **Ginkgo** *(Ginkgo triloba)* **p.382**

65. Bundle-scars 3 or more in a *single* curved line ................. 69
65. Bundle-scars more than 3, variously grouped or scattered, but not in a single line ............................................ 66

66. Stipule-scars absent; terminal bud present .................... 68
66. Stipule-scars present; terminal bud present or absent ......... 67

67. 2-3 bud-scales visible; bundle-scars not projecting; terminal bud present or generally absent. **Chestnut** *(Castanea dentata)* **p.430**
67. 4 or more bud-scales visible; bundle-scars projecting; terminal bud absent. ............................... **Mulberry** *(Morus)* 140

68. Buds large; twigs without resinous juice; fruit a nut; a tree. .... ............................................. **Hickory** *(Carya)* 101
68. Buds small; twigs with resinous juice; fruit a small white drupe; a shrub growing in swamps. **Poison Sumach** *(Rhus Vernix)* **p.528**

69. Bundle-scars 3 ............................................. 74
69. Bundle-scars 4 or more ..................................... 70

70. Terminal bud absent, but leaving a terminal scar on twig ..... 72
70. Terminal bud present ...................................... 71

71. Lateral buds mostly large, twig without resinous juice; fruit red, berry-like; a small tree .............. **Mountain Ash** *(Pyrus)* **p.488**

71. Lateral buds small, cut twig exuding watery, resinous juice; fruit small, whitish drupes; a shrub growing in swamps. . . . . . . . . . . . . .
. . . . . . . . . . . . . . . . . . . . . . . . . . . . . **Poison Sumach** (*Rhus Vernix*) **p.528**

72. Leaf-scars deeply V-shaped, almost entirely surrounding the buds 73
72. Leaf-scars, inversely triangular to heart-shaped, large, not more than half surrounding the bud; twigs stout; pith chocolate-brown.
. . . . . . . . . . . . . . . . . . . . . . . . . . . . **Ailanthus** (*Ailanthus glandulosa*)**p.524**

73. Pith yellowish-brown; twigs stout, exuding a milky juice when cut . . . . . . . . . . . . . . . . . . . . . . . . . . . . . . . . . . . . .**Sumach** (*Rhus*) 152
73. Pith whitish; twigs slender, without milky juice. . . . . . . . . . . . . . .
. . . . . . . . . . . . . . . . . . . . . . . . . **Yellow Wood** (*Cladrastis lutea*) **p.520**

74. Terminal buds on rapidly grown shoots absent, but leaving a terminal scar . . . . . . . . . . . . . . . . . . . . . . . . . . . . . . . . . . . . . . . . 83
74. Terminal buds present . . . . . . . . . . . . . . . . . . . . . . . . . . . . . . . . 75

75. Lateral buds flattened, appressed, about as broad as long . . . . . . 76
75. Lateral buds not distinctly flattened and appressed, mostly longer than broad . . . . . . . . . . . . . . . . . . . . . . . . . . . . . . . . . . . . . . . . 78

76. Terminal bud large, generally 12 mm. or more long; some of the lateral buds generally long, nearly equalling terminal bud; leaf-scars raised on dark red, polished ridges of the bark. . . . . . . . . . .
. . . . . . . . . . . . . . . . . . . . . . . . . . . . **Mountain Ash** (*Pyrus*) **p.488**
76. Terminal bud smaller, generally under 8 mm. long; all lateral buds small; leaf-scars not on specially colored ridges of the bark 77

77. Tree with bushy habit of growth; twigs with characteristic licorice-like taste, generally reddish-brown, more or less pale-woolly at least toward apex; lateral buds blunt, more or less pale-woolly. . . .
. . . . . . . . . . . . . . . . . . . . . . . . . . . . . . . . . . . . **Apple** (*Pyrus Malus*) **p.486**
77. Tree with upright habit of growth; twigs without characteristic taste, generally yellowish-green and generally smooth; lateral buds sharp-pointed, smooth or sometimes slightly downy. . . . . . . . . . . . . .
. . . . . . . . . . . . . . . . . . . . . . . . . . . . **Pear** (*Pyrus ccmmunis*) **p.484**

78. Buds spherical or nearly so, seldom pointed; bud-scales thick, shining; leaf-scars narrow; twigs more or less zigzag, branches generally thorny; fruit a small pome; small trees or shrubs. . . . . . .
. . . . . . . . . . . . . . . . . . . . . . . . . . . . **Hawthorn** (*Crataegus*) **p.494**
78. Buds not spherical; bud-scales thinner . . . . . . . . . . . . . . . . . . . . . 79

79. Leaf-scars narrow crescent-shaped, several times as broad as high . . . . . . . . . . . . . . . . . . . . . . . . . . . . . . . . . . . . . . . . . . . . . . 80
79. Leaf-scars semicircular to broadly crescent-shaped, seldom as much as 3 times as broad as high . . . . . . . . . . . . . . . . . . . . . . . . . . . . . 81

80. Buds long, narrow, elliptical, 3-4 times as long as wide. . . . . . . . . .
. . . . . . . . . . . . . . . . . . . . . . . . . . **Shad Bush** (*Amelanchier canadensis*)**p.492**
80. Buds conical, stout. . . . . . . . . . . . . . **Pear** (*Pyrus communis*) **p.484**

81. Twigs densely speckled with very minute pale dots, brightly colored, generally green-yellow below and more or less reddish above and highly polished; buds generally densely downy at least toward apex; collateral buds usually present. . . . . . . . . . . . . . . . . . . .
. . . . . . . . . . . . . . . . . . . . . . . . . . . . **Peach** (*Prunus Persica*) **p.512**
81. Twigs not densely speckled with minute dots; buds not densely downy, collateral buds generally not present . . . . . . . . . . . . . . . . . 82

82. Twigs without bitter taste; branchlets generally becoming corky-ridged; bud-scales downy-margined; leaf-scars large with conspicuous bundle-scars; fruit a spherical bur-like head generally present in winter . . . . . . **Sweet Gum** (*Liquidambar Styraciflua*) **p.480**
82. Twigs with bitter taste often resembling bitter almonds; branches without corky ridges; bud-scales not downy-margined; fruit a drupe. . . . . . . . . . . . . . . . . . . . . . . . . . . . . **Cherry or Plum** (*Prunus*) 144

83. Buds spherical or nearly so; bud-scales thick, shining; twigs more or less zigzag, often thorny; fruit a small pome. . . . . . . . . . . . . . . .
. . . . . . . . . . . . . . . . . . . . . . . . . . . . . . . **Hawthorn** (*Crataegus*)**p.494**
83. Buds not spherical, longer than broad . . . . . . . . . . . . . . . . . . . . . . 84
84. Twigs generally gray-woolly toward apex; buds blunt, brown-hairy at tip; stipule-scars at the sides of leaf-scar. . . . . . . . . . . . . . .
. . . . . . . . . . . . . . . . . . . . . . . . . . . . **Quince** (*Cydonia vulgaris*)**p.490**

84. Twigs smooth or downy but not woolly; buds pointed, generally smooth or somewhat downy; stipule-scars more or less behind leaf-scar. ................................... **Plum** *(Prunus)* 150

# THE PINES
## Pinus.

Needle-shaped leaves in many small clusters of 5 or less, each cluster surrounded by a persistent or deciduous sheath and borne on a rudimentary branch which is subtended by a scale-like primary leaf; fruit a cone with woody scales, maturing at the end of the second or third season; seeds winged. The position of the resin-ducts in the leaves is a distinctive character of some value and may be observed if a thin cross section is made with a sharp knife and viewed toward the light with a hand-lens. Twig photographs are about ¼ natural size.

85. 5 needles in a cluster. ............. **White Pine** *(Pinus Strobus)* p.344
85. Less than 5 needles in a cluster ............................... 86

86. 3 needles in a cluster. ............. **Pitch Pine** *(Pinus rigida)* p.346
86. 2 needles in a cluster ....................................... 87

87. Needles 3-6 in. long, cones at right angles to branch ........... 88
87. Needles ½-3½ in. long, cones pointing either backward or forward ...................................................... 89

88. Twigs reddish-brown, leaves slender and flexible, resin-ducts peripheral; native species. .............. **Red Pine** *(Pinus resinosa)* p.350
88. Twigs yellowish-brown, leaves thicker and stiff, resin-ducts between periphery and bundle; European species....................... .................. **Austrian Pine** *(Pinus Laricio,* var. *austriaca)* p.352

89. Cones pointing forward, leaves ½-1½ in. long, dark yellowish-green, resin-ducts between periphery and bundle; native species. ............................... **Jack Pine** *(Pinus Banksiana)* p.348
89. Cones pointing backward, leaves 1½-3½ in. long, bluish-green, resin-ducts peripheral; European species. ...................... ............................... **Scotch Pine** *(Pinus sylvestris)* p.354

# THE LARCHES
## Larix.

Pyramidal deciduous-leaved cone-bearing trees; twigs with resinous taste; rapidly-grown shoots with numerous scattered strongly decurrent leaf-scars with single bundle-scars; short stout wart-like branches with densely clustered leaf-scars abundant.

90. Cones ½-¾ inch long with few scales; twigs pale reddish-brown; a native tree growing in swamps. ............................... ............................ **American Larch** *(Larix laricina)* p.356
90. Cones 1 inch or more long with many scales; twigs yellowish, stouter; a European tree ....................................... .........**European Larch** *(Larix decidua)* under Comparisons p.356

# THE SPRUCES
## Picea.

Evergreen pyramidal trees with scaly bark, alternate scattered, 4-angled leaves without proper leaf-stalks but perched on persistent decurrent projections from the bark and ovate to cylindrical pendant cones which fall off the tree entire. The Spruces are distinguished from the Balsam Fir by the 4-sided scattered leaves, the projecting leaf-scars and the scaly bark. Twig photographs are about ⅛ natural size.

91. Twigs hairy ...................................................... 92
91. Twigs smooth or nearly so, cones cylindrical .................. 94

92. Cones cylindrical, more than 3 inches long; cultivated species. .... .................................. **Norway Spruce** *(Picea Abies)* p.366
92. Cones ovate to oblong, less than 3 inches long ................ 93

93. Leaves dark yellowish green, ½-¾ inch long. Cones ovate-oblong 1¼-2 inches long; a tree growing on uplands, rarely in wet places, reaching 40 ft. or more in height. .... **Red Spruce** *(Picea rubra)* p.360

93. Leaves bluish green, ¼-½ inch long, cones ovate, ½-1½ inches long, persistent on tree for more than a year; a tree growing chiefly in swamps or lowlands, generally under 30 ft. in height, sometimes fruiting when less than 5 ft. high. .................... ............................. **Black Spruce** *(Picea mariana)* **p.362**

94. Leaves green, cones 4-7 inches long, cultivated species. .......... .............................. **Norway Spruce** *(Picea Abies)* **p.366**
94. Leaves bluish green or silvery ................................ 95

95. Cones 2½-4 inches long, cone scales distinctly longer than broad with narrowed, ragged, blunt apex; cultivated western species. .... .............................**Blue Spruce** *(Picea Menziesii)* **p.364**
95. Cones 1½-2 inches long, cone scales rounded, not ragged; leaves generally with unpleasant odor, native in northern New England but cultivated further south. **White Spruce** *(Picea canadensis)* **p.358**

# THE POPLARS
## Populus.

Rapidly growing trees generally with erect more or less continuous trunk forming generally distinct whorls of branches at top of each year's growth by which the age of the tree may be estimated: branchlets brittle easily separating at point of attachment; young bark smooth, generally light colored; pith, 5-pointed star-shaped, upon drying generally turning brown or black; leaf-scars large, 3-lobed, inverted triangular, covered with a light colored corky layer; stipule-scars generally distinct, narrow; bundle-scars 3, simple or compound in 3 groups; buds with the first scale anterior (facing outward), the first pair of scales small and opposite; scale-scars marking annual growth persisting for several years; seeds downy, produced from catkins in spring, the tree often spreading widely by formation of root suckers. The Poplars resemble the Willows but are easily distinguished by the numerous scales to the bud. In addition to the native species here described a rare form, the Downy Poplar. [*Populus heterophylla* L.] occurs locally in swamps in southern New England.

96. Twigs of past season more or less slender, covered at least at apex with white cottony felt which may be readily rubbed off exposing the greenish bark below. ...... **Silver Poplar** *(Populus alba)* **p.386**
96. Twigs smooth, not at all covered with white felt .............. 97

97. Twigs yellowish ............................................... 98
97. Twigs not yellowish (generally reddish-brown). .............. 99

98. Lateral buds for the most part divergent, large, about 10 mm. or more in length, tree with more or less pyramidal head, but not narrowly spire-shaped. .... **Carolina Poplar** *(Populus deltoides)* **p.394**
:98. Lateral buds for the most part appressed, smaller, generally under 8 mm. long, tree narrowly spire-shaped. ........................ ................. **Lombardy Poplar** *(Populus nigra,* var. *italica)* **p.396**

99. Buds more or less pale dusty-downy. .......................... ............... **Large-toothed Aspen** *(Populus grandidentata)* **p.390**
99. Buds not downy .........................................100

100. Buds large, over 15 mm. long, covered with fragrant sticky gum. ...................... **Balsam Poplar** *(Populus balsamifera)* **p.392**
100. Buds small, under 10 mm. long, shiny, slightly sticky but not fragrant. .......... **Small-toothed Aspen** *(Populus tremuloides)* **p.388**

# THE HICKORIES
## Carya.

Trees with smooth gray tough bark in young trees, becoming rough-ened with age; twigs in the main stout, tough, flexible, but with difficulty broken, dark, sharply outlined against the sky; buds more or less naked to evidently scaly, frequently superposed, the lateral some-times enclosed in a sac soon splitting at the top and often stalked; leaf-scars alternate, more than 2-ranked, large, conspicuous, more or less 3-lobed inversely triangular; bundle-scars conspicuous, more than 3, irregularly scattered or collected in 3 more or less regular groups, rarely in a straight line; pith not chambered except at nodes, sometimes some-what star-shaped in cross section; lenticels oblong, conspicuous; fruit an unsculptured nut, inclosed in a husk which splits into four valves at least at the apex.

101.   Buds conspicuously bright yellow with minute glandular dots;
        terminal buds elongated, flattened; bud-scales 4-6, valvate in pairs.
        ............................... **Bitternut** *(Carya cordiformis)* **p.408**
101.   Buds not conspicuously bright yellow-dotted; terminal buds ovate;
        bud-scales, 10 or more, overlapping, or the outermost on lateral
        buds usually forming a closed sac soon splitting from the top;
        inner scales hairy. ....................................... 102

102.   Buds small, terminal buds 5-10 mm. long, their outer darker scales
        generally somewhat glandular dotted, but not conspicuously
        yellow; outer scales often falling and exposing downy scales
        beneath; twigs smooth, comparatively slender; bark not at all or
        but slightly shaggy. .................. **Pignut** *(Carya glabra)* **p.406**
102.   Buds large, the terminal buds 8-15 mm. long, ovate, nearly or
        quite glandless; twigs stout, often downy toward tip ........ 103

103.   Bark not shaggy; terminal buds broadly ovate to spherical, outer
        scales soon falling off entire, exposing pale yellowish-gray silky
        scales beneath. ..................... **Mockernut** *(Carya alba)* **p.404**
103.   Bark distinctly shaggy; terminal buds elongated ovate, outer
        scales persisting through winter but shagging off in pieces from
        their apex downward. ...... **Shag-bark Hickory** *(Carya ovata)* **p.402**

# THE BIRCHES
## Betula.

Bark smooth, in some species peeling into papery layers but not flaky;
lenticels becoming conspicuously horizontally elongated with age;
leaf-scars alternate, 2-ranked, semi-oval to crescent-shaped; stipule-
scars narrow, often inconspicuous; bundle-scars 3 rather inconspicuous;
fruit a flat seed-like body borne in catkins, staminate catkins generally
present on the tree in winter.

104.   Bark close, not easily separated into thin papery layers ..... 105
104.   Bark easily separated into thin papery layers and generally peel-
        ing spontaneously. ......................................... 106

105.   Bark dark reddish brown; twigs with strong wintergreen taste.
        ................................. **Black Birch** *(Betula lenta)* **p.414**
105.   Bark chalky-white; twigs without wintergreen taste, generally
        roughened with resinous dots.   **Gray Birch** *(Betula populifolia)* **p.420**

106.   Outer layers of bark chalky-white ........................ 107
106.   Outer layers of bark not chalky-white .................... 108

107.   Native species. ...... **Paper Birch** *(Betula alba,* var. *papyrifera)* **p.422**
107.   European species. ...... **European White Birch** *(Betula alba)* **p.424**

108.   Bark reddish-brown to light pink; rare and local in New Hamp-
        shire and Massachusetts, occasionally cultivated. ................
        ............................... **Red Birch** *(Betula nigra)* **p.418**
108.   Bark dirty-yellow; common throughout New England. .........
        ................................ **Yellow Birch** *(Betula lutea)* **p.416**

# THE OAKS
## Quercus.

The Oaks form a large genus, of which 52 are North American. Of
these, 12 are native to New England. Buds clustered at ends of twigs,
more or less 5-sided pyramidal, covered with 5 rows of closely overlapping brownish scales. Leaf-scars concave to rounded above, rounded
at base, generally broader than high and raised with a ridge more or
less well marked, decurrent from lower edge, the ridges from the 5
ranks of leaf-scars causing twig to be more or less 5-angled especially
when dried. Bundle-scars irregularly scattered, inconspicuous. Stipule-
scars inconspicuous. Pith of cut twig 5-pointed, star-shaped. Cross-
section of branch or trunk showing layers of large, porous spring wood
alternating with dense layers of summer wood. Medullary rays of wood
very prominent, showing as radial lines in cross section of a log,
also generally showing prominently, especially through a hand-lens, on
cut end of stout branchlet of several years growth. Fruit an acorn
inclosed in a scaly cup. Dead leaves often persistent on the tree
during winter.

## Key to Oaks based upon fruiting material.

109. Fruit maturing in autumn of second year, ripe acorns therefore borne upon parts of twig two years old; immature acorns to be found in winter on twigs of the past season's growth; shell of nut hairy inside; abortive ovules at the top of the nut; scales of acorn-cup broad and thin; lobes of leaves bristle-pointed. . . . . . .
. . . . . . . . . . . . . . . . . . . . . . . . . . . . . . . . . . . . . . . **Black Oaks** 110

109. Fruit maturing in one year, ripe acorns therefore borne upon past seasons growth; no immature acorns to be found upon twigs in winter; shell of nut smooth inside; abortive ovules at base of nut; lower scales at least of acorn cup more or less thickened at base giving a knobby appearance to surface of cup; scales more or less densely woolly; kernel commonly sweetish; lobes of leaves not bristle-pointed; bark flaky except in Chestnut Oak. . . . . . . . . . . .
. . . . . . . . . . . . . . . . . . . . . . . . . . . . . . . . . . . . . . **White Oaks** 114

110. Cup of acorn shallow saucer-shaped . . . . . . . . . . . . . . . . . . . . . . . . . 111
110. Cup top-shaped . . . . . . . . . . . . . . . . . . . . . . . . . . . . . . . . . . . . . . . . . 112

111. Cup thin, 15 mm. or less wide; buds 4 mm. or less long. . . . . . . . . . .
. . . . . . . . . . . . . . . . . . . . . . . . . . . **Pin Oak** *(Quercus palustris)* **p.448**
111. Cup thick, 20 mm. or more wide; buds over 4 mm. long. . . . . . . . . . .
. . . . . . . . . . . . . . . . . . . . . . . . . . . . **Red Oak** *(Quercus rubra)* **p.446**

112. Buds under 4 mm. long; twigs slender; shrubs. . . . . . . . . . . . . . . . . . .
. . . . . . . . . . . . . . . . . . . . . . . . **Bear Oak** *(Quercus ilicifolia)* **p.454**
112. Buds over 4.5 mm. long; twigs rather stout; trees . . . . . . . . . . . . 113

113. Upper scales of cup loosely overlapping; buds pointed, whole surface woolly; inner bark yellow. **Black Oak** *(Quercus velutina)* **p.452**
113. Upper scales of cup closely overlapping; buds blunt, downy above middle; inner bark pale red.   **Scarlet Oak** *(Quercus coccinea)* **p.450**

114. Upper scales of cup with thread-like outgrowths forming a fringe to cup; branchlets often with corky ridges; lateral buds frequently appressed. . . . . . . . **Bur Oak** *(Quercus macrocarpa)* **p.436**
114. Cup without distinct fringe; branchlets without corky ridges; lateral buds divergent . . . . . . . . . . . . . . . . . . . . . . . . . . . . . . . . . . . . 115

115. Bark on branchlets peeling back in dark stiff-papery layers; marginal scales of cup narrow awn-pointed; acorns long-stalked.
. . . . . . . . . . . . . . . . . . . . **Swamp White Oak** *(Quercus bicolor)* **p.438**
115. Bark on branchlets not peeling back in dark stiff-papery layers; acorns sessile or short-stalked (at times long-stalked in White Oak) . . . . . . . . . . . . . . . . . . . . . . . . . . . . . . . . . . . . . . . . . . . . . . . 116

116. Buds sharp-pointed . . . . . . . . . . . . . . . . . . . . . . . . . . . . . . . . . . . . . . 117
116. Buds blunt . . . . . . . . . . . . . . . . . . . . . . . . . . . . . . . . . . . . . . . . . . . . . 118

117. Nut 20-35 mm. long; buds 4-10 mm. long; bark thick, furrowed, not flaky. . . . . . . . . . . . . . . . . . . . . **Chestnut Oak** *(Quercus Prinus)* **p.444**
117. Nut 15-20 mm. long; buds 3-6 mm. long; bark thin, flaky. . . . . . . . .
. . . . . . . . . . . . . . . . . . . . . **Chinquapin Oak** *(Quercus Muhlenbergii)* **p.440**

118. Twigs slender, generally not over 2 mm. thick; shrubs. . . . . . . . . . . .
. . . . . . . . . . . . . . . . . . **Dwarf Chinquapin Oak** *(Quercus prinoides)* **p.442**
118. Twigs relatively stout, generally over 2 mm. thick; trees . . . . 119

119. Twigs, at least in part, covered with very fine close olive-green down; buds, generally nearly hemispherical, about as broad as long; scales of cup only slightly knobby, apex of nut generally downy. . . . . . . . . . . . . . . . . . . . . . . . **Post Oak** *(Quercus stellata)* **p.434**
119. Twigs smooth; buds distinctly longer than broad, broadly ovate; scales of cup thick-knobby at base, apex of nut generally smooth.
. . . . . . . . . . . . . . . . . . . . . . . . . . . . . **White Oak** *(Quercus alba)* **p.432**

## Key to Oaks without fruit.

NOTE.   (W) after name indicates that the tree belongs to the White Oak Group.
(B) after name indicates that the tree belongs to the Black Oak Group.
Immature acorns therefore may often be found on winter twigs of species marked with (B) but not on those marked with (W).

120. Buds large, those at tip of twig 4.5 mm. or more long . . . . . . . . 121
120. Buds smaller, less than 4.5 mm. long . . . . . . . . . . . . . . . . . . . . . . . 128

121. Bark of trunk flaky .......................................... 122
121. Bark of trunk not flaky ...................................... 124

122. Lateral buds generally appressed, buds downy; older twigs often with corky ridges. ...... **Bur Oak** (W) *(Quercus macrocarpa)***p.436**
122. Lateral buds divergent, buds smooth; twigs without corky ridges .......................................................... 123

123. Buds narrow conical, pointed. .................................. ................ **Chinquapin Oak** (W) *(Quercus Muhlenbergii)***p.440**
123. Buds shorter, blunt. .......... **White Oak** (W) *(Quercus alba)***p.432**

124. Surface of buds pale-woolly. ................................. 125
124. Surface of buds not woolly. .................................. 127

125. Inner bark of trunk orange-yellow; whole surface of bud woolly; buds large, ovate-conical. **Black Oak** (B) *(Quercus velutina)* **p.452**
125. Inner bark of trunk not yellow; not more than upper half of bud woolly ...................................................... 126

126. Buds sharp-pointed; ovate, the widest part about ¼-⅓ above base; slightly or not at all woolly toward apex. ................ ................................. **Red Oak** (B) *(Quercus rubra)***p.446**
126. Buds blunt-pointed; oval-ovate, the widest part at or slightly below middle; distinctly woolly above middle. .................... ...................... **Scarlet Oak** (B) *(Quercus coccinea)* **p.450**

127. Fissures of bark separated by long *flat* ridges; buds ovate, more or less constricted at base; twigs not bitter. ..................... .............................. **Red Oak** (B) *(Quercus rubra)***p.446**
127. Fissures of bark separated by long *rounded* ridges; buds narrower, conical, seldom constricted at base; twigs more or less bitter when chewed. ................**Chestnut Oak** (W) *(Quercus Prinus)* **p.444**

128. Buds narrow, conical ........................................ 129
128. Buds short, blunt .......................................... 132

129. Bark of trunk flaky ........................................ 130
129. Bark of trunk not flaky .................................... 131

130. Buds downy, lateral buds generally appressed; older twigs often with corky ridges....... **Bur Oak** (W) *(Quercus macrocarpa)***p.436**
130. Buds smooth, lateral buds divergent, twigs without corky ridges ...............**Chinquapin Oak** (W) *(Quercus Muhlenbergii)* **p.440**

131. Twigs of past season dull, finely downy; shrubs. ................. .......................... **Bear Oak** (B) *(Quercus ilicifolia)***p.454**
131. Twigs smooth, shining; slender pin-like twigs numerous, arising at nearly a right angle with the branchlets; trees. ................. .......................... **Pin Oak** (B) *(Quercus palustris)***p.448**

132. Bark on branchlets peeling into long, dark, stiff-papery layers. .................. **Swamp White Oak** (W) *(Quercus bicolor)***p.438**
132. Bark on branchlets not peeling into long, dark, stiff-papery layers ........................................................ 133

133. Twigs slender, generally not over 2 mm. thick; shrubs ...... 134
133. Twigs stout, generally over 2 mm. thick; trees ............. 135

134. Bark of trunk smooth; young acorns generally found on winter twigs; buds more generally conical. ............................ .......................... **Bear Oak** (B) *(Quercus ilicifolia)***p.454**
134. Bark of trunk flaky; young acorns never found on winter twigs. ..............**Dwarf Chinquapin Oak** (W) *(Quercus prinoides)***p.442**

135. Lateral buds generally appressed; buds densely downy; older twigs often with corky ridges. .............................. ..........................**Bur Oak** (W) *(Quercus macrocarpa)***p.436**
135. Lateral buds divergent; buds not densely downy; twigs without corky ridges .............................................. 136

136. Twigs at least in part covered with very fine close orange-brown down; buds generally nearly hemispherical and about as broad as long. ..................... **Post Oak** (W) *(Quercus stellata)***p.434**
136. Twigs smooth; buds broadly ovate, distinctly longer than broad. ........................... **White Oak** (W) *(Quercus alba)***p.432**

# THE ELMS
## Ulmus.

Leaf-scars alternate, 2-ranked, semi-circular, small, but conspicuous, covered with a light corky layer; bundle-scars prominent, 3 to several, sunken; terminal bud absent, lateral buds medium sized with 2 ranks of over-lapping bud-scales; twigs slender; bark ridged; fruit small, flat, winged, ripening in spring.

137.  Twigs gray and rough and strongly mucilaginous; tips of buds conspicuous with long rusty hairs. **Slippery Elm** *(Ulmus fulva)***p.456**
137.  Twigs neither gray and rough nor strongly mucilaginous; buds without long rusty hairs ................................. 138

138.  Buds chestnut brown; bud-scales with darker margins; bark ridged; native species ......................................... 139
138.  Buds smoky brown to almost black; bud-scales nearly uniform in color, bark firmer, roughened into dark oblong blocks; trunk mostly continuous into crown with stout limbs arising at a broad angle; head, "Oak-like;" European species. ....................
..........................  **English Elm** *(Ulmus campestris)* **p.458**

139.  Twigs often with corky ridges; trunk generally continuous into crown with stiff dependent lower branches; head narrow, "Hickory-like." ..........................  **Cork Elm** *(Ulmus racemosa)***p.462**
139.  Twigs without corky ridges; trunk dividing into several limbs, spreading gradually upward and gracefully recurving; head broad, "Elm like." ..................  **White Elm** *(Ulmus americana)* **p.460**

# THE MULBERRIES
## Morus.

Leaf-scars alternate, 2-ranked, nearly circular; stipule-scars narrow; bundle-scars projecting in a closed ring or irregularly scattered; terminal bud absent; bud-scales 2-ranked; twigs with milky juice.

140.  Buds about as long as broad, more or less flattened and appressed, generally under 4 mm. long; bud-scales reddish brown without darker margins. ............  **White Mulberry** *(Morus alba)* **p.468**
140.  Buds longer than broad, not at all or but slightly flattened, divergent, generally over 5 mm. long; bud-scales greenish brown with darker margins. ................  **Red Mulberry** *(Morus rubra)***p.466**

# THE MAGNOLIAS
## Magnolia.

Terminal bud much larger than lateral buds; bud-scales valvate, united in pairs to form a cap, corresponding to stipules, each pair enclosing in succession an erect folded leaf connected with the next inner pair of scales; the unmatured leaf which belongs to the outer pair of stipular scales falling off in autumn and leaving a scar on side of bud with a decurrent ridge below, representing its leaf stalk; stipule-scar narrow, encircling the twig; leaf-scars alternate, more than 2-ranked, broad, oval to narrow crescent-shaped, bundle-scars numerous, irregularly scattered or in a double row; twigs aromatic; fruit a cone made up of numerous follicles which split open in the autumn and let out the large flattish seeds.

141.  Buds large 25-50 mm. long, twigs stout, leaf-scars large ...... 142
141.  Buds small 10-20 mm. long; twigs slender; leaf-scars small ... 143

142.  Buds densely pale-downy; twigs light yellowish to bluish-green, more or less downy, fruit nearly spherical. **Large-leaved Magnolia,** Large-leaved Cucumber Tree, Large-leaved Umbrella Tree......
.........  *(Magnolia macrophylla* Michx.) under Comparisons **p.470**
142.  Buds smooth; twigs brown; fruit elongated. ....................
..........................  **Umbrella Tree** *(Magnolia tripetala)***p.472**

143.  Twigs brown; leaf-scars narrow, crescent to U-shaped; buds blunt, densely downy; bark flaky; a tree; in New England found only in cultivation. .............**Cucumber Tree** *(Magnolia acuminata)***p.470**

143.  Twigs and buds bright green; leaf-scars oval to broadly crescent-
      shaped; buds pointed, with long, silky hairs, often nearly smooth;
      pith with more or less distinct transverse woody partitions in the
      ground mass; bark smooth; in New England usually a shrub,
      growing wild in deep swamps in Eastern Massachusetts, also
      extensively cultivated.  **Sweet Bay,** Swamp Bay, Laurel Magnolia,
      Beaver Tree.  *(Magnolia virginiana* L.; M. *glauca* L.) ..............
      ...................................... under Comparisons **p.470**

# THE CHERRIES, PLUMS AND PEACH
## Prunus.

Leaf-scars alternate, more than 2-ranked; bundle-scars 3; stipule-scars
present, inconspicuous, or absent; buds with scales overlapping in several rows; terminal bud present or absent; fruit a drupe.

144.  Terminal bud present ........................................ 145
144.  Terminal bud absent.  (Plums) ........................... 150

145.  Twigs densely speckled with very minute pale dots, brightly
      colored, generally green-yellow below and more or less reddish
      above and highly polished; buds generally densely downy at least
      toward apex; collateral buds usually present. ...................
      ................................. **Peach.** *(Prunus Persica)* **p.512**
145.  Twigs not densely speckled with very minute dots; buds not
      densely downy; collateral buds absent (occasionally present in
      Wild Red Cherry) ........................................ 146

146.  Buds clustered at tips of all shoots; twigs under 2.5 mm. thick.
      .................... **Wild Red Cherry.** *(Prunus pennsylvanica)* **p.500**
146.  Buds not clustered, or clustered only on short fruit spurs; twigs
      over 2.5 mm. thick ........................................ 147

147.  Short stout slow-growing fruit spurs present with buds clustered
      at their tips; European species .......................... 148
147.  Short fruit spurs absent; native species .................... 149

148.  Habit erect, generally with a central leader. ..................
      ..........................**Sweet Cherry** *(Prunus avium)* **p.502**
148.  Habit spreading, without central leader; buds smaller; twigs more
      slender. .................... **Sour Cherry** *(Prunus Cerasus)* **p.504**

149.  Buds generally over 5 mm. long; bud-scales gray-margined; bark
      smooth; generally only a shrub. ...........................
      .......................... **Choke Cherry** *(Prunus virginiana)* **p.498**
149.  Buds generally under 5 mm. long; bud-scales uniform in color;
      bark becoming rough-scaly; a small to large tree. .............
      ....................... **Wild Black Cherry** *(Prunus serotina)* **p.496**

150.  Native species, growing wild ............................. 151
150.  Cultivated species.  Varieties chiefly of the American, European,
      ............................... or Japanese type of Plum.  **p.508**

151.  Buds generally under 4 mm. long. .............................
      .................... **American Wild Plum** *(Prunus americana)* **p.508**
151.  Buds generally over 4 mm. long. **Canada Plum** *(Prunus nigra)* **p.506**

# THE SUMACHS
## Rhus.

Shrubs or small trees with pithy twigs and milky or watery juice;
leaf-scars alternate, more than 2-ranked; bundle-scars numerous scattered or in a single curved line; stipule-scars absent; terminal bud
present or absent; fruit a small drupe borne on erect or drooping
clusters.

152.  Terminal bud present; fruit smooth white in loose drooping clus-
      ters. ...................... **Poison Sumach** *(Rhus Vernix)* **p.528**
152.  Terminal bud absent; fruit more or less hairy, red, in dense erect
      clusters ..................... ........................... 153

153.    Leaf-scars narrow, V-shaped, nearly encircling the buds; cut twig
        showing milky juice ........................................ 154
153.    Leaf-scars broader; inversely triangular to broadly crescent-
        shaped; twig with watery juice and resinous taste. ..............
        ........... Dwarf Sumach *(Rhus copallina)* under Comparisons **p.526**

154.    Twigs densely hairy. ....... Staghorn Sumach *(Rhus typhina)* **p.526**
154.    Twigs smooth. ................................................
        .......... Smooth Sumach *(Rhus glabra)* under Comparisons **p.526**

## THE MAPLES
### Acer.

Leaf-scars opposite, narrow U or V-shaped; bundle-scars conspicuous, typically 3, equidistant, though sometimes each of these becomes compounded; fruit winged, in pairs.

155.    Adjacent edges of leaf-scars meeting and prolonged upward into
        a conspicuous tooth ...................................... 156
155.    Adjacent edges not meeting, therefore not forming a tooth .... 158

156.    Buds white-downy, collateral buds generally present, twigs gener-
        ally with a bloom. .............. Box Elder *(Acer Negundo)* **p.546**
156.    Buds smooth, collateral buds never present, twigs without
        bloom ................................................... 157

157.    Buds with only one pair of scales visible, older branchlets white-
        streaked. .............. Striped Maple *(Acer pennsylvanicum)* **p.532**
157.    Buds with several pairs of scales visible, branchlets not white-
        streaked. ................. Norway Maple *(Acer platanoides)* **p.542**

158.    Outer single pair of bud-scales equalling the bud in length, their
        edges meeting and enclosing the bud, therefore generally only one
        pair of scales visible: pith brown; shrubs or at the most small
        trees. ................................................... 159
158.    Outer pair of scales shorter than bud, their edges not meeting,
        therefore several pairs of scales visible; trees ............... 160

159.    Buds and twigs stout, smooth; young bark with longitudinal white
        lines. .................. Striped Maple *(Acer pennsylvanicum)* **p.532**
159.    Buds and twigs more slender, both buds and twigs white-downy,
        white lines absent from bark. Mountain Maple *(Acer spicatum)* **p.534**

160.    Buds brown, narrow, sharp-pointed, generally 4-8 pairs of closely
        over-lapping scales visible, collateral buds absent. ..............
        ........................... Sugar Maple *(Acer saccharum)* **p.536**
160.    Buds red or green, broader, blunt-pointed, fewer scales visible 161

161.    Terminal buds small, red, generally under 5 mm. long and not
        distinctly larger than lateral buds; collateral buds generally
        present; pith pink; native trees ............................ 162
161.    Terminal buds large, stout, generally over 5 mm. long and gener-
        ally distinctly larger than lateral buds; collateral buds never
        present; European trees ................................... 163

162.    Broken twigs with rank odor, bark falling away in large, thin
        flakes on old trees. .......... Silver Maple *(Acer saccharinum)* **p.538**
162.    Broken twigs without rank odor, bark rough on old trees but gen-
        erally not flaking in large thin scales..........................
        ................................ Red Maple *(Acer rubrum)* **p.540**

163.    Buds red, inner scales covered with rusty wool; adjacent edges of
        leaf-scars meeting and forming a slight projection; bark close-
        ridged, not flaky. ............ Norway Maple *(Acer platanoides)* **p.542**
163.    Buds green, inner scales white-woolly, edges of leaf-scars not
        meeting; bark flaking off in squarish scales. ....................
        .................... Sycamore Maple *(Acer Pseudo-Platanus)* **p.544**

# THE ASHES
## Fraxinus.

Leaf-scars opposite, large, conspicuous, bundle-scars minute, forming
a curved line often more or less confluent; buds stout, scurfy, brown or
black with ovate bud-scales opposite in pairs; twigs stout and brittle;
fruit winged.

164. Leaf-scars deeply concave on upper margin. .....................
........................... **White Ash** *(Fraxinus americana)* **p.556**
164. Leaf-scars not deeply concave on upper margin, semicircular to
shield-shaped ............................................... 165

165. Bark soft-scaly; buds generally black; last pair of leaf-scars
generally some distance below end of twig giving a stalked-like
appearance to the terminal bud. ................................
............................. **Black Ash** *(Fraxinus nigra)* **p.560**
165. Bark ridged, not soft-scaly ................................. 166

166. Buds black; trees found only in cultivation. ...................
........**European Ash** *(Fraxinus excelsior)* under Comparisons **p.558**
166. Buds dark brown; trees native ........................... 167

167. Twigs downy. ............ **Red Ash** *(Fraxinus pennsylvanica)* **p.558**
167. Twigs smooth. **Green Ash** *(Fraxinus pennsylvanica,* var. *lanceolata)*
........................................under Comparisons **p.558**

# WHITE PINE
## Soft Pine, Weymouth Pine.
### Pinus Strobus L.

**HABIT**—The tallest conifer of New England, 50-80 ft. high with a trunk diameter of 2-4 ft., in virgin forests of northern New England trees have been found over 150 ft. in height with a trunk diameter of 7 ft.; trunk straight, tapering gradually, normally continuous into the crown, with wide-spreading, horizontal limbs, in young trees generally arising in whorls of five, and with secondary branches in the same plane, producing characteristic horizontal layers; head broadly conical, spray delicate, bluish-green.

**BARK**—On young trunks and branches, smooth, greenish-brown, becoming fissured into comparatively shallow, broad, flat-topped, longitudinal ridges.

**TWIGS**—Slender, light brown smooth or slightly hairy, resinous.

**LEAVES**—In clusters of 5, without sheaths in winter, soft, bluish-green, flexible, 3-5 inches long, slender, 3-sided. MICROSCOPIC SECTION—showing a single fibro-vascular bundle, 1 or 2 peripheral resin-ducts, a single layer of strengthening cells only beneath the epidermis, stomata only on the two inner sides.

**BUDS**—Ovate to oblong, about 1 cm. long, sharp-pointed, bud-scales long, pointed, yellowish-brown.

**FRUIT**—Cones, 4-10 inches long, stalked, drooping, cylindrical and more or less curved. SCALES—thin, not thickened at apex and without spines. Seeds winged.

**COMPARISONS**—The White Pine is the only Pine of New England that has 5 needles in a cluster. The layered arrangement of its secondary branches enables it to be recognized as far as it can be seen. Young trees can be further distinguished from the Pitch or Red Pines by the greater delicacy and bluer color of the leafage. Frequently the terminal bud of the central leader is killed by an insect, the Pine Weevil, thus interrupting the growth and causing one or more of the young lateral branches to grow erect to take its place. Gnarled old specimens which have many times in their lifetime suffered these insect injuries may present a rather picturesque appearance but are of little value for lumber. The tree photographed perhaps had its leader killed when young but despite the three erect limbs which have taken the place of the single leader it still shows the outline characteristic of the species.

**DISTRIBUTION**—In fertile soils; moist woodlands or dry uplands; often planted for ornament, wind-breaks and for reforestation. New-foundland and Nova Scotia, through Quebec and Ontario to Lake Winnipeg; south along the mountains to Georgia, ascending to 2,500 feet in the Adirondacks and to 4,300 feet in North Carolina; west to Minnesota and Iowa.

IN NEW ENGLAND—Common, from the vicinity of the sea coast to altitudes of 2,500 feet, forming extensive forests.

IN CONNECTICUT—Occasional near the coast becoming frequent northward and common in northeastern Connecticut.

**WOOD**—Light, not strong, straight-grained, easily worked, light brown often slightly tinged with red, largely manufactured into lumber, shingles and lathes, used in construction, for cabinet-making, the interior finish of buildings, woodenware, matches and the masts of vessels.

WHITE PINE

# PITCH PINE
## Hard Pine, Yellow Pine.
### Pinus rigida Mill.

**HABIT**—Generally a low tree 30-50 ft. in height with a trunk diameter of 1-2 ft. occasionally 70-80 ft. in height with trunk diameter of 2-4 ft.; trunk more or less tapering, branches thick, gnarled, often drooping, forming an open pyramidal or oblong head; foliage in coarse rigid, yellowish-green tufts. Dead branches and old persistent cones are frequent and the tree has generally a decidedly scraggly appearance.

**BARK**—On young trunks and branches rough, broken into reddish brown scales, with age becoming deeply furrowed into broad flat-topped ridges separating on the surface into rather loose dark reddish-brown scales. Clusters of leaves and short branches are not infrequently formed directly from the old trunk (see in photograph above the tape measure.)

**TWIGS**—Stout, light brown, not downy, roughened especially after the fall of the leaves by the decurrent bases of scales subtending the leaf-clusters.

**LEAVES**—In clusters of 3, with persistent sheaths, yellowish-green, 2-5 inches long, stout, stiff, spreading, with pointed tips. MICROSCOPIC SECTION—3-sided, showing 2 fibro-vascular bundles, resin-ducts located intermediate between bundles and periphery, strengthening cells beneath the epidermis in patches several layers thick, generally surrounding the resin-ducts and at one side of the vascular bundles, stomata on all three sides.

**BUDS**—Cylindrical to ovate, pointed, resin-coated, scales reddish-brown.

**FRUIT**—Cones 1½-4 inches long, without stalks, ovate becoming more or less spherical when opened, borne laterally, singly or in clusters at about a right angle to the twig, often remaining on the branches for ten or a dozen years and frequently found on trees only a few feet high. SCALES—thickened at tip and with a stiff recurved prickle.

**COMPARISONS**—The Pitch Pine is the only native Pine in New England that has three needles in a cluster. Its ragged appearance with frequent dead branches, persistent cones, and yellowish-green stiff foliage renders it easily distinguished from the White and Red Pines without examination of the needles.

**DISTRIBUTION**—Most common in dry, sterile soils, occasional in swamps. New Brunswick to Lake Ontario; south to Virginia and along the mountains to northern Georgia; west to western New York, Ohio, Kentucky, and Tennessee.

IN NEW ENGLAND—Maine—mostly in the southwestern section near the seacoast; as far north as Chesterville, Franklin county; scarcely more than a shrub near its northern limits; New Hampshire—most common along the Merrimac valley to the White Mountains and up the Connecticut valley to the mouth of the Passumpsic, reaching an altitude of 1,000 feet above the sea level; Vermont—common in the northern Champlain valley, less frequent in the Connecticut valley; common in the other New England states, often forming large tracts of woodland, sometimes exclusively occupying extensive areas.

IN CONNECTICUT—Rare or local in Litchfield county, frequent elsewhere.

**WOOD**—Light, soft, not strong, brittle, coarse-grained, very durable, light brown or red, with thick yellow or often white sapwood; largely used for fuel and in the manufacture of charcoal; occasionally sawed into lumber.

PITCH PINE

# JACK PINE
## Northern Scrub Pine, Gray Pine, Spruce Pine.
### Pinus Banksiana Lamb.
#### *P. divaricata* auth.

**HABIT**—Usually a low tree 15-30 ft. in height with a trunk diameter of 6-8 inches, under favorable conditions becoming 50-60 ft. high with a trunk diameter of 10-15 inches; with large spreading branches forming an open symmetrical head resembling somewhat the Spruce in regularity of outline or on exposed windy situations and in poor soil becoming stunted with gnarled stem and irregular scraggly distorted head.

**BARK**—Dark reddish-brown with irregular rounded ridges roughened with close scales.

**TWIGS**—Rather slender, reddish to purplish brown, not downy, roughened by scales subtending leaf-clusters.

**LEAVES**—In clusters of 2, with short persistent sheaths, dark yellowish-green, ½-1½ inches long, stout, stiff, generally curved and twisted, flattened or concave on one side, rounded on the other, tip pointed. MICROSCOPIC SECTION—showing 2 widely separated fibro-vascular bundles, resin-ducts located intermediate between bundles and periphery, a single layer of strengthening cells around the resin-ducts and one or more layers beneath the epidermis.

**BUDS**—Ovate, short-pointed, coated more or less thickly with resin.

**FRUIT**—Cones 1-2 inches long, without stalks, conic-oblong usually curved and pointing forward, appearing between or sometimes at the whorls of lateral branches, more or less distorted, remaining closed for several years, persisting on the tree often for a dozen years. SCALES—in young cones with an incurved prickle, when mature thickened at the apex without spines or prickles.

**COMPARISONS**—The short yellowish-green needles of the Jack Pine will distinguish this species from other Pines. The longest needles sometimes approach in size short needles of the Scotch Pine, but those of the Scotch Pine are of a bluish-green color and moreover their cones point backward instead of forward as in the Jack Pine.

**DISTRIBUTION**—Sterile, sandy soil; lowlands, boggy plains, rocky slopes. Nova Scotia, northwesterly to the Athabasca river, and northerly down the Mackenzie to the Arctic circle; west through northern New York, northern Illinois, and Michigan to Minnesota.

IN NEW ENGLAND—Maine—Traveller Mountain and Grand Lake; Beal's Island on Washington county coast, Harrington, Orland, and Cape Rosier; Schoodic peninsula in Gouldsboro, a forest 30 ft. high; Flagstaff; east branch of Penobscot; the Forks; Lake Umbagog; New Hampshire—around the shores of Lake Umbagog, on points extending into the lake, rare; Welch mountains; Vermont—rare, but few trees at each station; Monkton in Addison county; Fairfax, Franklin county; Starkesboro.

IN CONNECTICUT—Not reported.

**WOOD**—Light, soft, not strong, close-grained, clear pale brown or rarely orange color with a thick nearly white sapwood; used for fuel and occasionally for railroad ties and posts; occasionally manufactured into lumber.

JACK PINE

# RED PINE
## Norway Pine.
### Pinus resinosa Ait.

**HABIT**—A tree 50-75 ft. in height with a trunk diameter of 2-3 ft., in Maine, reaching a height of over 100 ft.; trunk erect, continuous into the crown with stout spreading branches often dependent and ascending at their tips, more distinctly whorled than in the Pitch Pine, in young trees clothing the trunk to the ground, forming a broadly pyramidal head becoming irregularly round-topped with age. Foliage in long flexible dark green tufts.

**BARK**—Reddish-brown, with shallow flat ridges, separating off in irregular thin flaky scales.

**TWIGS**—Stout, light reddish brown, not downy, roughened by decurrent scales subtending leaf clusters especially toward base of each year's growth.

**LEAVES**—In clusters of 2, with long persistent sheaths, dark green, shining, 3-6 inches long, slender, soft, flexible, flattened on one side, rounded on the other, with pointed tip. MICROSCOPIC SECTION —showing 2 fibro-vascular bundles, peripheral resin-ducts, a single layer of strengthening cells beneath the epidermis and around the resin-ducts, stomata all around.

**BUDS**—Oblong to conical, pointed; scales reddish-brown.

**FRUIT**—Cones about 2 inches long, without stalks, ovate-conical, when opened more or less spherical, making a right angle with the stem, ripened cones remaining on the tree during winter. SCALES—thickened at apex but without spines or prickers.

**COMPARISONS**—The Red Pine with two long needles in a cluster is not to be confused with our native New England Pines. It resembles however, the Austrian Pine, but may be distinguished from this species by its more slender flexible needles (see under Austrian Pine).

**DISTRIBUTION**—In poor soils; sandy plains, dry woods. Newfoundland and New Brunswick, throughout Quebec and Ontario, to the southern end of Lake Winnipeg; south to Pennsylvania; west through Michigan and Wisconsin to Minnesota.

IN NEW ENGLAND—Maine—common, plains, Brunswick, (Cumberland county); woods, Bristol (Lincoln county); from Amherst (western part of Hancock county) and Clifton (southeastern part of Penobscot county) northward just east of the Penobscot river the predominant tree, generally on dry ridges and eskers, but in Greenbush, and Passadunkeag growing abundantly on peat bogs with Black Spruce: hillsides and lower mountains about Moosehead, scattered: New Hampshire—ranges with the Pitch Pine as far north as the White Mountains, but is less common, usually in groves of a few to several hundred acres in extent; Vermont—less common than the White or the Pitch Pine, but not rare; Massachusetts—still more local, in stations widely separated, single trees or small groups; Rhode Island—occasional.

IN CONNECTICUT—Rare or local; Granby, Salisbury.

**WOOD**—Light, hard, very close-grained, pale red, with thin yellow often nearly white sapwood; largely used in the construction of bridges and buildings, for piles, masts and spars. The bark is occasionally used for tanning leather.

RED PINE

# AUSTRIAN PINE
## Black Pine.
### Pinus Laricio, var. austriaca Endl.

**HABIT**—A tall tree reaching 60-80 ft. in height; trunk erect continuous into the crown, branches in young trees regularly whorled, foliage in rigid dark green tufts.

**BARK**—Grayish-brown, roughened with scaly ridges, reddish-brown within.

**TWIGS**—Stout, yellowish-brown, not downy, roughened by decurrent scales subtending leaf-clusters especially toward base of each year's growth.

**LEAVES**—In clusters of 2, with relatively short persistent sheaths, dark dullish green, 3-5 inches long, rigid, flattened on one side, rounded on the other, sharp-pointed. MICROSCOPIC SECTION—showing 2 fibro-vascular bundles, resin-ducts located intermediate between bundles and periphery, strengthening cells beneath the epidermis in patches several layers thick also surrounding the resin-ducts and on one side of the fibro-vascular bundles, stomata all around.

**BUDS**—Oblong-conical, pointed, sometimes covered with a white resin.

**FRUIT**—Cones 2¼-3 inches long, without stalks, ovate-conical, becoming broadly ovate when opened, making about a right angle with the stem. SCALES—thickened at apex, generally with a short dull spine.

**COMPARISONS**—The Austrian Pine resembles most closely the Red Pine among our New England species. The stiff character of its sharp-pointed leaves in distinction to the soft flexible leaves of the Red Pine may be observed by striking the open hand against a tuft of the needles. The winter twigs of the Austrian Pine are yellowish-brown, those of the Red Pine are bright red. The microscopic sections of the leaves of the two species are very distinct.

**DISTRIBUTION**—A native of Europe but frequently cultivated in this country as an ornamental tree and to some extent used in forest planting.

**WOOD**—Light, soft, rich in turpentine and very durable. In Europe the wood is used as a building timber and turpentine is obtained from the tree.

AUSTRIAN PINE

# SCOTCH PINE
## Scotch "Fir."
### Pinus sylvestris L.

---

**HABIT**—A tree up to 70 ft. or occasionally 120 ft. in height; as cultivated in this country in the open, often a low branching tree with more or less pendant limbs and inclined trunk presenting a rather straggling unkempt appearance; frequently of more erect habit, especially in company with other trees.

**BARK**—Grayish-brown, scaly, upper part of trunk and branches characteristically smoothish in appearance by flaking off of the outer bark in thin papery light-reddish layered scales.

**TWIGS**—Of medium thickness, dull grayish-yellow, not downy, roughened by scales subtending leaf clusters.

**LEAVES**—In clusters of 2, persistent, sheaths becoming lacerated, dull bluish-green 1½-3½ inches long, stiff, generally twisted, flat or concave on one side, rounded on the other, pointed. MICROSCOPIC SECTION—showing 2 fibro-vascular bundles, peripheral resin-ducts, strengthening cells around resin-ducts, at one side of the bundles and beneath the epidermis, stomata all around.

**BUDS**—Oblong-conical, brown, often somewhat resinous-coated.

**FRUIT**—Cones 1½-2½ inches long, short-stalked, grayish or reddish brown, conic-oblong, generally appearing with the whorls of lateral branches, usually pointing backward. SCALES—in young cones with a short projection which when mature may persist as a short weak inconspicuous point or is deciduous, apex of scale thickened with a more or less prominent four-sided boss often recurved especially toward base of cone.

**COMPARISONS**—The Scotch Pine often improperly called Scotch "Fir" may be distinguished from the other Pines native or cultivated in New England by the bald reddish appearance of the upper part of trunk and branches, the short bluish-green leaves and the backward-pointing cones.

**DISTRIBUTION**—A European tree cultivated abroad in extensive forests for its timber. In this country more or less planted as an ornamental tree, and sparingly escaped from cultivation. In Connecticut rare or local as an escape; New London, Lyme, Southington, Bridgeport.

**WOOD**—Light, soft, reddish-brown with thick light yellowish or reddish sapwood, easily split and durable, corresponding in importance abroad to the White Pine in this country.

SCOTCH PINE

# AMERICAN LARCH

## Tamarack, Hackmatack, Black Larch, "Juniper."

### Larix laricina (Du Roi) Koch.

#### *L. americana* Michx.

---

**HABIT**—A tree 30-70 ft. in height, with a trunk diameter of 1-3 ft., at high altitudes reduced to 1-2 ft. in height; trunk erect continuous into the crown, branches irregular or indistinctly whorled, in young age and when crowded and in swamps forming a narrow symmetrical pyramidal head, in old age becoming broader and of irregular form. The Larch is the only New England cone-bearing tree that sheds its leaves in the fall; specimens in winter consequently are frequently mistaken for dead trees.

**BARK**—On young trunks smooth, with age becoming roughened with thin, close, reddish-brown, roundish scales.

**TWIGS**—Slender, smooth, pale orange colored to reddish-brown with short lateral wart-like branches, with resinous taste.

**LEAF-SCARS**—Scattered on rapidly grown shoots, very numerous and strongly decurrent, minute, triangular, with a single bundle-scar; also on short wart-like branches, smaller and densely clustered.

**BUDS**—Scattered along last season's twigs, on older growth at the ends of the short lateral branches, small, about 1 mm long, spherical, reddish, shining.

**FRUIT**—Ovate, oblong cones, about ½-¾ inch long on short, stout, incurved stalks, persistent on trees throughout winter. SCALES—thin, about a dozen or fewer in number.

**COMPARISONS**—The American Larch or Tamarack as it is more commonly called by woodsmen is hardly to be confused with any other tree except the European Larch [*Larix decidua* Mill.; *L. europaea* DC.]. The European Larch is a species adapted to dryer situations than the American form. It is readily distinguished by its stouter, yellower twigs, larger cones, about 1 inch long, with numerous cone scales (see lower twig in plate).

**DISTRIBUTION**—Low lands, shaded hillsides, borders of ponds; in New England preferring cold swamps; sometimes far up mountain slopes. Labrador. Newfoundland, and Nova Scotia, west to the Rocky mountains; from the Rockies through British columbia, northward along the Yukon and Mackenzie systems, to the limit of tree growth beyond the Arctic circle; south along the mountains to New Jersey and Pennsylvania; west to Minnesota.

IN NEW ENGLAND—Maine, New Hampshire and Vermont—abundant, filling swamps acres in extent, alone or associated with other trees, mostly Black Spruce; growing depressed and scattered on Katahdin at an altitude of 4,000 ft.; Massachusetts—rather common at least northward; Rhode Island—not reported.

IN CONNECTICUT—Absent near the coast; rare in the eastern part of the state; Union, Tolland; becoming occasional westward and frequent in Litchfield county.

**WOOD**—Very heavy, hard and strong, rather coarse-grained, very durable in contact with soil, bright light red with thin nearly white sapwood; largely used for the upper knees of small vessels, fence posts, telegraph poles, railroad ties, in cabinet making and for interior finish of buildings.

AMERICAN LARCH
EUROPEAN LARCH (lower twig only)

# WHITE SPRUCE
## Cat, Skunk or Labrador Spruce.
### Picea canadensis (Mill.) BSP.
#### *P. alba* Link.

**HABIT**—A tree 40-75 feet in height with a trunk diameter of 1-2 ft.; trunk straight, slowly tapering, branches numerous, slightly ascending or nearly horizontal, with numerous lateral, generally somewhat pendant branchlets, spread in more or less well marked dense planes, forming a broad-based pyramidal head; foliage bluish-green.

**BARK**—Grayish to pale reddish-brown; on young trunks and branches smoothish or slightly roughened becoming in a relatively late stage flaky with small closely appressed scales.

**TWIGS**—Light, yellowish-brown, smooth.

**LEAF-SCARS**—Alternate, more than 2-ranked, on strongly projecting, decurrent ridges of the bark. BUNDLE-SCARS—single.

**LEAVES**—Bluish-green, 4-angled, 10-25 mm. long, blunt or sharp-pointed, straight or incurved, without proper leaf-stalks with a strong rank odor when bruised which is responsible for some of the common names.

**BUDS**—Ovate, blunt-pointed, light brown.

**FRUIT**—Oblong-cylindrical cones, 1½-2½ inches long, generally falling the first winter. SCALES—thin, flexible and elastic; margin rounded or straight-topped, generally entire.

**COMPARISONS**—The White Spruce differs from our other native Spruces, the Red and the Black, by its smooth twigs, less scaly bark, rather longer and more nearly cylindrical cones and usually by the rank odor of its leaves; from the Red Spruce further by its bluish-green foliage. From the smooth-twigged Blue Spruce it is distinguished by its smaller cones and less distinctly layered arrangement of branches.

**DISTRIBUTION**—Low, damp, but not wet woods; dry, sandy soils, high, rocky slopes and exposed hilltops, often in scanty soil. Newfoundland and Nova Scotia, through the provinces of Quebec and Ontario to Manitoba and British Columbia, northward beyond all other trees, within 20 miles of the Arctic sea; west through the northern sections of the northern tier of states to the Rocky mountains. Sometimes cultivated as an ornamental tree.

**IN NEW ENGLAND**—Maine—frequent in sandy soils, often more common than the Red Spruce, as far south as the shores of Casco bay; New Hampshire—abundant around the shores of the Connecticut river, disappearing southward at Fifteen-Mile falls; Vermont—restricted mainly to the northern sections, more common in the northeast; Massachusetts—occasional in the mountainous regions of Berkshire county; a few trees in Hancock; as far south as Amherst, and Northampton, probably about the southern limit of the species; Rhode Island—not reported.

**IN CONNECTICUT**—Rare. Waterford, a few trees in a pasture as an escape from cultivation.

**WOOD**—Light, soft, not strong, straight-grained, light yellow, with hardly distinguishable sapwood; manufactured into lumber in the eastern provinces of Canada and used in construction for the interior finish of buildings and for paper pulp.

WHITE SPRUCE

# RED SPRUCE

Picea rubra (Du Roi) Dietr.

*P. nigra,* var. *rubra* Engelm. ; *P. rubcns* Sarg.

**HABIT**—A tree 40-75 ft. in height with a trunk diameter of 1-2½ ft.; trunk straight, slowly tapering; branches toward the middle of the tree horizontal with upward tips, more or less strongly declined toward the base forming a narrow conical head somewhat broader than that of the Black Spruce; foliage dark yellowish-green.

**BARK**—Reddish-brown, flaky with thin scales.

**TWIGS**—Brown, more or less densely covered with short rusty to black hairs.

**LEAF-SCARS**—Alternate, more than 2-ranked, on strongly projecting decurrent ridges of the bark.  BUNDLE-SCARS—single.

**LEAVES**—Dark yellowish-green, 4-angled, 10-20 mm. long, blunt-pointed, straight or curved, without proper leaf-stalks.

**BUDS**—Ovate, pointed, reddish-brown.

**FRUIT**—Ovate-oblong cones, 1¼-2 inches long, with short stalks not at all or but slightly recurved, falling the first autumn or sometimes remaining on the tree a year longer.  SCALES—stiff, thin; margin rounded, entire or slightly toothed.

**COMPARISONS**—The Red Spruce from its close resemblance to the Black Spruce is considered by some authors as merely a variety of this latter species (see Black Spruce under Comparisons).  It differs from the White and the Blue Spruce by its hairy twigs and yellowish-green foliage and from the Norway Spruce by its shorter cones.

**DISTRIBUTION**—Cool, rich woods, well-drained valleys, slopes of mountains not infrequently extending down to the borders of swamps. Prince Edward Island and Nova Scotia along the valley of the St. Lawrence; south along the Alleghanies to Georgia, ascending to an altitude of 4,500 feet in the Adirondacks, and 4,000-5,000 feet in West Virginia; west through the northern tier of states to Minnesota.

IN NEW ENGLAND—Maine—throughout; most common towards the coast and in the extreme north, thus forming a belt around the central area, where it is often quite wanting except on cool or elevated slopes; New Hampshire—throughout; the most abundant conifer of upper Coos, the White Mountain region where it climbs to the alpine area, and the higher parts of the Connecticut-Merrimac watershed; Vermont —throughout; the common Spruce of the Green mountains, often in dense groves on rocky slopes with thin soil; Massachusetts—common in the mountainous regions of Berkshire county and on uplands in the northern sections, occasional southward; Rhode Island—not reported.

IN CONNECTICUT—Rare.  Litchfield, Canaan, Salisbury.

**WOOD**—Light, soft, close-grained, not strong, pale, slightly tinged with red, with paler sapwood generally about 2 inches thick; largely manufactured into lumber in the northeastern states and used for the flooring and construction of houses, for the sounding-boards of musical instruments and in the manufacture of paper pulp.

RED SPRUCE

# BLACK SPRUCE
## Swamp, Bog, Water or Double Spruce.
### Picea mariana (Mill.) BSP.
*P. nigra* Link ; *P. brevifolia* Peck.

---

**HABIT**—In New England usually a small slender tree 10-30 ft. in height with a trunk diameter of 5-8 inches, much larger northward and westward, reduced to a shrub 2-5 ft. in height at high altitudes; with relatively short, generally scattered branches, horizontal or usually declined and curving upward at the ends; in open-grown trees, basal branches frequently resting on the ground, taking root and sending up shoots; crown an irregular open narrow-based cone; foliage bluish-green.

**BARK**—Grayish-brown, flaky, with thin scales.

**TWIGS**—Brown or yellowish-brown, more or less densely covered with short rusty to black hairs.

**LEAF-SCARS**—Alternate, more than 2-ranked on strongly projecting decurrent ridges of the bark.   BUNDLE-SCARS—single.

**LEAVES**—Bluish-green, 4-angled, 5-15 mm. long, blunt-pointed, straight or slightly incurved, without proper leaf-stalks.

**BUDS**—Ovate, pointed, reddish-brown.

**FRUIT**—Ovate cones, ½ to 1½ inches long becoming nearly spherical when open, on short strongly recurved stalks generally remaining on the tree for many years.   SCALES—stiff, thin; margin rounded, uneven, ragged, toothed or rarely entire.

**COMPARISONS**—The Black Spruce closely resembles the Red Spruce from which it may be distinguished by its shorter, more nearly spherical cones which generally remain for many years on the tree, by the more ragged edging of the cone-scales, by the bluish-green color of its foliage and by its habitat in swampy land.   Extreme forms of the two species are sufficiently distinct but they are often difficult to distinguish even in the fruiting condition.

**DISTRIBUTION**—Swamps, sphagnum bogs, shores of rivers and ponds, wet, rocky hillsides; not uncommon, especially northward, on dry up-lands and mountain slopes.   Labrador, Newfoundland, and Nova Scotia, westward beyond the Rocky mountains, extending northward along the tributaries of the Yukon in Alaska.

IN NEW ENGLAND—Maine—common throughout, covering extensive areas almost to the exclusion of other trees in the central and northern sections, occasional on the top of Katahdin (5,215 ft.); New Hampshire and Vermont—common in sphagnum swamps of low and high altitudes; the dwarf form, var. *semiprostrata*, occurs on the summit of Mt. Mans-field; Massachusetts—frequent; Rhode Island—not reported.

IN CONNECTICUT—Swamps and sphagnum bogs.   Rare or local over most of the state but absent near the coast.   Usually a small stunted tree 5 to 15 ft. high but growing much larger in the cool swamps of Litchfield county.   In open bogs the trees often produce cones when not more than 5 ft. high, and the cones persist on the tree for many years.

**WOOD**—Light, soft, not strong, pale yellowish-white, with thin sap-wood probably rarely used outside of Manitoba and Saskatchewan except in the manufacture of paper pulp.   Spruce gum is gathered from this and the other New England spruces.   Spruce beer is made by boiling the branches of the Black and Red Spruces.

BLACK SPRUCE

# BLUE SPRUCE
## Colorado Blue Spruce, Silver Spruce.
### Picea Menziesii Engelm.
*P. Parryana* (Andre) Sarg. ; *P. pungens* Engelm.

**HABIT**—A tree reaching in Colorado a height of 100 ft. and a trunk diameter of 2-3 ft., much smaller in cultivation; branches rigid, horizontal with short, stout, stiff, lateral branchlets arranged in horizontal planes giving a layered effect to the tree, especially in the young stages; older trees becoming less regular with a thin, ragged, pyramidal crown; foliage bluish-green to silvery-white or rarely dull green.

**BARK**—Grayish-brown, scaly becoming deeply ridged toward the base.

**TWIGS**—Bright yellowish to reddish-brown, smooth.

**LEAF-SCARS**—Alternate, more than 2-ranked, on strongly projecting decurrent ridges of the bark.   BUNDLE-SCARS—single.

**LEAVES**—Bluish-green to silvery-white or rarely dull green, 4-angled, 25-30 mm. long on sterile branches, often not over half as long on fruiting branches, stout, stiff, sharp-pointed, incurved, without proper leaf-stalks, with a pungent somewhat disagreeable odor when bruised.

**BUDS**—Ovate, blunt-pointed, light brown.

**FRUIT**—Oblong-cylindrical cones 2½ to 4 inches long, generally not remaining on the tree after the second winter.   SCALES—thin, distinctly longer than broad with narrowed, flexible, ragged, blunt tips.

**COMPARISONS**—The Blue Spruce as cultivated as an ornamental tree is strikingly distinct from other Spruces in its bluish-green or silvery foliage and the horizontally layered arrangement of its branchlets.   The long stiff sharp-pointed needles and the narrowed elongated scales of the large cones are further characteristic.

**DISTRIBUTION**—Along or near streams.   Colorado and eastern Utah, northward to the Wind River mountains of Wyoming.   Often planted as an ornamental tree in the eastern and northern states and also in Europe, especially individuals with blue foliage.

**WOOD**—Light, soft, close-grained, weak, pale brown, or often nearly white with hardly distinguishable sapwood.

BLUE SPRUCE

# NORWAY SPRUCE
## Picea Abies (L.) Karst.
### *P. excelsa* Link.

---

**HABIT**—A large rapidly growing tree, 50-100 ft. or more in height with a trunk diameter up to 2 ft.; with spreading horizontal or ascending branches and in mature trees generally with strongly drooping lateral branchlets, forming a rather broad pyramidal head; foliage dark green. The tree usually has a single erect trunk continuous into the crown but although the tree photographed shows a double stem it is typical in general outline.

**BARK**—Reddish-brown, on young trunks and branches smoothish with very fine flaky scales becoming with age roughened with larger thicker flaky scales.

**TWIGS**—Brown, smooth or hairy.

**LEAF-SCARS**—Alternate, more than 2-ranked, on strongly projecting decurrent ridges of the bark.

**LEAVES**—Dark green and usually shining, 4-angled, 15-25 mm. long, sharp-pointed, without proper leaf-stalks.

**BUDS**—Ovate, pointed, light brown.

**FRUIT**—Cylindrical-oblong, pendant cones, 4-7 inches long, light reddish-brown, falling after the first winter. SCALES—thin, stiff, generally broader than long, margin more or less irregular and finely toothed.

**COMPARISONS**—The large cones form the most distinctive character of the Norway Spruce, and when present easily separate this species from all others with which it might be confused. The pendant lateral branches generally strikingly noticeable on the older trees together with the vigor of growth furnish good habit characters of distinction.

**DISTRIBUTION**—A large tree of Europe especially abundant in Norway: largely cultivated in this country as ornamental individual trees, in hedges and for windbreaks.

**WOOD**—Light, soft, close-grained, reddish to yellowish-white; used for spars, oars and masts to small vessels.

NORWAY SPRUCE

# DOUGLAS FIR
## Red Fir, Douglas Spruce.
### Pseudotsuga taxifolia (Lam.) Britton.
*P. mucronata* (Raf.) Sudw. ; *P. Douglasii* (Lindl.) Carr.

**HABIT**—A tree under favorable conditions in the west reaching a height of 200 ft. or over and a trunk diameter up to 10 or 12 ft.; branches horizontal with more or less pendulous branchlets forming a pyramidal head. A number of varieties are in cultivation varying somewhat in habit and color of foliage.

**BARK**—On young trunks dark gray, smooth, with few resin blisters, soon becoming roughened, with reddish-brown scales and eventually deeply ridged.

**TWIGS**—Reddish to yellowish-brown, more or less downy, becoming with age smooth and dark grayish-brown. Photograph of twig is about ⅓ natural size.

**LEAVES**—Scattered, sometimes appearing somewhat 2-ranked but less distinctly so than leaves of the Balsam Fir, dark green above, pale below with grayish lines of minute dots, flattened, generally blunt, ¾ inch or more long, slightly narrowed at base but not distinctly stalked, arising at about a right angle to the twig and leaving in falling a round scar slightly raised at the base, and slightly fragrant and aromatic when crushed. MICROSCOPIC SECTION—showing a single fibro-vascular bundle, 2 resin-ducts next to the epidermis, strengthening cells beneath the epidermis and generally around the resin-ducts, giant thick walled irregularly lobed cells frequently appearing in cross-sections of the leaf on either side of the bundle, stomata on the under side.

**BUDS**—Comparatively large, narrowly ovate to conical, sharp pointed, reddish brown, 7-12 mm. long, loosely clustered at tips of twigs; bud-scales not resinous-coated, often with reflexed tips.

**FRUIT**—A cone maturing in one season, pendant, stalked, 2-4⅓ inches long. SCALES—persistent, rounded on edges with conspicuous protruding bracts which are long-pointed and laterally winged like the feathering on an arrow.

**COMPARISONS**—The Douglas Fir resembles the Balsam Fir but may be readily distinguished by its large dark brown buds, free from resin, by the slightly projecting leaf-scars and especially by the cones with persistent scales and lobed bracts. Further a thin knife section held toward the light and looked at with a hand-lens shows the two resin-ducts on the edge of the leaf while those of the Balsam Fir are located between the edge and the bundle.

**DISTRIBUTION**—Throughout the Rocky mountain system south of latitudes 55 degrees north to the Pacific coast, forming extensive forests. Planted for ornament in the eastern states where, however, only plants grown from seed obtained from the interior of the continent are successful.

**WOOD**—Light red or yellow, with nearly white sapwood, very variable in density, quality and in the thickness of the sapwood; largely manufactured into lumber in British Columbia, western Washington and Oregon and used for all kinds of construction, fuel, railroad ties and piles. The bark is sometimes used in tanning leather.

Douglas Fir

# BALSAM FIR

## Balsam, Fir, Balm of Gilead Fir.

### Abies balsamea (L.) Mill.

**HABIT**—A medium sized tree, 25-60 ft. in height with a trunk diameter of 1-2 ft., becoming a shrub toward the tops of high mountains; branches usually arising in distinct whorls and throughout horizontal, ascending or declining, or declining toward the base horizontal in the middle and ascending toward the top of the tree forming a symmetrical broad-based conical head. A rapidly growing comparatively short-lived tree losing its lower branches at an early period.

**BARK**—Grayish-brown, smooth with raised blisters containing a fragrant oily resin; in old trees becoming somewhat roughened with small scales at base of trunk.

**TWIGS**—Grayish and more or less downy, becoming with age grayish-brown and smooth, branchlets mostly opposite arising at a wide angle. Photograph of twig is about ⅓ natural size.

**LEAVES**—Scattered, on young trees and sterile twigs generally twisting so as to appear 2-ranked as in the Hemlock, on upper fruiting branches and leading shoots generally covering the upper side of the twigs; dark green and shining on upper side, pale below with grayish lines of minute dots, flattened, generally blunt about ¾ inch or more long, slightly narrowed at base but not stalked, arising at about a right angle to the twig, leaving after falling a flat, round scar, fragrant, aromatic when crushed. MICROSCOPIC SECTION—showing 2 fibro-vascular bundles closely adjacent and appearing as one in a knife section, 2 resin-ducts between the bundles and the epidermis with stomata chiefly on the under side.

**BUDS**—Small, broadly ovate to spherical, generally less than 5 mm. long, closely grouped at tips of main twigs; bud-scales varnished and glued together by resinous coating.

**FRUIT**—Erect cones ripening in the autumn of the first season. SCALES—falling and leaving only the erect central axes to which they were attached persistent through winter.

**COMPARISONS**—The Balsam Fir is distinguished from our native New England evergreens by its smooth blistery bark and by its leaves which are attached directly to the twig and leave a round, flat scar on falling. From the Hemlock it is further distinguished by the absence of leaf stalks and from the Spruce by the flattened apparently 2-ranked leaves. See under Douglas Fir for Comparisons with this species.

**DISTRIBUTION**—Rich, damp, cool woods, deep swamps, mountain slopes. Occasionally cultivated as an ornamental tree. Labrador, Newfoundland, and Nova Scotia, northwest to the Great Bear Lake region; south to Pennsylvania and along high mountains to Virginia; west to Minnesota.

IN NEW ENGLAND—Maine—very generally distributed, ordinarily associated with White Pine, Black Spruce, Red Spruce, and a few deciduous trees, growing at an altitude of 4,500 feet upon Katahdin; New Hampshire—common in upper Coos county and in the White Mountains, where it climbs up to the alpine area; in the southern part of the state, in the extensive swamps around the sources of the Contoocook and Miller's rivers it is the prevailing timber; Vermont—common; not rare on mountain slopes and even summits; Massachusetts—not uncommon on mountain slopes in the northwestern and central portions of the state, ranging above the Red Spruces upon Graylock; a few trees here and there in damp woods or cold swamps in the southern and eastern sections, where it has probably been accidentally introduced; Rhode Island—not reported.

IN CONNECTICUT—Rare. Cold swamps and woods. Middlebury, Goshen, Cornwall, Salisbury. Also occurs as an escape from cultivation at Woodstock, Andover and Farmington.

**WOOD**—Light, soft, not strong, coarse-grained, perishable, pale brown, streaked with yellow, with thick lighter colored sapwood, occasionally made into lumber, principally used for packing cases, used largely in manufacture of wood pulp. From the blisters in the bark Canada balsam is obtained which is used in medicine and as a medium for mounting microscopic preparations. The fragrant leaves and small twigs are used to stuff balsam or so-called "pine"-pillows.

BALSAM FIR

# HEMLOCK
## Hemlock Spruce.
### Tsuga canadensis (L.) Carr.

**HABIT**—A large tree 50-80 ft. in height with a trunk diameter of 2-4 ft.; branches long, slender, horizontal or drooping at base, ascending above, forming a broad-based pyramidal head with fine feathery spray giving a delicate airy appearance to the tree. The apex is plume-like and generally bent to one side indicating, so woodsmen claim, the direction of prevailing winds.

**BARK**—Reddish to grayish-brown, with shallow broad connecting ridges somewhat scaly on the surface.

**TWIGS**—Slender, yellowish-brown, more or less downy, branchlets generally not opposite and arising at less than a right angle. Photograph of twig is about ⅓ natural size.

**LEAVES**—Scattered but generally twisting so as to appear 2-ranked, dark, slightly yellowish-green above, pale green below with grayish lines of minute dots on either side of midrib, flattened generally blunt at the apex, about ½ inch long with a distinct short stalk, borne upon a reddish-brown decurrent projection of the bark which is left as a raised scar at the fall of the leaf. MICROSCOPIC SECTION—showing a single fibro-vascular bundle and a large resin-duct filling the space between the bundle and the epidermis.

**BUDS**—Small, about 2mm. long, ovate, reddish-brown, not resinous-coated.

**FRUIT**—Small, stalked, pendant cones, ripening the first season, and generally persistent through winter, about ¾ inch long.

**COMPARISONS**—In its flattened, apparently 2-ranked leaves the Hemlock resembles the Balsam Fir, but aside from the difference in habit and bark, the leaves of the Hemlock are shorter, distinctly stalked and leave projecting scars when they fall off. From the Spruces it is distinguished by its distinctly flattened and stalked leaves and flattened spray.

**DISTRIBUTION**—Cold soils, borders of swamps, deep woods, ravines, mountain slopes, and also cultivated as an ornamental tree. Nova Scotia, New Brunswick, through Quebec and Ontario; south to Delaware and along the mountains to Georgia and Alabama, ascending to an altitude of 2000 feet in the Adirondacks; west to Michigan and Minnesota.

IN NEW ENGLAND—Maine—abundant, generally distributed in the southern and central portions, becoming rare northward, disappearing entirely in most of Aroostook county and the northern Penobscot region; New Hampshire—abundant, from the sea to a height of 2,000 feet in the White Mountains, disappearing in upper Coos county; Vermont—common especially in mountain forests; Massachusetts and Rhode Island—common.

IN CONNECTICUT—Usually frequent but rather local in its distribution.

**WOOD**—Light, soft, not strong, brittle, coarse-grained, difficult to work, liable to wind-shake and splinter, not durable when exposed to the air, light brown tinged with red, with thin somewhat darker sapwood; largely manufactured into coarse lumber, employed for the outside finish of buildings. The astringent inner bark furnishes the largest part of the material used in the northeastern states and Canada in tanning leather. Oil of Hemlock is distilled from the young branches.

Hemlock

# COAST WHITE CEDAR
## White Cedar, Cedar.
### Chamaecyparis thyoides (L.) BSP.
*C. sphaeroidea* Spach ; *Cupressus thyoides* L.

**HABIT**—A small tree, 20-50 ft. in height with a trunk diameter of 1-2 ft., further south reaching 90 ft. in height and a trunk diameter of 4 ft.; trunk tall, erect, tapering gradually, branches short, slender, more or less horizontal, with delicate feathery secondary branches and branchlets loosely enveloping the narrow conical head and surmounted by an airy, pliant, plume-like terminal shoot.

**BARK**—Grayish-brown, separating off in narrow shreddy strips, more or less spirally twisted; on younger and sometimes also on older trunks the bark separates off in broader reddish-brown strips, (see photograph of young trunk).

**TWIGS**—Generally less than 1.5 mm. thick, slightly but not prominently flattened, arranged in more or less fan-shaped clusters in planes at various angles, the last season's growth bluish-green from the complete covering of minute leaves, with death of leaves the second season becoming reddish-brown, older growth slowly losing its leaves and marked by scars of deciduous branchlets. Photograph of twig is about ⅘ natural size.

**LEAVES**—Minute, scale-like, 1-2 mm. long, appressed and closely overlapping, opposite in 4 ranks, but not giving a conspicuously 4-sided appearance to the twigs, more or less keeled and with a raised glandular dot at least on leaves of rapidly grown shoots, with spicy aromatic odor when crushed.

**FRUIT**—Small, spherical cones, 5-8 mm. in diameter, inconspicuous in winter, opening toward the center never toward the base, maturing the first season and persistent through the winter. SCALES—thickened, woody, shield-shaped, with a slight projection in middle, each perched on a stalk connecting it with the center of the cone; seeds winged.

**COMPARISONS**—The Coast White Cedar resembles the Arbor Vitae as indicated under this species but its twigs are only slightly flattened, the clusters of twigs are less distinctly fan-shaped, the twigs and leaves are smaller and the leaves are of a bluish rather than of a yellowish-green. The cones are distinctive being spherical and with thickened shield-shaped scales perched on stalks connecting them with the center. Aside from the fruit characters which separate them, the Coast White Cedar is distinguished from the Red Cedar by the more or less distinct fan-shaped arrangement of its twigs, the absence of two kinds of leaves, the more distinct glandular dot generally present on the leaf and by the fact that the twigs are round or slightly compressed in section and not distinctly 4-sided as are those of the Red Cedar.

**DISTRIBUTION**—In deep swamps and marshes, which it often fills to the exclusion of other trees, mostly near the seacoast. Cape Breton island and near Halifax, Nova Scotia, perhaps introduced in both; southward, coast region to Florida and west to Mississippi.

IN NEW ENGLAND—Maine—reported from the southern part of York county; New Hampshire—limited to Rockingham county near the coast; Vermont—no station known; Massachusetts—occasional in central and eastern parts, very common in the southeast; Rhode Island—common.

IN CONNECTICUT—Rare in western and central districts; Danbury and New Fairfield, becoming occasional or frequent eastward.

**WOOD**—Light, soft, not strong, close-grained, slightly fragrant, light brown, tinged with red, largely used in boat building, and cooperage and for woodenware, shingles, the interior finish of houses, fence posts and railroad ties.

COAST WHITE CEDAR

# ARBOR VITAE
## White Cedar, Cedar.
### Thuja occidentalis L.

**HABIT**—Commonly 25-50 ft. in height with trunk diameter of 1-2 ft., in northern Maine occasionally reaching a height of 70 ft. and a trunk diameter of 3-5 ft.; trunk more or less lobed and buttressed at base, often inclined and twisted, frequently dividing into two or more stout erect stems; branches short, horizontal, lower branches often strongly declined, branchlets numerous, forming a dense, conical head clothed with foliage to near the base.

**BARK**—Ashy-gray to light reddish-brown, separating off in long, narrow, flat, shreddy strips, often more or less spirally twisted.

**TWIGS**—Generally more than 2 mm. wide, decidedly flattened, arranged in fan-shaped clusters, placed vertically or in planes at various angles, often mistaken for the true leaves which are minute and completely cover the last season's growth, dark yellowish-green, paler on the underside, with the death of the leaves in the second season becoming pale cinnamon brown and later shining reddish-brown, round in section, swollen at place of attachment to main branch, and marked by scars of deciduous branchlets. Photograph of twig is about ⅚ natural size.

**LEAVES**—Minute, 3-6 mm. long, scale-like, appressed and closely overlapping, opposite in 4 ranks; on the flattened spray those in the side pairs keeled, those in the other pair flat, ovate, each with a single raised glandular spot especially conspicuous on leaves of leading shoots; with a characteristic camphor-like aromatic odor when crushed.

**FRUIT**—Small, oblong cones, about ½ inch long, pale reddish-brown, opening to the base when mature, maturing the first season and persistent through the winter. SCALES—6-12, thin, oblong, dry with margins mostly entire.

**COMPARISONS**—The Arbor Vitae is often called White Cedar and resembles the Coast White Cedar, which likewise is often known as White Cedar, in its bark, its habit of growth and its flattened fan-shaped spray. The twigs of the Arbor Vitae are much more flattened and larger and the clusters of twigs more decidedly fan-shaped; the leaves are also larger and of a yellowish-green color. The cones of the two species are decidedly different, those of the Arbor Vitae being oblong with thin scales opening to the base of the cone, those of the Coast White Cedar being spherical with thickened shield-shaped scales, perched on stalks attached to the center of the cone.

**DISTRIBUTION**—Low, swampy lands, rocky borders of rivers and ponds. Often cultivated as single ornamental trees and in hedges. Southern Labrador to Nova Scotia; west to Manitoba; south along the mountains to North Carolina and East Tennessee; west to Minnesota.

IN NEW ENGLAND—Maine—throughout the state; most abundant in the central and northern portions, forming extensive areas known as "Cedar Swamps"; sometimes bordering a growth of Black Spruce at a lower level; New Hampshire—mostly confined to the upper part of Coos county, disappearing at the White river narrows near Hanover; seen only in isolated localities south of the White Mountains; Vermont—common in swamps at levels below 1,000 ft.; Massachusetts—Berkshire county; occasional in the northern sections of the Connecticut river valley; Rhode Island—not reported.

IN CONNECTICUT—Rare; Canaan, on a limestone ridge and in a nearby swamp, Salisbury, rocky hillsides and at another locality in a deep swamp; apparently native at these three localities. Escaped from cultivation to fields and roadsides at Norwich, East Hartford, Killingly and Windsor.

**WOOD**—Light, soft, brittle, very coarse-grained, durable, fragrant, pale yellowish-brown, largely used in Canada and the northern states for fence posts, rails, railroad ties, spools and shingles.

ARBOR VITAE

# COMMON JUNIPER
## Dwarf Juniper.
### Juniperus communis L.

**HABIT**—A shrub or small tree 5-15 ft. high; in the type form with generally several erect stems, bearing erect branches densely clothed with foliage, forming a narrow or rather broad compact plume-like erect growth (habit picture at the right); in the more common dwarf variety; [*Juniperus communis*, var. *depressa* Pursh; *J. nana* of Britton's Manual in part; *J. communis*, var. *canadensis* Loud.; J. *communis*, var. *alpina* Gray's Manual ed. 6 in part] with low-lying branches, frequently rooting below, radiating from the center and curving upwards to form low, broad, round mats resembling gigantic birds' nests 1 to 3 ft. high and often 10 to 20 ft. in diameter (habit picture at the left).

**BARK**—Grayish-brown, breaking on the surface into thin papery shreddy longitudinal layers, which lift at the ends and edges exposing the reddish bark below.

**TWIGS**—Smooth, light yellow, turning to red, prominently 3-angled the first two years by decurrent ridges from below the leaves. Photograph of twig is about ⅘ natural size.

**LEAVES**—All alike in whorls of 3, separated by short internodes, spreading from the twigs at a broad angle, 7-20 mm. long, awl-shaped, stiff and sharp-pointed, free from glandular dots, compressed, the upper side concave and conspicuously streaked with a broad white line, the dark green under side appearing uppermost by the bending over of the twigs and leaves; persistent for several seasons.

**BUDS**—Distinct, scaly.

**FRUIT**—About the size of a pea, fleshy, berry-like, dark blue, covered with a bloom, sweetish with a resinous flavor, remaining on the plant during winter, but as the species is dioecious, to be found only on a part of the plants.

**COMPARISONS**—The Common Juniper is distinguished from its near relative the Red Cedar by its lower habit of growth, by the fact that its leaves are all alike and without glandular dots; in distinction from the typically appressed leaves of the Red Cedar, the leaves of the Common Juniper are spreading at a wide angle. They thus resemble the juvenile type of leaves found on young specimens of the Red Cedar and on rapid-growing twigs of older trees of the same species but may be distinguished by being almost always in 3's, wider and longer, more distinctly whitened above, with a greater separation between the nodes and by the presence of distinct scaly buds. A number of forms are described but not always recognized. The dwarf variety (var. *depressa*) is described as having leaves 8-13 mm. long, and the type as having leaves 12-21 mm. long but they are best distinguished by their different habits of growth as shown in the photographs.

**DISTRIBUTION**—In poor rocky soil, pastures and waste open places. Widely distributed through the colder regions and mountains of the northern part of the U. S., in a broad band extending westward from Newfoundland on the north and New Jersey and Pennsylvania on the south. The dwarf form (var. *depressa)* occurs throughout New England. The type is reported as less common and as occurring in Massachusetts and southward.

IN CONNECTICUT—The type is listed as rare and is reported only from Norwich. It is not uncommon, however, about Storrs. The variety *depressa* is frequent throughout this state.

**WOOD**—Hard, close-grained, very durable in contact with soil, light brown, with pale sapwood. In northern Europe the fruit is extensively used in giving its peculiar flavor to Holland gin.

COMMON JUNIPER

# RED CEDAR
## Savin, Cedar, Red Juniper.
### Juniperus virginiana L.

**HABIT**—A medium sized tree 25-40 ft. in height with trunk diameter of 8-20 inches, much larger in the southern states; trunk more or less ridged and buttressed at base, with slender branches horizontal below erect above, forming in young trees a narrow, conical head, becoming in old age wider, spreading, ovate, round-topped, or on bleak situations especially near the sea shore more or less irregularly distorted.

**BARK**—Light reddish-brown separating off in long narrow shreddy strips more or less fringed at the edges, frequently somewhat spirally twisted.

**TWIGS**—Generally 4-sided in mature trees, green from covering of minute leaves, not flattened nor arranged in fan-shaped clusters, becoming reddish-brown after the fall of the leaves. Photograph of twig is about ⅘ natural size.

**LEAVES**—Dark green or reddish-brown with aromatic odor when crushed, persistent for several years, of two kinds:—
1. The form typical of the species; about 2 mm. or less long, scale-like, opposite in pairs, forming 4 ranks, closely overlapping and appressed, rounded, with or without an inconspicuous glandular dot on the back, ovate, sharp or blunt-pointed. (See left hand twig.)
2. The juvenile form; occurring often exclusively on very young trees and also frequently together with the typical form on older trees; narrow, awl-shaped to needle-shaped, sharp-pointed without glands, spreading, scattered and not overlapping, opposite or in 3's, 5-20 mm. long. (See right hand twig.)

**BUDS**—Inconspicuous.

**FRUIT**—About the size of a small pea, fleshy, berry-like, dark blue, covered with a bloom, sweetish with a resinous flavor, containing generally 1-2 bony seeds. The fruit remains on the tree during winter but the species is dioecious and consequently not all the trees bear fruit.

**COMPARISONS**—The Red Cedar resembles the Coast White Cedar but it fails to show a flattened fan-shaped arrangement of its twigs, its twigs further are generally 4-sided when bearing typical leaves and on young trees and generally on some twigs of older trees leaves of the juvenile type may be found. The berry-like fruit of the Red Cedar when present is the most distinctive character separating this species from the Coast White Cedar. The Common Juniper is not to be confused with Red Cedar trees that have typical leaves. It resembles somewhat the juvenile leaved form of the Red Cedar, however, but the growth of the former is generally less upright, the leaves always in 3's and generally more whitened above and the buds are more conspicuous.

**DISTRIBUTION**—Dry, rocky hills but not at great altitudes, borders of lakes and streams, sterile plains, peaty swamps. Nova Scotia and New Brunswick to Ontario; south to Florida; west to Dakota, Nebraska, Kansas and Indian Territory.

IN NEW ENGLAND—Maine—rare, though it extends northward to the middle Kennebec valley, reduced almost to a shrub; New Hampshire —most frequent in the southeast part of the state; sparingly in the Connecticut valley, as far north as Haverhill; found also in Hart's location in the White Mountain region; Vermont—not abundant; occurs here and there on hills at levels less than 1,000 feet; frequent in the Champlain and lower Connecticut valleys; Massachusetts—west and center occasional, eastward common; Rhode Island—common.

IN CONNECTICUT—Common.

**WOOD**—Light, close-grained, brittle, not strong, dull red with thin nearly white sapwood, very fragrant, easily worked; largely used for posts, the sills of buildings, the interior finish of houses, the lining of chests and closets as a protection of woolen garments against attacks of moths, and for pails and other small articles of wooden-ware. A decoction of the fruit and leaves is used medicinally and oil of Red Cedar is distilled from the leaves and wood as a perfume.

RED CEDAR

# GINKGO
## Maidenhair Tree.
### Ginkgo biloba L.
*Salisburia adiantifolia* Smith.

***

**HABIT**—A tree reaching a height of 60-80 ft., with generally a single erect trunk (a double trunk in tree photographed) continuous into the crown with straight, slender branches, making an angle of about 45 degrees with the trunk and regularly parallel except those below which are more or less declined, forming in mature specimens a very regular symmetrical broadly ovate to pyramidal head.     There are several horticultural varieties including one weeping form.

**BARK**—Ashy gray, on younger trunks and branches smooth, becoming with age seamy and longitudinally roughened.

**TWIGS**—Rather stout, smooth, yellowish-brown, shining, a thin grayish skin separating off in narrow shreds on older twigs; rapidly-grown twigs of one year's growth, comparatively rare, with scattered leaf-scars; stout lateral or terminal spurs with thickly crowded leaf-scars common.     PITH—pale yellowish, with ragged outline.

**LEAF-SCARS**—Alternate, 2-ranked or more than 2-ranked, semi-oval, raised, upper margin generally fringed.     STIPULE-SCARS—absent. BUNDLE-SCARS—2, often most distinct in recent leaf-scars on short spurs.

**BUDS**—Light chestnut brown, short, conical, generally under 4 mm. long, isolated lateral buds on rapidly grown shoots divergent, on short spurs generally only terminal buds developed.     BUD-SCALES—about 5 visible, broader than long, thickened and dotted toward the middle with small reddish transparent lumps.

**FRUIT**—A stone-fruit with a sweet ill-smelling flesh.     The tree is dioecious, there being separate male and female individual trees.     On account of the disagreeable odor of the fruit the male trees are more frequently planted.     The two sexes are said to differ in their growth forms, the male tree being more narrowly pyramidal while the female forms a broad head.

**COMPARISONS**—The Ginkgo belongs to the Gymnosperms, an order of plants which are mostly cone-bearing like the Pines and Spruces.     It has a peculiarity with the Larch in that it is not evergreen as are most of its relatives but sheds its leaves in the fall.     Like the Larch, too, it has numerous stubby spurs with crowded leaf-scars.     It differs from the Larch in that its large leaf-scars are not strongly decurrent and are relatively far apart on the rapidly grown shoots and further have 2 bundle-scars.

**DISTRIBUTION**—A native of northern China, introduced into America early in the century and generally successful in the eastern states as far north as eastern Massachusetts and central Michigan and along the St. Lawrence River in parts of Canada.

GINKGO

# YELLOW WILLOW
## Golden Osier.
### Salix alba, var. vitellina (L.) Koch.
#### *S. vitellina* Koch.

**HABIT**—A large tree reaching 50-80 ft. in height with a trunk diameter of 3-5 ft.; trunk short, rarely erect, generally inclining to one side, dividing low down into a number of stout spreading limbs, forming an irregular broad rounded head.

**BARK**—On young stems smooth, becoming with age dark gray and deeply furrowed.

**TWIGS**—Rather slender, bright yellow, smooth and shining or dull with more or less dense covering of fine silky hairs, bitter to taste. LENTICELS—scattered, inconspicuous. PITH—more or less 5-pointed.

**LEAF-SCARS**—Alternate, more than 2-ranked, narrow, raised, broadly V-shaped, more or less swoolen at the bundle-scars. STIPULE-SCARS—oblique, close to leaf-scars and often appearing connected with them. BUNDLE-SCARS—3.

**BUDS**—Terminal bud absent, lateral buds about 5 mm. long, oblong, rounded at apex, smooth or more or less silky-downy, flattened and appressed against twig.   BUD-SCALES—a single bud-scale visible, rounded on back, flattened toward the twig, forming a cap to silky-hairy green leaves within.

**FRUIT**—A catkin of small capsules, containing numerous hairy seeds ripening in spring. The willows are dioecious and the male trees of the Yellow Willow are seldom planted in this country.

**COMPARISONS**—The species of Willows are closely related and have hybridized abundantly. Their classification is based largely upon differences in the pistils and stamens but since the Willows are dioecious and therefore bear the male and female flowers upon separate trees their determination even when in flower is often a matter of considerable difficulty.   The Yellow Willow here described, a yellow twigged variety of the less common European White Willow [*Salix alba* L.], is one of the most common tree Willows in New England.   The European Weeping Willow [*Salix babylonica* L.] was formerly much planted for ornament especially in cemeteries and may be distinguished by the drooping habit of its branches.   The Black Willow [*Salix nigra* Marsh.], a small-budded species is the one sizable native Willow in New England.   The Willows may be most readily separated from the other trees by the single cap-like scale to the bud in connection with the 3 bundle-scars in the narrow leaf-scar.

**DISTRIBUTION**—A European tree much planted in this country for ornament.   It has become naturalized throughout the populated regions of New England, in moist places. near streams and ponds.

**WOOD**—Very light, soft, tough, light brown in color with thick nearly white sapwood, easily worked and taking a beautiful polish; used in this country for charcoal and for fuel.

YELLOW WILLOW

# SILVER POPLAR
## White Poplar, Silver-leaf Poplar, Abele.
### Populus alba L.

**HABIT**—A good sized tree 40-75 ft. high, with a trunk diameter of 2-4 ft.; branches wide-spreading, developing a large, irregular, open, broad, round-topped head; spreading abundantly by means of root suckers.

**BARK**—On young trunks and limbs smooth, characteristically light greenish-gray or whitish, often with dark blotches; base of older trunk at length deeply furrowed into firm dark ridges. The Silver Poplar retains its smooth light colored bark longer than our other members of the genus.

**TWIGS**—Slender or sometimes stout, greenish-gray, densely covered with thick whitish-cottony wool which can be readily rubbed off and often remains throughout the winter only toward the apex; where wool is removed the surface is shiny; short spurs numerous with conspicuous raised leaf-scars and with terminal buds only. LENTICELS—pale, round, raised dots. PITH—5-pointed, star-shaped.

**LEAF-SCARS**—Alternate, more than 2-ranked, semi-circular to inversely triangular; on short spurs narrower. STIPULE-SCARS—distinct. BUNDLE-SCARS—3, simple or compound.

**BUDS**—Small, ovate to conical, light chestnut brown; neither sticky nor fragrant; shining or more or less covered especially toward base with cottony wool; lateral buds 5-7 mm. long, terminal buds somewhat larger, thicker. BUD-SCALES—margined with very minute hairs; the first scale of lateral buds anterior. This first scale in front has a scale directly above it, the edges of the two being essentially parallel; likewise the first scale in back generally has a scale directly above it with similarly parallel edges. The first four scales therefore form two ranks facing respectively front and back. This condition seems constant for typical buds, but does not hold for abnormally small buds.

**COMPARISONS**—The Silver Poplar, acquires a roughened trunk later than the other Poplars, retaining the smooth whitish-green appearance of its bark as a distinctive character. Its generally delicate twigs, greenish-gray when not covered with cottony wool which generally can be found at least at the apex, furnish further characters that distinguish this species from the other poplars. The two rows of scales with parallel edges in the lateral buds are found to a less striking degree in the larger buds of the Small-toothed Aspen and the Large-toothed Aspen.

**DISTRIBUTION**—Widely distributed in the Old World. Introduced from England by the early settlers and soon established in the colonial towns on the western shore of Massachusetts Bay. Planted or spontaneous over a wide area. New Brunswick and Nova Scotia, occasional; southward to Virginia.

**IN NEW ENGLAND**—Occasional throughout, local, sometimes common.

**IN CONNECTICUT**—Occasional, escaped from cultivation to roadsides and waste places.

**WOOD**—Light, soft, weak, reddish-yellow with nearly white sapwood; difficult to split and to ignite; used in Europe for rollers, packing cases and flooring.

SILVER POPLAR

# SMALL-TOOTHED ASPEN

## American or Quaking Aspen, Popple, Poplar, Aspen.

### Populus tremuloides Michx.

---

**HABIT**—As generally found a small tree 35-40 ft. high though not infrequently reaching 50-60 ft. in height with a trunk diameter of 1½ ft. or more; trunk tapering, continuous into top of tree; main branches slender, scattered, often drooping at the ends forming an open, narrow, round-topped head; spreading by means of root suckers.

**BARK**—On young trunks and branches thin, pale yellowish-brown, orange-green or nearly white with dark blotches below the branches, smooth with horizontal raised ridges (often encircling limbs); on older trunks especially toward the base, thick, furrowed and nearly black.

**TWIGS**—Slender, round, bright reddish-brown, smooth, shining. Older twigs grayish-brown, roughened by elevated leaf-scars and by swollen bases of detached branchlets. LENTICELS—light reddish-orange, scattered, oblong. PITH—5-pointed, star-shaped.

**LEAF-SCARS**—Alternate, more than 2-ranked, large, inversely triangular, covered with light colored corky layer, upper edge of scar more or less depressed. STIPULE-SCARS—blackish, more or less conspicuous. BUNDLE-SCARS—3, simple or each compounded.

**BUDS**—Narrowly conical, sharp-pointed, generally appressed especially toward apex of twig or incurved, about 5-7 mm. long, shining, slightly sticky but not fragrant; flower buds larger, ovate. BUD-SCALES—6 or 7 in number, smooth, reddish-brown, shining, scarious along the margins; the first scale of lateral buds anterior (i.e. facing outward), reaching about ⅓ of the way to the apex, often splitting at the top.

**COMPARISONS**—In general habit and bark characters the Small-toothed resembles the Large-toothed Aspen. It is readily distinguished from the latter by its shining reddish-brown, often slightly sticky, mostly appressed buds which are free from down. Those of the Large-toothed Aspen are thicker, dull dusty-looking, more or less gray-downy, and for the most part divergent. The bark of the Small-toothed Aspen is generally somewhat lighter in color, often nearly white and generally earlier and more deeply roughened at the base; the larger branches of the Large-toothed Aspen have a tendency to grow out at a wider angle with the trunk than those of the Small-toothed Aspen. The buds resemble somewhat those of the Balsam Poplar but are much smaller, only slightly sticky and not fragrant. It is separated from the Carolina Poplar and Lombardy Poplar by its reddish twigs, those of the latter two species being yellow; from the Silver Poplar by absence of down on twigs.

**DISTRIBUTION**—In practically all soils and situations except in deep swamps though more often in dry ground; one of the first trees to take possession of clearings or burnt lands. Newfoundland, Labrador, and Nova Scotia to the Hudson Bay region and Alaska; south to New Jersey, along the mountains in Pennsylvania and Kentucky, ascending 3,000 feet in the Adirondacks; west to the slopes of the Rocky mountains, along which it extends to Mexico and lower California.

IN NEW ENGLAND—Common, reaching in the White Mountain region, an altitude of 3,000 ft.

IN CONNECTICUT—Frequent.

**WOOD**—Light brown, with nearly white sapwood of 25-30 layers of annual growth, soft, weak and soon decaying; used in great quantities for paper pulp and in the manufacture of excelsior.

SMALL-TOOTHED ASPEN

# LARGE-TOOTHED ASPEN
## Popple, Poplar.
### Populus grandidentata Michx.

**HABIT**—Generally a small tree 30-45 ft. in height with trunk diameter of up to 1½ ft., at times reaching much greater dimensions; resembling the Small-toothed Aspen; spreading by means of root suckers.

**BARK**—Resembling that of Small-toothed Aspen though generally with more yellow or buff color to young trunks and limbs. The older trunks seem to be rather less deeply furrowed.

**TWIGS**—Stout, round, reddish-brown or somewhat yellowish-brown, in early winter often more or less pale-downy in protected portions, older twigs greenish-gray, otherwise resembling Small-toothed Aspen.

**LEAF-SCARS**—Resembling Small-toothed Aspen though the rather larger stipule-scars are often indistinct or absent.

**BUDS**—Averaging larger than those of Small-toothed Aspen, ovate to conical, pointed, generally divergent, dull, dusty-looking, due to fine, close, pale wool, especially at margins of scales; flower buds larger and thicker. BUD-SCALES—light chestnut brown with scarious margins; first scale of bud anterior.

**COMPARISONS**—The Large-toothed Aspen resembles the Small-toothed Aspen with which it is frequently confused. For points of distinction see under the latter species. The Lombardy and Carolina Poplars are distinguished by their yellow twigs and smooth buds; the Balsam Poplar by its shining fragrant resinous buds; the Silver Poplar by its generally more delicate, greenish twigs which are cottony-woolly at least toward the apex.

**DISTRIBUTION**—In rich or poor soils; woods, hillsides, borders of streams. Nova Scotia, New Brunswick, southern Quebec, and Ontario; south to Pennsylvania and Delaware, along the mountains to Kentucky, North Carolina, and Tennessee; west to Minnesota.

IN NEW ENGLAND—Common, occasional at altitudes of 2,000 feet or more.

IN CONNECTICUT—Frequent.

**WOOD**—Light brown, with thin nearly white sapwood of 20-30 layers of annual growth, weak and soft, used in manufacture of paper, excelsior, and to a small extent for woodenware.

LARGE-TOOTHED ASPEN

# BALSAM POPLAR
## Balsam, Tacamahac, Balm of Gilead.
### Populus balsamifera L.

**HABIT**—A medium sized tree, 30-75 ft. in height with trunk diameter of 1-3 ft.; head open, comparatively narrow, with spire-like tendency; spreading by means of root suckers.

**BARK**—On young trunks and branches smooth, light brown tinged with red, on older trunks dark gray tinged with red, broken into broad, firm, rounded ridges.

**TWIGS**—Stout, round, bright reddish-brown, smooth, shining; older twigs dark orange colored becoming gray tinged with yellowish-green, roughened by thickened leaf-scars; short spurs numerous with terminal but without lateral buds. LENTICELS—oblong, light reddish-orange, scattered. PITH—5-pointed, star-shaped.

**LEAF-SCARS**—Alternate, more than 2-ranked, large, 3-lobed, inversely triangular, rather narrow for the group. STIPULE-SCARS—distinct. BUNDLE-SCARS—3, simple or compound.

**BUDS**—Large, dark red, resinous, sticky, fragrant especially if crushed, narrowly ovate to conical long-pointed, 15-25 mm. long, terminal larger and relatively wider than lateral buds. BUD-SCALES—thick, smooth, oblong, pointed, red or green, saturated with fragrant amber-colored resin which on the outside, where exposed to the air, forms a dark reddish, shining varnish to the bud; the first scale of lateral bud anterior.

**COMPARISONS**—The Balsam Poplar with its varieties is distinguished from all other forms by the fragrance of its large resinous buds. Twigs and buds resemble those of the Small-toothed Aspen in color but are much larger and are distinctly fragrant especially if crushed. The Balm of Gilead [*Populus candicans* Ait.] is considered a distinct species by some and by others only a variety. It is extensively planted. It differs from the typical Balsam Poplar in its more spreading branches forming a broader and more open head but the twig characters are closely similar. The photographs were all taken from this latter variety, the descriptions from the type.

**DISTRIBUTION**—Alluvial soils; river banks, valleys, borders of swamps, woods. Newfoundland and Nova Scotia; west to Manitoba; northward to the coast of Alaska and along the Mackenzie River to the Artic circle; west through northern New York, Michigan, Minnesota, Dakota (Black Hills), Montana, beyond the Rockies to the Pacific coast.

IN NEW ENGLAND—Maine—common; New Hampshire—Connecticut river valley, generally near the river, becoming more plentiful northward; Vermont—frequent; Massachusetts and Rhode Island—not reported.

IN CONNECTICUT—Local. River banks, wet woods and roadsides, usually as an escape from cultivation; Southington, Milford, Wilton, Sherman, New Milford and Kent. Apparently native at Norfolk.

**WOOD**—Light, soft and weak; light brown, with thick nearly white sapwood; used for pails, boxes and paper pulp.

BALSAM POPLAR

# CAROLINA POPLAR
## Cottonwood, Necklace Poplar.
### Populus deltoides Marsh.
#### *P. monilifera* Ait. ; *P. canadensis* Moench.

---

**HABIT**—A large tree, the largest of the Poplars, 75-100 ft. in height with a trunk diameter of 3-5 ft.; lower branches massive nearly horizontal, those above arising at a sharper angle and forming altogether in old trees a broad-spreading, rather open head, often as broad as high; in younger individuals forming a more pyramidal head; of very rapid growth hence much planted for quick effects.  The form cultivated under the name Carolina Poplar and considered by some distinct from the Cottonwood, is of pyramidal habit of growth with erect tapering trunk continuous to the top of the tree and producing branches in whorls at the upper limit of each year's growth.  The figures in the plate were all taken from the more commonly cultivated form.

**BARK**—On young trunks and branches thin, smooth, light yellowish-green.  On older trunks thick, ashy-gray, deeply divided into long, broad, flattish or eventually rounded ridges of characteristic appearance in native-grown trees.

**TWIGS**—Stout, yellowish to greenish-yellow, smooth, round or marked especially on vigorous trees with more or less prominent wings running down from the two sides and bases of the leaf-scars.  LENTICELS—large, pale, elongated longitudinally.

**LEAF-SCARS**—Alternate, more than 2-ranked, large, 3-lobed, inversely triangular.  STIPULE-SCARS—generally conspicuous, blackish.  BUNDLE-SCARS—3, simple or compound.

**BUDS**—Conical, large, the lateral buds reaching 15 mm. and the terminal buds reaching 20 mm. in length, frequently much smaller; lateral buds, especially the larger flower buds, generally divergent and often strongly recurved; terminal bud more or less distinctly 5-sided.  BUD-SCALES—smooth, light chestnut brown, shining; first scale of lateral bud anterior; outer scales slightly resinous-sticky, inner scales thickly coated with a light yellow sticky resin which is scarcely fragrant.

**COMPARISONS**—The Carolina Poplar is distinguished from our other Poplars except the Lombardy Poplar by its light yellow twigs.  The Lombardy has somewhat similar twigs but they are more slender, the buds are generally much smaller and typically appressed.  Appressed buds do occur on the Carolina Poplar and divergent buds on the Lombardy but they are more typical on each tree as indicated.  The distinct habit of the Lombardy Poplar is however a sufficient criterion of this latter species.

**DISTRIBUTION**—In moist soil, river banks and basins, shores of lakes, not uncommon in drier locations, often cultivated.  Throughout Quebec and Ontario to the base of the Rocky mountains; south to Florida; west to the Rocky mountains.

IN NEW ENGLAND—Maine—not reported; New Hampshire—restricted to the immediate vicinity of the Connecticut river, disappearing near the northern part of Westmoreland; Vermont—western sections, abundant along the shores of the Hoosac river in Pownal and along Lake Champlain; in the Connecticut valley as far north as Brattleboro; Massachusetts—along the Connecticut and its tributaries; Rhode Island —occasional.

IN CONNECTICUT—Frequent in the valleys of the Connecticut, Farmington, and Housatonic rivers; rare or occasional elsewhere.

**WOOD**—Dark brown, with thick nearly white sapwood, light and soft, warping badly in drying and difficult to season, used for paper pulp and in the manufacture of boxes.

Carolina Poplar

# LOMBARDY POPLAR

Populus nigra, var. italica Du Roi.

*P. dilatata* Ait. ; *P. pyramidalis* Rozier ; *P. fastigiata* Desf.

**HABIT**—A tall tree reaching over 100 ft. in height with a buttressed tapering, continuous trunk, sometimes as much as 6-8 ft. in diameter at base; branches numerous, arising low on the trunk, bending upward at a sharp angle with numerous branchlets also sharply ascending to form a very narrow spire-shaped tree of decidedly characteristic appearance; spreading by means of root suckers. It tends to retain its leaves on the lower part of the tree. (See bark picture.)

**BARK**—On old trees gray to brown, deeply furrowed.

**TWIGS**—Resembling those of Carolina Poplar but slender, round and appressed.

**LEAF-SCARS**—Resembling those of Carolina Poplar but smaller.

**BUDS**—Resembling those of Carolina Poplar but for the most part appressed, distinctly smaller, terminal buds seldom over 10 mm. long and lateral buds generally under 8 mm. in length.

**COMPARISONS**—The Lombardy Poplar is readily distinguished from all our other trees by its striking spire-shaped habit of growth. In twig characters it resembles the Carolina Poplar but the twigs are slender and the buds average smaller and are more characteristically appressed.

**DISTRIBUTION**—A European tree much planted in this country for ornament, escaping to a certain extent to roadsides and river banks.

**WOOD**—Light, soft, weak, close-grained, reddish-brown with thick nearly white sapwood, used to a slight extent in the manufacture of boxes and wooden ware

LOMBARDY POPLAR

# BUTTERNUT
## Oilnut, White Walnut.
### Juglans cinerea L.

**HABIT**—A small to medium-sized tree 20-45 ft. in height, with trunk diameter of 1-4 ft.; comparatively large for the height; soon dividing into a few stout spreading branches with lower branches somewhat drooping forming a symmetrical, broad, low, round-topped head of inversely pyramidal outline.

**BARK**—On young trunks and branches smooth, light gray, on older trunks deeply divided into long, rather broad, flat-topped, whitish ridges separated by smoothish, broader fissures, which are likewise gray or frequently become black in striking contrast to the whitish ridges; inner bark becoming yellow on exposure to air, bitter.

**TWIGS**—Stout, reddish-buff to greenish-gray, downy or nearly smooth, round or somewhat angled from lobes of leaf-scars, bitter to taste, and coloring saliva yellow when chewed. LENTICELS—small, pale, raised dots. PITH—somewhat 5-pointed, star-shaped, dark brown, chambered, the narrow chambers a little wider than the intervening diaphragms.

**LEAF-SCARS**—Large, conspicuous, 3-lobed, inversely triangular; margins elevated, upper margin generally convex seldom slightly notched, surmounted by a raised, downy pad. BUNDLE-SCARS—dark, conspicuous in 3 U-shaped clusters.

**BUDS**—Densely pale-downy; terminal buds large, conical-oblong, 10-20 mm. long, longer than broad, flattened oblong to conical, obliquely blunt-pointed; lateral buds smaller, ovate, rounded at apex, 1-3 superposed buds generally present above axillary bud, the uppermost the largest, often far above the leaf-scar and more or less stalked or developing into a twig the first season, especially on rapidly grown shoots; staminate flower buds lateral, rather spherical, protruding the undeveloped catkins like miniature scaly cones from the envelope of short scales. BUD-SCALES—thick, outer scales of terminal bud lobed at apex.

**FRUIT**—Elongated, 4-10 cm. long, husk thickly covered with sticky hairs, not regularly splitting. NUT—light brown, elongated-ovate, 4-ribbed, pointed, rough, deeply sculptured; within, 2-celled at base, 1-celled above; seed sweet, edible, very oily, soon becoming rancid.

**COMPARISONS**—In twig characters the Butternut most nearly resembles the Black Walnut but is easily distinguished from this species (see Comparisons under Black Walnut). Its points of dissimilarity to the Bitternut are given under this latter species.

**DISTRIBUTION**—Roadsides, rich woods, river valleys, fertile, moist hillsides, high up on mountain slopes. New Brunswick, throughout Quebec and eastern Ontario; south to Delaware, along the mountains to Georgia and Alabama; west to Minnesota, Kansas, and Arkansas.

IN NEW ENGLAND—Maine, common, often abundant; New Hampshire—throughout the Connecticut valley, and along the Merrimac and its tributaries, to the base of the White Mountains; Vermont—frequent; Massachusetts—common in the eastern and central portions, frequent westward; Rhode Island—common.

IN CONNECTICUT—Frequent.

**WOOD**—Light, soft, not strong, coarse-grained, light brown, turning darker with exposure, with thin, light-colored sapwood, composed of 5 or 6 layers of annual growth; largely employed in the interior finish of houses and for furniture. The inner bark possesses mild cathartic properties. Sugar is made from the sap and the green husks of the fruit are used to dye cloth yellow or orange color.

BUTTERNUT

# BLACK WALNUT
## Juglans nigra L.

**HABIT**—A large tree, 50-75 ft. high with a trunk diameter of 2-5 ft., reaching a height of 150 ft. and a trunk diameter of 6-8 ft. in the Ohio valley; trunk straight, tapering, giving off stout branches, those below often nearly horizontal or declined, those above arising at a sharper angle, spreading, forming an open, symmetrical, round-topped head.

**BARK**—Thick, dark, rough, deeply furrowed into rounded ridges; inner bark becoming yellow on exposure to air.

**TWIGS**—Stout, densely gray-downy to smooth and reddish-buff; bitter to taste and coloring saliva yellow when chewed. LENTICELS—small, pale, raised dots, rather inconspicuous. PITH—buff, paler than that of Butternut, chambered, the open chambers several times wider than the intervening diaphragms.

**LEAF-SCARS**—Large, conspicuous, elevated, 3-lobed inversely triangular to heart-shaped, upper margin distinctly notched enclosing the axillary bud; no downy pad above leaf-scar. BUNDLE-SCARS—dark, conspicuous in 3 U-shaped clusters.

**BUDS**—Pale, silky-downy; terminal buds ovate, generally under 10 mm. long and scarcely longer than broad, slightly flattened, obliquely blunt-pointed; lateral buds smaller, their outer scales opening at apex during winter, frequently a single superposed accessory bud above axillary bud. BUD-SCALES—thick, outer scales of terminal bud generally not evidently lobed.

**FRUIT**—Round-oval, 4-10 cm. in diameter, husk smooth not regularly splitting. NUT—dark brown, round-oval, slightly flattened, sculptured with interrupted, irregular, thick ridges; within 4-celled below the middle, 2-celled above; seed sweet, edible, oily, soon becoming rancid.

**COMPARISONS**—The Black Walnut is most closely related to the Butternut which it resembles in its chambered pith and the general twig appearance. The Butternut, however, has terminal buds longer than broad, downy pads above leaf-scars which are not notched as are leaf-scars of the Black Walnut and it further has elongated rather than spherical nuts. The pith is dark brown while that of Black Walnut is pale buff and the chambers are not much wider than the diaphragms. In habit it is a lower, more spreading tree than the Black Walnut and the light gray color especially of the flat ridges of the bark is further characteristic. The points of dissimilarity to the Bitternut are mentioned under this latter species.

**DISTRIBUTION**—Rich woods, largely destroyed for its valuable timber and now scarce; occasionally cultivated as an ornamental tree in the eastern United States. Massachusetts; south to Florida; west to Minnesota, Kansas, Arkansas and Texas.

IN NEW ENGLAND—Maine, New Hampshire, and Vermont—not reported native; Massachusetts—rare east of the Connecticut river, occasional along the western part of the Connecticut valley to the New York line; Rhode Island—doubtfully native, Apponaug, and elsewhere.

IN CONNECTICUT—Rare. Roadsides and rocky hillsides, in most localities derived from planted trees: Norwich, East Hartford, Newington, Southington, Seymour and Southbury, Trumbull and Easton. Probably native at North Canaan.

**WOOD**—Heavy, hard, strong, rather coarse-grained, very durable, rich dark brown, with thin lighter colored sapwood of 10-20 layers of annual growth; largely used in cabinet-making, the interior finish of houses, gun-stocks, and in boat and ship building.

BLACK WALNUT

# SHAG-BARK HICKORY
## Shell-bark Hickory, Walnut.
### Carya ovata (Mill.) K. Koch.
*C. alba* Nutt. ; *Hickoria ovata* Britton.

**HABIT**—A large tree, the tallest of the Hickories 50-75 ft. high, with trunk diameter of less than 2 ft.; in the forest producing a tall, straight trunk often free from branches for 50 ft. or more, surmounted by a narrow head of few limbs; in the open generally forking low down or below the middle of the tree into stout ascending limbs forming an irregular open narrow oblong or inversely conical round-topped head.

**BARK**—On young trunks and limbs smooth, light gray, becoming seamy; on old trunks shagging characteristically into long flat plates which are free at the base or both ends.

**TWIGS**—Stout, somewhat downy or smooth and shining, reddish-brown to light gray. LENTICELS—numerous, pale, conspicuous, longitudinally elongated. PITH—obscurely 5-pointed, star-shaped.

**LEAF-SCARS**—Alternate, more than 2-ranked, large, conspicuous, pale, slightly elevated, 3-lobed, heart-shaped to semi-circular. STIPULE-SCARS—absent. BUNDLE-SCARS—numerous, irregularly scattered or arranged in 3 more or less definite circular groups.

**BUDS**—Large, terminal bud 10-20 mm. long, broadly ovate, rather blunt-pointed. BUD-SCALES—the 3-4 outer scales dark brown, slightly downy or nearly smooth, fine-hairy on margins, broadly triangular, sharp-pointed, the outermost keeled and often with apex prolonged into a long, rigid point, persistent through winter but cracking and shagging off from the apex downward; inner scales yellowish-green, often tinged with red, densely downy on outer surface, shining within.

**FRUIT**—Nearly spherical, 3-5 cm. long, depressed at apex; husk 5-8 mm. thick, with small pale lenticels, splitting to the base into four pieces. NUT—whitish, variable in size and shape, generally oblong, flattened, 4-ridged, rounded or pointed at base and apex; seed sweet.

**COMPARISONS**—The Shag-bark Hickory is distinguished from other trees by the distinct shagging of its bark. The bark especially of one variety of the Pignut shags to a certain extent but not so extensively. From the Pignut, however, it is distinguished by its larger buds, and stouter twigs. From the Mockernut it is distinguished by its relatively longer buds, the darker, comparatively smooth, outer scales of which remain throughout the winter though shagging away more or less completely from the tip toward the base.

**DISTRIBUTION**—In various soils and situations, fertile slopes, brooksides, rocky hills. Valley of the St. Lawrence; south to Delaware and along the mountains to Florida; west to Minnesota, Kansas, Indian Territory, and Texas.

IN NEW ENGLAND—Maine, along or near the coast as far north as Harpswell; New Hampshire—common as far north as Lake Winnepesaukee; Vermont—occasional along the Connecticut to Windsor, rather common in the Champlain valley and along the western slopes of the Green mountains; Massachusetts and Rhode Island—common.

IN CONNECTICUT—Frequent or common.

**WOOD**—Heavy, very hard and strong, tough, close-grained, flexible, light brown with thin nearly white sapwood; largely used in the manufacture of agricultural implements, carriages, wagons, and for axe-handles, baskets and fuel. The nut is the common hickory nut of commerce.

SHAG-BARK HICKORY

# MOCKERNUT
## Big Bud Hickory, White-heart Hickory.
### Carya alba (L.) K. Koch.
*C. tomentosa* Nutt. ; *Hickoria alba* Britton.

**HABIT**—A tall tree 50-70 ft. high with trunk diameter of 2-3 ft.; lower branches more or less drooping, those above ascending at a sharp angle, forming a narrow oblong or broad round-topped head, trunk somewhat swollen at base.

**BARK**—Light to dark gray, not shaggy, broken by irregular interrupted fissures into shallow rounded and smooth-topped ridges which are transversely cracked at intervals; the smoothness of the furrows and of the rounded ridges together with the grayness of the bark is quite characteristic, giving an appearance as if the roughness of the bark had been sandpapered down or as if a thin veil had been drawn over the trunk.

**TWIGS**—Very stout, generally more or less finely-downy, reddish-brown to gray. LENTICELS—numerous, pale, conspicuous, longitudinally elongated. PITH—obscurely 5-pointed, star-shaped.

**LEAF-SCARS**—Alternate, more than 2-ranked, similar to those of Shag-bark Hickory but rather tending to be more distinctly 3-lobed with basal lobe elongated.

**BUDS**—Terminal buds pale, densely hairy, broadly ovate, blunt or sharp-pointed, 10-20 mm. long, outermost scales falling in early autumn, exposing the yellowish-gray silky inner scales, some of which fall during the winter.

**FRUIT**—Spherical to obovate, 4-6 cm. long, more or less narrowed at the ends; husk 3-4 mm. thick, splitting to middle or nearly to base. NUT—brown, variable in size and shape, spherical to oblong, more or less flattened and angled and generally pointed at both ends; shell very thick; seed comparatively small, sweet.

**COMPARISONS**—The Mockernut, so named from the disappointingly small kernel obtained from the relatively large nut, is distinguished by its large, fat, pale, downy buds, which do not retain the outer dark scales as do the narrower buds of the Shag-bark Hickory. The peculiar smoothness of the ridges and furrows of the gray bark is also a distinctive characteristic.

**DISTRIBUTION**—In various soils; woods, dry, rocky ridges, mountain slopes. Niagara peninsula and westward; south to Florida, ascending 3,500 feet in Virginia; west to Kansas, Nebraska, Missouri, Indian Territory, and Texas.

IN NEW ENGLAND—Maine and Vermont not reported; New Hampshire—sparingly along the coast; Massachusetts—rather common eastward; Rhode Island—common.

IN CONNECTICUT—Occasional or frequent.

**WOOD**—Very heavy, hard, tough, strong, close-grained, flexible, rich dark brown, with thick nearly white sapwood; used for the same purpose as that of the Shag-bark Hickory.

MOCKERNUT

# PIGNUT
## Pignut or Broom Hickory.
### Carya glabra (Mill.) Spach.
*C. porcina* Nutt.; *Hickoria glabra* Britton.

---

**HABIT**—A good sized tree, 50-60 ft. in height with a trunk diameter of 2-5 ft.; branches slender, more or less contorted, the lower ones especially usually strongly pendulous, forming a narrow oblong head, well shown in the tree photographed, or broader in other specimens.

**BARK**—Dark gray, fissured into irregular diamond-shaped areas somewhat suggesting bark of White Ash, but narrow ridges flattened, tough, tending to become detached at ends; sometimes somewhat shaggy especially in one of the varieties mentioned below, which has a bark approaching that of the Shag-bark Hickory.

**TWIGS**—Comparatively slender for the genus, smooth, reddish-brown, to gray. LENTICELS—numerous, longitudinally elongated, more or less conspicuous. PITH—obscurely 5-pointed, star-shaped.

**LEAF-SCARS**—Alternate, more than 2-ranked, obscurely 3-lobed, heart-shaped to semi-circular or oblong. BUNDLE-SCARS—numerous, irregularly scattered or collected in 3 more or less definite groups.

**BUDS**—Reddish-brown to gray, small, terminal bud under 10 mm. long, oval, blunt or sharp-pointed, becoming subglobose toward spring. BUD-SCALES—outer scales dark, smooth or finely downy, generally slightly yellow glandular-dotted, more or less keeled, and sometimes long pointed, often falling before the end of winter and exposing the pale-silky inner scales.

**FRUIT**—Pear-shaped to oblong to nearly spherical, 3-5 cm. long; very variable in size and shape; husk under 2 mm. thick, in some forms splitting only at the apex and enclosing the nut after it has fallen to the ground, in other forms splitting to the middle or to the base. NUT—thick or rather thin shelled, generally not ridged nor sharp-pointed; seed sweet or sometimes bitter.

**COMPARISONS**—The Pignut is a very variable species and there are several varieties described, some of which have been recognized as distinct species, as for instance *Carya microcarpa* Nutt.,—the Small-fruited Hickory—which is perhaps the most conspicuous. It has a somewhat shaggy bark and a nearly spherical fruit with the husk splitting to the base. The most distinctive feature of the whole species is the small size of the buds, which before the outer dark scales drop off resemble buds of the Shag-bark Hickory except for size, and after these outer scales have been shed may be compared with miniature Mockernut buds. Its bark is not smoothed off like that of the Mockernut nor except in extreme cases shaggy like that of the Shag-bark.

**DISTRIBUTION**—Woods, dry hills and uplands. Niagara peninsula and along Lake Erie; south to the Gulf of Mexico; west to Minnesota, Nebraska, Kansas, Indian Territory, and Texas.

IN NEW ENGLAND—Maine—frequent in the southern corner of York county; New Hampshire—common toward the coast and along the lower Merrimac valley; abundant on hills near the Connecticut river, but only occasional above Bellows Falls; Vermont—Marsh Hill, Ferrisburgh, W. Castleton and Pownal; Massachusetts—common eastward; along the Connecticut river valley and some of the tributary valleys, more common than the Shag-bark; Rhode Island—common.

IN CONNECTICUT—Occasional or frequent.

**WOOD**—Heavy, hard, very strong and tough, flexible, light or dark brown, with thick, lighter colored or often nearly white sapwood; used for the handles of tools and in the manufacture of wagons and agricultural implements, and largely for fuel.

PIGNUT

# BITTERNUT
## Swamp Hickory.
Carya cordiformis (Wang.) K. Koch.

*C. amara* Nutt. ; *Hickoria minima* (Marsh.) Britton.

---

**HABIT**—A tall tree 50-75 ft. in height, with a trunk diameter of 1-2½ ft.; trunk generally early developing several stout ascending and somewhat diverging branches to form a broad spreading head generally widest toward the top.

**BARK**—Thin, light gray, close, with shallow fissures and narrow ridges rarely flaking off in small thin scales.

**TWIGS**—Slender, buff or gray or reddish, smooth or slightly downy toward apex, generally yellow-glandular above. LENTICELS—more or less distinct, pale, numerous, longitudinally elongated. PITH—infrequently star-shaped, brown.

**LEAF-SCARS**—Alternate, more than 2-ranked, obscurely 3-lobed, heart-shaped, inversely triangular to elliptical, pale, raised, large, prominent, the upper margin generally rounded, convex to sharp-pointed, often 2-toothed at apex. BUNDLE-SCARS—prominent, irregularly scattered or collected into 3 more or less regular groups or sometimes apparently in single curved line.

**BUDS**—Slender, strikingly yellow with crowded glandular dots, slightly hairy between the scales; terminal bud 5-15 mm. long, flattened, obliquely blunt-pointed; lateral buds more or less 4-angled, the axillary bud generally minute with one or more larger superposed buds above it, often considerably separated from each other, the uppermost of the series stalked or developing into a twig the first season. BUD-SCALES—4, valvate in pairs.

**FRUIT**—Nearly spherical to pear-shaped 2-3.5 cm. long, generally 4-winged from the apex to about the middle; husk about 1 mm. thick, yellow glandular-dotted, tardily splitting to about the middle into 4 valves. NUT—usually thin-shelled, sometimes broader than long, smooth, short-pointed; seed deeply and irregularly roughened, sweetish at first, becoming intensely bitter.

**COMPARISONS**—The Bitternut is not to be confused with any other tree if due notice is taken of the narrow bright yellow, glandular-dotted often superposed buds. The Butternut has superposed buds but they are pale greenish-yellow and very downy, not bright yellow nor glandular dotted and the pith though similarly brown is distinctly chambered.

**DISTRIBUTION**—In varying soils and situations; wet woods, low, damp fields, river valleys, along roadsides, occasional upon uplands and hill slopes. From Montreal west to Georgian bay; south to Florida, ascending 3,500 feet in Virginia; west to Minnesota, Nebraska, Kansas, Indian Territory, and Texas.

IN NEW ENGLAND—Maine—southward, rare; New Hampshire—eastern limit in the Connecticut valley, where it ranges farther north than any other of our Hickories, reaching Well's river; Vermont—occasional west of the Green mountains and in the southern Connecticut valley; Massachusetts—rather common, abundant in the vicinity of Boston; Rhode Island—common.

IN CONNECTICUT—Occasional.

**WOOD**—Heavy, very hard, strong, tough, close-grained, dark brown, with thick light brown or often nearly white sapwood; largely used for hoops and ox-yokes and for fuel.

BITTERNUT

# HOP HORNBEAM
## Ironwood, Leverwood, Deerwood.
### Ostrya virginiana (Mill.) K. Koch.

**HABIT**—A small tree 25-40 ft. in height with a trunk diameter of generally less than 1 ft.; branches long, slender, those below widely spreading and often drooping but with branchlets tending upward forming an irregular oblong or broadly ovate head often as broad as tall with slender, stiff spray.

**BARK**—Thin, flaky, light grayish-brown broken into narrow flattish pieces, loose at the ends.

**TWIGS**—Slender, 1-2 mm. in thickness, dark reddish-brown, often zigzag, for the most part smooth and shining. LENTICELS—scattered, pale.

**LEAF-SCARS**—Alternate, 2-ranked, minute, 1.75 mm. or less in diameter, flattened, elliptical, projecting. STIPULE-SCARS—triangular, rather inconspicuous. BUNDLE-SCARS—generally 3, inconspicuous; if scar is surface-sectioned, 5 bundle-scars are evident.

**BUDS**—Small, 3-7 mm. long, narrowly ovate, pointed, light reddish-brown, smooth or somewhat finely downy, slightly gummy especially within, generally strongly divergent; terminal bud absent. BUD-SCALES —in 4 ranks, about 8 scales visible, increasing in size from below upwards, longitudinally striate if viewed toward light.

**FRUIT**—A small seed-like nutlet, enclosed in an inflated sac-like, veiny bract, long-hairy at base; the fruits aggregated together in a hop-like cluster about 7 cm. long, with stalks often hairy, generally falling before winter. Young staminate catkins abundantly present, cylindrical, usually in 3's, their scales bristle-pointed.

**COMPARISONS**—The Hop Hornbeam from its general appearance and bark character is sometimes mistaken for a young Elm. The scales of the bark, however, are narrower and more flaky, the leaf-scars are smaller and the bundle-scars are not sunken, the bud-scales are in 4 ranks and the staminate flowers are borne in catkins which are generally present on the tree in winter. For differences between the Hop Hornbeam and the American Hornbeam, see under latter species.

**DISTRIBUTION**—In rather open woods and along highlands. Nova Scotia to Lake Superior, scattered throughout the whole country east of the Mississippi, ranging through western Minnesota to Nebraska, Kansas, Indian Territory and Texas.

IN NEW ENGLAND—Common in all parts.

IN CONNECTICUT—Frequent.

**WOOD**—Strong, hard, tough, durable, light brown and tinged with red or often nearly white, with thick pale sapwood of 40-50 layers of annual growth, used for fence posts, levers, handles of tools, mallets and other small articles.

HOP HORNBEAM

# AMERICAN HORNBEAM
## Hornbeam, Blue Beech, Ironwood, Water Beech.
### Carpinus caroliniana Walt.

**HABIT**—A low tree or shrub 10-30 ft. high with a trunk diameter generally under 1 ft.; with long, slender, tough, more or less zigzag branches not easily broken, which are somewhat pendulous at ends forming a bushy wide spreading, flat or round-topped head; the trunk is frequently zigzag above giving appearance of being forked with broad rounded crotches.

**BARK**—Smooth, thin, dark bluish-gray, close-fitting, sinewy-fluted with smooth, rounded, longitudinal ridges. The smooth ridges of the bark are very characteristic and may be compared to the appearance of the wrist which becomes similarly ridged by the protrusion of the sinews when the hand is clenched.

**TWIGS**—Slender, about 1 mm. thick or less toward apex, dark red, and shining, smooth, or often somewhat hairy. LENTICELS—scattered, pale, generally conspicuous.

**LEAF-SCARS**—Alternate, 2-ranked, minute, flattened, elliptical, projecting. STIPULE-SCARS—narrow, triangular, rather inconspicuous. BUNDLE-SCARS—generally 3, inconspicuous, up to 5 visible when surface-sectioned.

**BUDS**—Small, usually 2-4 mm. long, narrowly ovate to oblong, pointed, reddish-brown, more or less hairy especially the buds containing staminate catkins which are larger and oval to obovate; leaf buds more or less appressed or only slightly divergent, terminal bud absent. BUD-SCALES—in 4 ranks about 8-12 scales visible, increasing in size from below upward white-scarious and often downy on edges, frequently with a woolly patch of down on tip; longitudinally striate when viewed toward light.

**FRUIT**—A small ribbed seed-like nutlet enclosed by a veiny generally 3-lobed bract about 2.5 cm. long, which is saw-toothed on one side of larger lobe and often has one of lower lobes lacking, usually falling before winter. Staminate catkins entirely enclosed in the larger buds therefore not visible during winter.

**COMPARISONS**—The American Hornbeam is often confused with the Hop Hornbeam perhaps chiefly from their unfortunate similarity in common names. The smooth, close, bluish-gray bark together with the habitat in which it grows has given it the name of Water Beech. The sinewy-fluting to the bark is unique among our trees and readily distinguishes the American Hornbeam from the Hop Hornbeam, the bark of which is flaky in narrow scales. Further the American Hornbeam never shows any catkins in winter while they are generally abundant on the Hop Hornbeam; the buds of the American Hornbeam are smaller, and have whitish down on the edges; those of the Hop Hornbeam are for the most part smooth and slightly gummy. The Beech which the American Hornbeam resembles in its bark has much larger and relatively longer buds.

**DISTRIBUTION**—Low, wet woods, and margins of swamps. Province of Quebec to Georgian bay; south to Florida; west to Minnesota, Nebraska, Kansas, Indian Territory, and Texas.

IN NEW ENGLAND—Rather common throughout, less frequent towards the coast.

IN CONNECTICUT—Frequent or common.

**WOOD**—Light brown with thick, nearly white sapwood, sometimes used for levers, the handles of tools and other small articles.

AMERICAN HORNBEAM

# BLACK BIRCH
## Cherry Birch; Sweet Birch.
### Betula lenta L.

**HABIT**—A medium to large sized tree 50-75 ft. high, with a trunk diameter of 1-4 ft.; branches long and slender, in young specimens upper branches ascending at sharp angle, lower branches horizontal or drooping with delicate spray forming a narrow head; in older trees becoming wide spreading, ovate in outline.

**BARK**—On young trunks and branches smooth, close, not peeling, dark reddish-brown, shining, with horizontally elongated pale lenticels resembling the bark of the cultivated Cherry whence the common name; in older trunks tardily broken into large thick irregular plates; inner bark with distinct wintergreen taste.

**TWIGS**—Slender, light reddish-brown, smooth, shining, with strong wintergreen flavor when chewed; short spur-like lateral shoots abundant, bearing two leaves each season, much roughened by leaf-scars of numerous past seasons. LENTICELS—pale, raised dots, becoming horizontally elongated with age. PITH—elliptical.

**LEAF-SCARS**—Alternate, 2-ranked, small, semi-oval to depressed inversely triangular to crescent-shaped, projecting. STIPULE-SCARS— present, narrow, inconspicuous. BUNDLE-SCARS—generally 3 and inconspicuous.

**BUDS**—Medium, 5-10 mm. long, conical, sharp-pointed, reddish-brown, divergent; terminal bud absent on long shoots; buds on short spurs terminal. BUD-SCALES—downy on margins, overlapping with more than 2 ranks; in buds of long shoots 3 scales visible, two lateral of equal size reaching half way up and a third with edges rolled around the bud; scales of terminal buds on short spurs more numerous, about 7 visible.

**FRUIT**—An erect, stalkless, oval-oblong catkin, 2-4 cm. long, with smooth scales about 4-6 mm. long, equally 3-lobed above the middle and with seed-like winged nutlets about as broad as their wings.

**COMPARISONS**—The Black Birch differs from other Birches in its close dark cherry-like bark. It is most closely related to the Yellow Birch in the character of its fruit and the aromatic flavor of the young bark. Besides the bark differences, however, the twigs of the Black Birch have a more decided wintergreen flavor. It has in general a somewhat less spreading habit of growth, the buds are divergent and the catkins are downy.

**DISTRIBUTION**—Moist grounds; rich woods, old pastures, fertile hill slopes, banks of rivers. Maine; south to Delaware, along the mountains to Florida; west to Minnesota and Kansas.

**IN NEW ENGLAND**—Maine—frequent; New Hampshire—in the highlands of the southern section, and along the Connecticut river valley to a short distance north of Windsor; Vermont—frequent in the western part of the state, and in the southern Connecticut valley; Massachusetts and Rhode Island—frequent throughout, especially in the highlands, less often near the coast.

**IN CONNECTICUT**—Widely distributed, especially in the Connecticut river valley, frequent or common.

**WOOD**—Heavy, very strong and hard, close-grained, dark brown tinged with red, with thin light brown or yellow sapwood of 70-80 layers of annual growth; largely used in the manufacture of furniture and for fuel, and occasionally in ship and boat building. Oil of wintergreen, used medicinally and as a flavor, is distilled from the wood, and beer is abtained by fermenting the sugary sap.

BLACK BIRCH

# YELLOW BIRCH
## Silver or Gray Birch.
### Betula lutea Michx. f.

**HABIT**—A large tree 60-90 ft. in height with trunk diameter of 2-4 ft., reaching its largest size in northern New England; in the open branching low down with long slender wide spreading somewhat pendulous branches forming a broadly ovate to hemispherical head. Older trees than the one photographed generally show a broader outline with the trunk less conspicuously continuous into the head.

**BARK**—On young trunks and branches close, bright, silvery-yellowish gray, generally at length peeling into thin ribbon-like layers which roll back and extend up the trunk in long lines of ragged fringe. There is considerable variation in the amount of peeling of the outer bark. A well marked condition of peeling is shown in the bark photographed; the bark of the tree used for the habit showed scarcely any peeling. On older trunks especially toward the base the silvery bark is entirely shed and the bark below shows reddish-brown and becomes rough and fissured into irregular plate-like scales.

**TWIGS**—Slender, light yellowish-brown, becoming darker, smooth or somewhat hairy; with only slight wintergreen flavor when chewed; short spur-like lateral branches abundant, similar to those of Black Birch. LENTICELS—pale, raised dots, inconspicuous, becoming horizontally elongated with age.

**LEAF-SCARS**—Alternate, 2-ranked, similar to those of Black Birch.

**BUDS**—Similar to those of Black Birch, more or less appressed. BUD-SCALES—more or less downy.

**FRUIT**—An erect, stalkless or short-stalked downy catkin, ovate to oblong, 2-4 cm. long and about 2 mm. wide and relatively wider than fruit of Black Birch; scales downy on the back and edges, 8-10 mm. long, longer than broad, nearly equally 3-lobed to the middle; with seed-like winged nutlets about as broad as their wings.

**COMPARISONS**—The Yellow Birch differs from the Black Birch as indicated in Comparisons under the latter species. In the peeling of the outer bark it resembles the Paper and the Red Birch. Its outer bark, however, is a dingy yellow and not a chalky white as is that of the exposed layers of the Paper Birch; moreover, in peeling the thin layers tend to curl back to form longitudinal lines of ragged fringe. The fringes of bark are larger and more ragged than in the Red Birch but the color alone is sufficient to distinguish the two forms.

**DISTRIBUTION**—Low, rich woodlands, mountain slopes. Newfoundland and Nova Scotia to Rainy river; south to the middle states, and along the mountains to Tennessee and North Carolina; west to Minnesota.

**IN NEW ENGLAND**—Abundant northward; common throughout, from borders of lowland swamps to 1,000 feet above the sea level; more common at considerable altitudes, where it often occurs in extensive patches or belts.

**IN CONNECTICUT**—Occasional or frequent.

**WOOD**—Heavy, very strong, hard, close-grained, light brown tinged with red, with thin nearly white sapwood; largely used in the manufacture of furniture, button and tassel moulds, boxes, the hubs of wheels and for fuel.

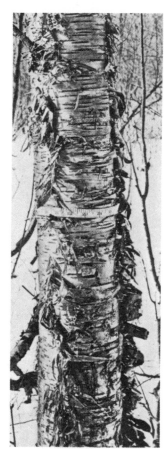

YELLOW BIRCH

# RED BIRCH
## River Birch.
### Betula nigra L.

**HABIT**—A medium sized tree, 30-50 ft. in height with a trunk diameter of 1-1½ ft., much larger southward; trunk often divided relatively low down as shown in photographs into a few slightly spreading limbs beset with numerous slender more or less pendulous branchlets, forming a rather narrow oblong head, becoming irregular and broader with age.

**BARK**—On young trunks and branches, thin, shining, light reddish-brown, peeling freely into thin papery layers of various shades of red and brown which curl back and remain for several years as ragged fringes and show the light pinkish tints of the freshly exposed inner layers; at base of older trunks, dark reddish-brown, deeply furrowed and broken into thick irregular plate-like scales.

**TWIGS**—Slender, dark red, for the most part smooth. LENTICELS—pale, becoming horizontally elongated.

**LEAF-SCARS**—Alternate, 2-ranked.

**BUDS**—Small, about 6 mm. long, shining, light chestnut brown, smooth or more or less hairy, ovate, pointed, more or less appressed.

**FRUIT**—Ripening in late spring or summer, a stalked, downy, cylindrical, erect, catkin, 2-5 cm. long; scales downy, with 3 narrow lobes; seed-like nutlet about as wide as the downy margined wings.

**COMPARISONS**—The Red Birch resembles the Yellow Birch in the more or less persistent ragged fringes of papery layers into which the outer bark peels. Its bark, however, is dark reddish to light cinnamon color and is rather less ragged in peeling than that of the Yellow Birch which, moreover, is of a dirty yellowish color. The Black Birch with its dark bark and the white barked species cannot be confused with the tree under discussion. This tree is rare and local in New England and except as planted for ornament is found along river banks.

**DISTRIBUTION**—Along rivers, ponds, and woodlands inundated a part of the year. Doubtfully and indefinitely reported from Canada; south, east of the Alleghany mountains, to Florida; west, locally through the northern tier of states to Minnesota and along the Gulf states to Texas; western limits, Nebraska, Kansas, Indian Territory, and Missouri.

**IN NEW ENGLAND**—Not reported in Maine, Vermont, Rhode Island or Connecticut; New Hampshire—found sparingly along streams in the southern part of the state; abundant along the banks of Beaver Brook, Pelham; Massachusetts—along the Merrimac river and its tributaries, bordering swamps in Methuen and ponds in North Andover.

**IN CONNECTICUT**——Not reported.

**WOOD**—Light, rather hard, strong, close-grained, light brown with pale sapwood of 40-50 layers of annual growth; used in the manufacture of furniture, wooden ware, wooden shoes and in turnery.

RED BIRCH

# GRAY BIRCH
## Old-field, White, Poverty, Small White or Poplar Birch.
### Betula populifolia Marsh.

---

**HABIT**—A small short-lived tree, 20-35 ft. in height with a trunk diameter of generally less than 1 ft., commonly growing in clumps; trunk slender, generally inclined to one side, continuous into top of tree, with a fringe from top to bottom of short slender branches which grow upward for a short distance but soon bend downward, with delicate spray forming a narrow, open, pyramidal, pointed head.

**BARK**—Dull chalky-white, close, not peeling, with distinct dark triangular patches below insertion of branches; inner bark reddish-orange yellow; base of older trees nearly black and roughened by irregular fissures; young trunks and branches bright reddish-brown.

**TWIGS**—Slender, bright reddish-brown or grayish, becoming with age dull chalky-white, much roughened by warty resinous exudations. **LENTICELS**—pale, raised dots becoming with age conspicuous and horizontally elongated.

**LEAF-SCARS**—Alternate, 2-ranked, small, with characters of the genus.

**BUDS**—Small, about 5 mm. or generally less in length, smooth, somewhat resinous especially within, ovate, pointed, divergent. **BUD-SCALES**—finely downy on margins, 3-4 visible.

**FRUIT**—An erect or pendant, slender-stalked, narrow-cylindrical catkin, 1.5 to 3.5 cm. long; scales minute 2-4 mm. long, finely downy with broad lateral recurved lobes, and narrow middle lobe suggesting the silhouette of a soaring bird; seed-like nutlet, minute, narrower than the wings. Staminate catkin usually solitary.

**COMPARISONS**—The Gray Birch resembles the Paper Birch in having a whitish outer bark. The bark however is a dingier gray and does not peel into thin papery layers as does that of the Paper Birch. A close inspection of its bark sometimes may show a certain breaking away of the outer part in minute inconspicuous scales, but this is not to be confused with a natural peeling. The bark, moreover, cannot be separated into thin papery layers. The slender twigs are generally conspicuously roughened with resinous dots while those of the twigs of the Paper Birch are in general not so roughened except slightly in certain varieties. The Gray Birch is less inclined to produce large limbs and the numerous small branches are rather strongly pendant after leaving the trunk. The species is short lived, never forming a large tree, and is most frequently met with as a waste-land tree.

**DISTRIBUTION**—Dry, gravelly soils, occasional in swamps and frequent along their borders, often springing up on burnt lands and usually the first tree to take possession of abandoned or neglected fields; often difficult to eradicate as it sprouts readily from the cut stump. Nova Scotia to Lake Ontario; south, mostly in the coast region, to Delaware; west to Lake Ontario.

IN NEW ENGLAND—Maine—abundant; New Hampshire—abundant eastward, as far north as Conway and along the Connecticut to Westmoreland; Vermont—common in the western and frequent in the southern sections; Massachusetts and Rhode Island—common.

IN CONNECTICUT—Common.

**WOOD**—Light, soft, not strong, close-grained, not durable, light brown, with thick nearly white sapwood; used in the manufacture of spools, shoe pegs and wood pulp, for the hoops of barrels and largely for fuel.

GRAY BIRCH

# PAPER BIRCH
## Canoe or White Birch.
### Betula alba, var. papyrifera (Marsh.) Spach.
#### *B. papyrifera* Marsh.

**HABIT**—A large tree, 50-75 ft. or occasionally more in height with a trunk diameter of 1-3 ft.; developing when not crowded an open, irregular, rounded head, with numerous branches and erect branchlets.

**BARK**—Trunk and older branches chalky-white, peeling or easily separated into thin paper-like layers of a delicate pinkish to yellowish tinge where not exposed to the sun, with conspicuous, horizontally elongated, raised lenticels; inner bark reddish-orange yellow. With age the outer bark rolls back in ragged sheets and the trunk becomes more or less black-streaked and blotched and the base rough and fissured into large irregular thick scales. The bark of the Paper Birch is much sought after by visitors in the woods for use as letter paper, small picture frames and other souvenir articles. In consequence trees of this species in the neighborhood of picnic grounds generally are despoiled of their bark and even its close-barked relative the Gray Birch is not immune from attacks of those who are ignorant of the difference in bark characters between the two species.

**TWIGS**—Stouter than those of the Gray Birch; smooth or somewhat hairy, reddish-brown. LENTICELS—pale, orange colored dots becoming horizontally elongated. LEAF-SCARS—2-ranked, resembling those of the Gray Birch.

**BUDS**—About 5-10 mm. long, ovate, pointed, divergent. BUD-SCALES —downy on margins.

**FRUIT**—A short-stalked, cylindrical, smooth catkin 2-5 cm. long; scales 4-6 mm. long, with thick lateral lobes, hairy-margined; seed-like nutlet, narrower than the wings; staminate catkins in 2's or usually in 3's.

**COMPARISONS**—The Paper Birch, as known to woodsmen, is distinguished by its chalky-white bark peeling into thin papery layers. A number of botanically more or less distinct separate varieties and species have been recognized but *Betula alba*, var. *papyrifera* is the most common. The peeling of its bark distinguishes it from the Gray Birch. The exposed outer bark is more distinctly white and the dark triangular patches noticeable at the insertion of branches in the Gray Birch are often absent especially on older trunks or less distinct. The bark does not typically form the ragged fringe characteristic of the Yellow Birch and while it may not show the characteristic chalky-white where it has peeled, the color is not a dingy yellow but some delicate shade, generally of cinnamon.

**DISTRIBUTION**—Deep, rich woods, river banks, mountain slopes. Canada, Atlantic to Pacific, northward to Labrador and Alaska to the limit of deciduous trees; south to Pennsylvania and Illinois; west to the Rocky mountains and Washington on the Pacific coast.

IN NEW ENGLAND—Maine—abundant; New Hampshire—in all sections, most common on highlands up to the alpine area of the White Mountains, above the range of the Yellow Birch; Vermont—common; Massachusetts—common in the western and central sections, rare towards the coast; Rhode Island—not reported.

IN CONNECTICUT—Rare near the coast, Lyme, Huntington, becoming occasional northward and frequent in Litchfield county.

**WOOD**—Light, strong, hard, tough, very close-grained, light brown, tinged with red, with thick nearly white sapwood; largely used for spools, shoe-lasts, pegs and in turnery, the manufacture of wood pulp and for fuel. The tough resinous durable bark impervious to water is used by all the northern Indians in their canoes, and for baskets, bags, drinking cups and other small articles, and often to cover their wigwams in winter.

PAPER BIRCH

# EUROPEAN WHITE BIRCH
## European Paper Birch.
### Betula alba L.

The European Birch of which our American Paper Birch is considered a variety is closely related to this latter species. There are many horticultural varieties. Aside from the weeping variety the forms most frequently seen in cultivation are erect with fine drooping spray. The bark is often slashed at the base of the trunk with deep "gusset"-like furrows exposing the dark inner bark in sharp contrast to the whiteness of the outer layers. The outer bark is separable into thin papery layers but does not seem so inclined to peel spontaneously as our native Paper Birch.

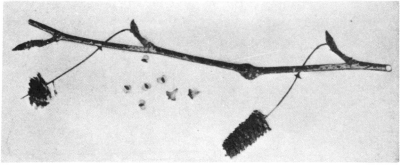

EUROPEAN WHITE BIRCH

# SPECKLED ALDER
## Hoary Alder, Alder.
### Alnus incana (L.) Moench.

**HABIT**—A small tree, or more frequently a shrub 8-25 ft. high with a trunk diameter generally under 5 inches; generally growing in clumps of several stems.

**BARK**—Grayish-brown, smooth, with prominent whitish lenticels somewhat elongated horizontally.

**TWIGS**—Rather slender, more or less zigzag, finely downy, grayish-brown, becoming hoary white toward the tips especially of fruiting twigs. LENTICELS—scattered, whitish, conspicuous. PITH—dark green, 3-cornered.

**LEAF-SCARS**—Alternate, 2-ranked, or sometimes apparently more than 2-ranked, conspicuous, inversely triangular, raised, light yellowish-brown.    STIPULE-SCARS—narrow,   triangular.    BUNDLE-SCARS—3, often compounded.

**BUDS**—Distinctly stalked, about 8 mm. long, reddish, more or less whitened with fine down, slightly sticky within; terminal buds scarcely larger than laterals.    BUD-SCALES—3 scales visible, closely stuck together.

**FRUIT**—A woody cone-like catkin, 6-12 mm. long, remaining on the plant during winter, often distorted by strap-shaped projections caused by a fungus. Staminate catkins of the coming season pendant at the ends of reflexed branchlets with the young fertile catkins appearing lateral and pointing downward; seed-like nutlets, round, flattened.

**COMPARISONS**—The Speckled Alder is distinguished from its most common relative, the Smooth Alder [*Alnus rugosa* (Du Roi) Spreng.], by position of the fertile catkins which in the Smooth Alder are erect and seem to be terminal and in the Speckled Alder point downward and seem to be lateral. These two common species occur throughout New England but intermediate forms are found especially near their northern limits. The European Black Alder [*Alnus vulgaris* Hill.] is somewhat planted for ornament in this country and is reported in several localities as escaped from cultivation. In contrast to our native Alders it has an erect, distinctly tree-like habit of growth and reaches in Europe a height of 70 ft.

**DISTRIBUTION**—Swamps and borders of streams. Newfoundland to Saskatchewan, south to Pennsylvania and Nebraska.

**IN NEW ENGLAND**—Throughout, more or less common especially toward the north, local in sections toward the south.

**IN CONNECTICUT**—Local or occasional except in the southeastern part of the state where it is rare.

**WOOD**—Soft, used as a source of gunpowder charcoal and said to be further valuable because of its durability in water.

SPECKLED ALDER

# BEECH
## American Beech.
### Fagus grandifolia Ehrh.

*F. ferruginea* Ait.; *F. americana* Sweet; *F. atropunicea* Sudw.

---

**HABIT**—A tall tree 50-75 ft. or more in height with a trunk diameter of 1½-4 ft.; in the forest with a tall slender trunk free of branches for more than half its length; in the open low-branched with numerous long, slender, widely spreading or drooping branches, forming a symmetrical, broad, dense, rounded, oblong or obovate head; roots near the surface, widely spreading and sending up shoots which often surround the parent plant with a thicket of small trees.

**BARK**—Close, smooth, steel-gray; more or less dark mottled and covered with lichens in the country; in or about cities where lichen growth is prevented by injurious gases in the air, a clear, lighter bluish-gray; from the ease with which it is carved, generally adorned with initials and coventionalized outlines of the human heart.

**TWIGS**—Slender, somewhat zigzag, smooth, shining, reddish-brown, becoming gray on older growth. Spray flattish from 2-ranked position of the buds; slow-growing branchlets numerous, leafy at tips, elongating each season only a small fraction of an inch, and growing but slightly in thickness; thus one of the twigs in photograph is 29 years old and had grown only 4½ inches in length and acquired a thickness of less than 3 mm. during this time. LENTICELS—numerous, conspicuous, orange to gray, elongated longitudinally. LEAVES—frequently remaining on tree in winter, pale yellow, oval, sharp-pointed, with prominent, straight veins, ending in teeth.

**LEAF-SCARS**—Small, raised, elliptical to semi-circular. STIPULE-SCARS—narrow, distinct, nearly encircling twig. BUNDLE-SCARS—inconspicuous, best seen by cutting surface section, 5 or more in double row or scattered.

**BUDS**—Conspicuously long and very slender, 10-20 mm. long, about 5 times as long as wide, gradually tapering to sharp-pointed apex; terminal bud present not conspicuously larger than laterals. BUD-SCALES—numerous, 10-20 in 4 ranks, increasing in length from base to apex, reddish-brown, their margins more or less finely hairy and often with a woolly patch of down at tip, leaving a rather long and distinct set of scale-scars marking each year's growth.

**FRUIT**—A stalked bur, densely downy and covered with soft spreading and more or less recurved prickles, 4-valved, splitting to near the base, remaining on the tree into winter, after the nut has fallen. NUT—brown, shining, 1.0-1.5 cm. long, 3-sided pyramidal; seed sweet, edible.

**COMPARISONS**—The long narrow buds and the smooth, bluish-gray bark of the Beech make it an easy tree to identify in the winter. The pale persistent dead leaves in connection with the habit may frequently be used to distinguish the tree from a distance, the Oaks being about the only other trees that have a similar retention of their withered leaves. The European Beech [*Fagus sylvatica* L.] with weeping and purple-leaved varieties is frequently planted for ornament. It has a darker bark than the American tree but quite closely resembles it.

**DISTRIBUTION**—Moist, rocky soil. Nova Scotia through Quebec and Ontario: south to Florida; west to Wisconsin, Missouri, and Texas.

IN NEW ENGLAND—Maine—abundant; New Hampshire—throughout the state; common on the Connecticut-Merrimac watershed, enters largely into the composition of the hardwood forests of Coos county; Vermont—abundant; Massachusetts—in western sections abundant, common eastward; Rhode Island—common.

IN CONNECTICUT—Occasional or frequent, rarely maturing perfect fruit.

**WOOD**—Hard, strong, tough, very close-grained, not durable, difficult to season, dark or often light red, with thin nearly white sapwood of 20-30 layers of annual growth; largely used in the manufacture of chairs, shoe lasts, plane stocks, the handles of tools and for fuel.

BEECH

# CHESTNUT

Castanea dentata (Marsh.) Borkh.

*C. sativa*, var. *americana* Sarg. ; *C. vesca*, var. *americana* Michx.

---

**HABIT**—A large tree 60-80 ft. in height with trunk diameter of 5-6 ft. or larger; in the forest, trunk tall and slender, in the open trunk short and thick generally tapering rapidly from point of branching into top of tree; lower branches horizontal or declining, often gnarled and twisted, upper branches arising at a sharper angle, forming a low, open, broad, spreading, rounded, ovate head often as broad as high. Young branches tend to bend up from all sides and give an even-edged outline to the tree as if the head had been trimmed like a round-topped hedge. The Chestnut when cut sprouts readily from the stump and in consequence in wood-lots Chestnut trees are most commonly to be found in groups of 2-4 or even more surrounding the old stump from which they originally sprouted. (See plate).

**BARK**—On young trunks and branches smooth, reddish-bronze, often shining; with age broken by shallow fissures into long, broad, flat, more or less oblique ridges.

**TWIGS**—Stout, generally straight, greenish-yellow or reddish-brown, smooth, round or somewhat angled from base and outer edges of leaf-scars; somewhat swollen at nodes. LENTICELS—Numerous, conspicuous, forming minute, raised, white dots. PITH—5-pointed, star-shaped.

**LEAF-SCARS**—Sometimes distinctly 2-ranked, generally more than 2-ranked, raised, semioval. STIPULE-SCARS—narrow, triangular, often inconspicuous. BUNDLE-SCARS—scattered, inconspicuous, if leaf-scar is surface-sectioned bundle-scars are found in two small lateral clusters and a large more or less circular basal cluster.

**BUDS**—Small, ovate, light to dark chestnut brown, 4-6 mm. long, often oblique to the leaf-scar; terminal bud generally absent, the end of the twig being marked by a small scar and the bud at end of twig being in the axil of the uppermost leaf-scar. BUD-SCALES—2-3 only visible, thin-margined.

**FRUIT**—A large, round bur, sharp-spiny without and hairy within, opening by 4 valves. Photograph of bur reduced to about ½ natural size. NUTS—generally 3 (1-5), dark brown, white-downy at apex, ovate, flattened where in contact with other nuts; seed—sweet, edible.

**COMPARISONS**—From the appearance of gnarled old specimens grown in the open, the Chestnut might be taken for one of the Oaks. Its pith, further, is star-shaped but its buds are not clustered at ends of the twigs as in Oaks and have only 2-3 scales visible. At times the buds of the Chestnut have a 2-ranked arrangement and in this condition the twigs alone might be confused with those of the Linden (which see under Comparisons). Since the tree begins bearing early and the characteristic burs remain on the ground, the fruit is a valuable winter character. The bark in middle-aged trees resembles somewhat that of the Red Oak. If the bark is blazed the wood exposed does not show the short clear lines representing medullary rays in tangential section seen in Oaks under similar treatment.

**DISTRIBUTION**—In strong, well-drained soil; pastures, rocky woods, and hillsides. Ontario, common; south to Delaware, along the mountains to Alabama; west to Michigan, Indiana, and Tennessee.

IN NEW ENGLAND—Maine—southern sections, probably not indigenous north of latitude 44° 20'; New Hampshire—Connecticut valley near the river, as far north as Windsor, Vt.; most abundant in the Merrimac valley south of Concord, but occasional a short distance northward; Vermont—common in the southern sections, especially in the Connecticut valley; occasional as far north as Windsor, West Rutland, Burlington; Massachusetts—rather common throughout the state, but less frequent near the sea; Rhode Island—common.

IN CONNECTICUT—Common.

**WOOD**—Light, soft, not very strong, liable to check and warp in drying, easily split, durable in contact with the soil, reddish-brown with thin lighter colored sapwood of 3 or 4 layers of annual growth; used largely in the manufacture of cheap furniture and in the interior finish of houses, for railroad ties, piling, fence posts, and rails. The nuts which are superior to those of the Old World Chestnut in flavor and sweetness are gathered in great quantities in the forest and sold in the cities.

CHESTNUT

# WHITE OAK
## Quercus alba L.

**HABIT**—A large tree with average height of 50-75 ft. and trunk diameter of 1-6 ft., somewhat various in habit, tending in the open to show a broad outline, sometimes 2-3 times as broad as high, with short trunk and lower limbs horizontal or declined, characteristically gnarled and twisted.

**BARK**—Light gray or nearly white, whence its name; broken by shallow fissures into long, irregular, thin scales which readily flake off. On some trees ridges broken into short oblongs giving a rougher appearance to bark. Bark up to 2 inches thick in older trees; inner bark light. The bark is rich in tannin, is of medicinal value and is used in tanning.

**TWIGS**—Of medium thickness, greenish-reddish to gray, smooth, sometimes covered with a bloom. LENTICELS—forming conspicuous, light-colored, minute, rounded, raised dots. LEAVES—frequently remaining on tree throughout winter, oblong to obovate with generally 7 large blunt lobes. PITH—5-pointed, star-shaped.

**BUDS**—Broadly ovate, blunt, about 3 mm. long (2-6 mm.), reddish-brown, sometimes slightly hairy.

**FRUIT**—Maturing in autumn of first year singly or in pairs, sessile or sometimes on slender stalks. NUT—ovoid to oblong, rounded at apex, shiny, light chestnut brown, 1.5-2.5 cm. long, enclosed ⅓-¼ of its length by deep saucer-shaped to hemispherical cup. Scales of cup white-woolly, thick-knobby at base, with short, blunt tips becoming thinner and flatter at rim of cup. Meat, sweet edible sometimes roasted and used as substitute for coffee, or when boiled said to be a good substitute for chestnuts.

**COMPARISONS**—The White Oak is the most common of the White Oak group. Its light flaky bark resembles that of several other oaks. It is readily distinguished from the Swamp White Oak by absence of peeling of bark on young branches and by its larger and more pointed buds; from the Post Oak by absence of greenish down on twigs and by generally larger, narrower buds; from the Chinquapin Oak by its blunt buds; from the Dwarf Chinquapin Oak by its larger stature, larger twigs and buds.

**DISTRIBUTION**—On moist or dry ground and in various soils, sometimes forming nearly pure forests. Quebec and Ontario; south to the Gulf of Mexico; west to Minnesota, Nebraska, Kansas, Arkansas and Texas.

IN NEW ENGLAND—Maine—southern sections; New Hampshire—most abundant eastward; in the Connecticut valley confined to the hills in the immediate vicinity of the river, extending up the tributary streams a short distance and disappearing entirely before reaching the mouth of the Passumpsic; Vermont—common west of the Green Mountains, less so in the southern Connecticut valley; Massachusetts, Rhode Island —common.

IN CONNECTICUT—Common throughout.

**WOOD**—Strong, very heavy, hard, tough, close-grained, durable, light brown, with thin lighter colored sapwood; the most valuable of the Oaks for timber, used in shipbuilding, for construction and in cooperage, the manufacture of carriages, agricultural implements, baskets, the interior finish of houses, cabinet making, for railroad ties and fences, and largely as fuel.

WHITE OAK

# POST OAK
## Box White Oak, Iron Oak.
### Quercus stellata Wang.
*Q. minor* Sarg.; *Q. obtusiloba* Michx.

**HABIT**—In New England a small tree with height in southern section up to 60 ft., with trunk diameter of 3 ft.; at northern limit a shrub 10-35 ft. high with trunk diameter of ½-1 ft.; in the open forming a broad dense, round-topped head with stout spreading branches.

**BARK**—Flaky; similar to that of White Oak but rather darker, rougher, corresponding more to type of White Oak bark with short oblong ridges; ½-1 inch in thickness. Twigs when ½ inch to 1 inch in diameter begin to acquire a flaky bark with loose, dark gray scales lifting at sides and ends.

**TWIGS**—Stout, light orange, reddish-brown; the younger growth by its light color, in striking contrast with darker, older growth which is often almost black; young twigs covered, at least in part, with short, dense orange-brown down, rough to the touch, often not easily noticed without a hand-lens. Late in season down may become almost black and disappear from the more exposed parts of twig. Bases of leaf-scars projecting with a sudden curve from the twig. LENTICELS—pale, minute. LEAVES—often persistent, oblong, obovate, thick with generally 5 rounded lobes, the middle pair much the largest. PITH—5-pointed, star-shaped.

**BUDS**—Broadly ovate, often as broad as long and hemispherical, blunt, rarely acute, generally under 3 mm. long, sometimes up to 6 mm. in length. BUD-SCALES—bright reddish-brown, sparingly downy.

**FRUIT**—Maturing in autumn of first year, single or in pairs or clustered; sessile or short-stalked. NUT—ovate, to oblong 1.5-2 cm. long, generally covered with pale down at apex. CUP—covering ⅓-½ the nut, top-shaped or cup-shaped, scales rather thin and flat, only slightly knobby, pale, woolly. Meat sweet.

**COMPARISONS**—Readily distinguished from White Oak which it most nearly resembles by rough, dirty orange-brown down which is to be found more or less completely covering twigs. Buds are blunter, shorter, generally more nearly hemispherical and of a brighter reddish tinge.

**DISTRIBUTION**—Doubtfully from southern Ontario; south to Florida; west to Kansas, Indian Territory and Texas.

IN NEW ENGLAND—Mostly in sterile soil near the sea-coast; Massachusetts—southern Cape Cod from Falmouth to Brewster, the most northern station reported, occasional; the islands of Naushon, Martha's Vineyard where it is rather common, and Nantucket where it is rare; Rhode Island—along the shore of the northern arm of Wickford harbor.

IN CONNECTICUT—Local. Usually in rocky ground on and near the coast; East Lyme and Old Lyme, Branford, New Haven, Orange and Milford, and westward; extending inland as far as Hamden; on Mt. Carmel and Huntington at 350 ft. elevation.

**WOOD**—Very heavy, hard, close-grained, durable in contact with soil, difficult to season, light or dark brown, with thick lighter colored sapwood; used for fuel, fencing, railroad ties and sometimes in the manufacture of carriages, for cooperage and in construction.

Post Oak

# BUR OAK
## Mossy-cup or Over-cup Oak.
### Quercus macrocarpa Michx.

**HABIT**—Although one of our largest Oaks in the central states, in New England of medium size only 40-60 ft. in height with a trunk diameter of 1-3 ft.; in the open forming a broad, round top with thick spreading limbs and numerous often drooping branchlets.

**BARK**—Flaky, resembling that of White Oak but rather darker and with ridges rather firmer.

**TWIGS**—Stout, yellowish-brown, smooth or downy, twigs on some trees after the first year developing corky ridges. LENTICELS—minute, pale, raised dots, inconspicuous. LEAVES—which sometimes persist, obovate-oblong, divided by deep indentations into 5-7 rounded lobes, the terminal lobe the largest. PITH—5-pointed, star-shaped.

**BUDS**—Conical to broadly ovate, sharp-pointed or blunt, 3-5 mm. long, reddish-brown, covered with pale wool; lateral buds more or less strongly appressed and flattened against the twig. Stipules often persisting at tips of twigs, long, downy thread-like. BUD-SCALES—relatively few to a bud.

**FRUIT**—Maturing in autumn of first year, very variable, sessile or stalked, generally single. NUT—ovate to oval, 2-5 cm. long, apex rounded or depressed, covered with pale down. CUP—thick hemispherical to top-shaped enclosing from ¼ to the entire nut; scales of cup, pale, woolly, thickened at base with pointed tips, tips of upper scales prolonged into a more or less distinct fringe.

**COMPARISONS**—The Bur Oak is sharply distinguished from our other Oaks by a number of well-marked characters such as the presence of corky ridges on the young branchlets, the copious fringe to the large acorn, the appressed and downy buds. These characters however are not always present in a given specimen; thus the corky ridges may fail to appear throughout an entire tree; the acorns may be reduced in size and in the distinctness of the fringe; and the lateral buds may be more or less divergent.

**DISTRIBUTION**—Low rich bottom lands. Nova Scotia to Manitoba; south to Pennsylvania and Tennessee; west to Montana, Nebraska, Kansas, Indian Territory and Texas.

IN NEW ENGLAND—Maine—known only in the valleys of the middle Penobscot and the Kennebec; Vermont—lowlands, about Lake Champlain, especially in Addison County, not common; Massachusetts—valley of the Ware river, Stockbridge and towns south along the Housatonic river; Rhode Island—no station reported.

IN CONNECTICUT—Rich bottom lands or swampy places; rare or local and confined to the northwestern part of the state; reported from Canaan and Salisbury.

**WOOD**—Similar to that of White Oak from which it is not generally distinguished commercially, although superior in strength.

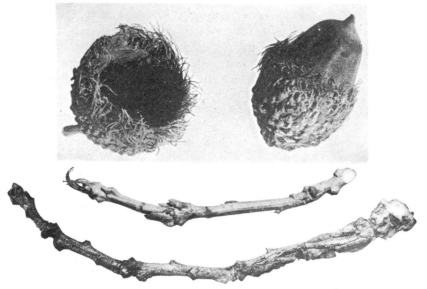

BUR OAK

# SWAMP WHITE OAK

Quercus bicolor Willd.

*Q. platanoides* Sudw.

**HABIT**—A medium sized tree, 40-60 ft. high, with trunk diameter of 2-3 ft.; in the open with round-topped open head, sometimes broader than high, upper limbs ascending, lower limbs rather small, horizontal or declined even to the ground, with numerous tufted, small, scraggly, lateral, pendant branchlets. The scraggly branchlets in connection with the peeling of the bark give a very rough unkempt appearance to the tree. Trunk erect, generally continuous, sometimes forking above to give somewhat the aspect of an Elm in respect to main limbs.

**BARK**—Flaky, grayish-brown, divided by deep longitudinal fissures into rather long, flat ridges. Bark on small branchlets, dark reddish-brown to black, peeling into long, persistent, stiff-papery layers, which curl back and expose the lighter bark beneath.

**TWIGS**—Mediumly stout to slender, yellowish-green to reddish-brown, smooth (seldom slightly downy). Medullary rays generally absent in branchlets even of 6 to 8 years growth. LENTICELS—pale, raised. LEAVES—which may persist obovate-oblong, wedge-shaped at base, wavy-margined to blunt-lobed, with 6-8 pairs of primary veins. PITH—5-pointed, star-shaped.

**BUDS**—Broadly ovate to oval to spherical; blunt-pointed; small, 2-4 mm. long. BUD-SCALES—brown, at times slightly hairy above middle.

**FRUIT**—Maturing in one year, single or in pairs or groups of 3, generally with long stalks, 2.5 to 10 cm. long. NUT—light chestnut, ovate to oblong, 2-3 cm. long, apex covered with pale down, rounded or pointed. CUP—thick, cup-shaped, about ⅓ enclosing nut; scales pale woolly, those at base more or less thickened, at rim of cup tips of scales elongated, narrow, awn-pointed, often forming short fringe. Meat sweet, edible.

**COMPARISONS**—The sycamore-like peeling of the bark from the young branchlets easily distinguishes this species from all other Oaks. The bark somewhat resembles that of White Oak but is somewhat darker and the ridges are longer.

**DISTRIBUTION**—Borders of swamps and streams. Quebec to Ontario where it is known as the Blue Oak; south to Delaware along the mountains to northern Georgia; west to Minnesota, Iowa, East Kansas and Arkansas.

IN NEW ENGLAND—Maine—York county; New Hampshire—Merrimac valley as far as the mouth of the Souhegan, and probably throughout Rockingham county; Vermont—low grounds about Lake Champlain; Massachusetts—frequent in the western and central sections, common eastward—Rhode Island—common.

IN CONNECTICUT—Frequent.

**WOOD**—Similar to that of White Oak, and used for same general purposes; sapwood, thin, hardly distinguishable from heartwood.

SWAMP WHITE OAK

# CHINQUAPIN OAK

## Chestnut Oak, Yellow Oak.

### Quercus Muhlenbergii Engelm.

#### *Q. acuminata* Houba.

---

**HABIT**—Small to medium sized tree 30-40 ft. high with a trunk diameter of 1-2 ft.; in basin of the Mississippi reaching an exceptional height of 160 feet; trunk buttressed at base in older specimens, branches comparatively small forming narrow, round-topped head.

**BARK**—Thin, flaky, broken into loose grayish or sometimes slightly brownish scales.

**TWIGS**—Rather slender, light orange to reddish-brown, smooth. LENTICELS—pale, inconspicuous. LEAVES—resembling those of Chestnut with large incurved, glandular-tipped teeth or rarely with wavy margin resembling the leaf of the Chestnut Oak. PITH—5-pointed, star-shaped.

**BUDS**—Narrowly ovate to conical, sharp-pointed, 3-5 mm. long. BUD-SCALES—light chestnut brown, slightly hairy on edges, appearing longitudinally striate if held toward light and viewed with a hand-lens. Buds similar to those of Chestnut Oak but smaller.

**FRUIT**—Maturing the first season, sessile or short-stalked, singly or in pairs. NUT—broadly ovate to oval, 1 -20 mm. long, narrowed and rounded at pale downy apex, light chestnut brown. CUP—thin, rather shallow cup-shaped enclosing about ½ or less of the nut; scales pale brown, woolly, slightly knobby at base of cup, the brownish tips of the scales sometimes forming a slight fringe at rim of cup. Meat sweet, edible.

**COMPARISONS**—The Chinquapin Oak resembles the Chestnut Oak on the one hand and the Dwarf Chinquapin Oak on the other. It is distinguished from the former by its flaky, gray bark, and the smaller size of buds and acorns; from the latter by its sharp-pointed buds and larger size.

**DISTRIBUTION**—Rare and local in the Atlantic states, usually on limestone soil, on dry hillsides, rocky ridges and rich bottoms. Ontario; south to Delaware and District of Columbia, along the mountains to northern Alabama; west to Minnesota, Nebraska, Kansas, Indian Territory and Texas.

IN NEW ENGLAND—Vermont—Gardner's Island, Lake Champlain; Ferrisburg.

IN CONNECTICUT—Rare. Calcareous ridges in the northwestern part of the state: Canaan, Salisbury, also along the Housatonic river in Kent, New Milford and bordering tide water in Milford.

**WOOD**—Heavy, very hard, strong, close-grained, durable, with thin light-colored sapwood, largely used in cooperage, for wheels, fencing and railroad ties.

CHINQUAPIN OAK

# DWARF CHINQUAPIN OAK
## Scrub Chestnut Oak, Chinquapin Oak, Scrub Oak.
### Quercus prinoides Willd.

**HABIT**—A low shrub generally 2-4 ft. high or occasionally reaching 15 ft. in height, forming broad clumps by prolific stolons.

**BARK**—Light brown, scaly; scaliness evident when trunk reaches a diameter of 1½ inches.

**TWIGS**—Slender; generally not over 2 mm. thick, orange to reddish-brown; generally smooth; a variety, *rufescens* Rehder with yellowish hairs on twigs. LENTICELS—pale, rather conspicuous. LEAVES—oblanceolate to obovate-oblong, coarsely wavy-toothed. PITH—5-pointed, star-shaped.

**BUDS**—Spherical to ovate, rounded or slightly narrowed at apex, about 3 mm. long. SCALES—chestnut brown, thin, scarious and slightly hairy on edges; small collateral buds sometimes present on either side of axillary bud.

**FRUIT**—Maturing the first season, produced in great abundance, sessile or short-stalked, singly or in pairs. NUT—oval, light chestnut brown and shiny, apex blunt-pointed and covered with pale down, 15 to 25 mm. long. CUP—thin, deep cup-shaped, covering ½ or more of nut; scales pale woolly, more or less knobby, thickened at base of cup, thinner toward rim. Meat sweet.

**COMPARISONS**—In habit the Dwarf Chinquapin Oak most nearly resembles the Bear Oak but is smaller when of the same age; has flaky bark, after reaching a trunk diameter of 1½ inches or more, while the bark of the Bear Oak is close, for the most part smooth, even on old specimens not flaky though developing small close scales. It further belongs to the White Oak group (see page 338) and since both these two Scrub Oaks produce fruit in great abundance acorns are generally accessible and easily distinguished. The Bear Oak generally has redder, sharp-pointed buds while those of the Dwarf Chinquapin Oak are blunt with edges of scales ashy with fine wool or mealy scurfiness. Moreover, except in variety *rufescens*, twigs of the Dwarf Chinquapin Oak are smooth. The Chestnut Oak and the Chinquapin Oak are distinguished by their larger and sharp-pointed buds. The buds of the Swamp White Oak are somewhat similar to those of the Dwarf Chinquapin Oak but the larger size of the tree and peeling of the bark on branchlets of the Swamp White Oak are distinctive. Further west apparently the species inter-grades into the Chinquapin Oak.

**DISTRIBUTION**—Dry woods, rocky slopes and hillside pastures, sometimes in open sandy soil. From Maine south to North Carolina, west to Kansas, Nebraska and Texas.

IN NEW ENGLAND—More or less common throughout.

IN CONNECTICUT—Occasional or frequent.

**WOOD**—From small size of plant, of no economic value except as fuel.

Dwarf Chinquapin Oak

# CHESTNUT OAK
## Rock Chestnut Oak, Rock Oak.
### Quercus Prinus L.

---

**HABIT**—A medium sized or small tree, 25-50 ft. high with a trunk diameter of 1-2½ ft.; further south much larger reaching 100 ft. in height; trunk tall, straight, continuous, or divided rather low down into large spreading limbs, forming broad open head, sometimes broader than high.

**BARK**—Brown to black, deeply fissured into long, more or less continuous, thick, rough ridges which are somewhat flattened on surface or on older trees more characteristically rounded or sharp-edged, a section through one of the ridges forming thus an inverted letter "V" with its apex somewhat rounded or in younger specimens flattened; bark of young trees and of smaller branches smooth.

**TWIGS**—Stout, light orange to reddish-brown, smooth with somewhat bitter taste. LENTICELS—pale, generally inconspicuous. LEAVES —oblong, lanceolate to obovate, wavy-margined with 10-16 pairs of primary veins. PITH—5-pointed, star-shaped.

**BUDS**—Narrowly ovate-conical, sharp-pointed, 4-10 mm. long. BUD-SCALES—light chestnut brown, slightly hairy toward apex and on margins, appearing longitudinally striate if viewed toward light with a hand-lens. Margins of scales tend to lose their brown color and to become light or dark gray.

**FRUIT**—Maturing the first season, short-stalked, singly or in pairs. NUT—shiny, light chestnut brown, oval to ovate to nearly cylindrical, variable in size and relative thickness; 20-35 mm. long; from three times to less than twice as long as broad. CUP—thin, deep, top-shaped to hemispherical, covering ⅓ or less of nut; scales reddish-brown, woolly, more or less knobby especially toward base of cup. **Meat** sweet.

**COMPARISONS**—The Chestnut Oak is readily distinguished from the other members of the White Oak group by the fact that its bark is not flaky. Its firm, round-ridged bark is definitely characteristic when typically developed. The buds resemble somewhat those of the Red Oak, but are somewhat lighter in color with edges of scales bleached, are much narrower and for the most part conical, with the widest part at or very near the base, whereas the buds of the Red Oak, when typically developed, are much fatter, with the widest part about a third of the distance from the base. The bark of the Red Oak, moreover, has flat ridges.

**DISTRIBUTION**—Woods, rocky ridges and hillsides. Along the Canadian shore of Lake Erie; south to Delaware and along the mountains to Georgia, extending nearly to the summit of Mt. Pisgah in North Carolina; west to Kentucky, Tennessee, and Alabama.

IN NEW ENGLAND—Maine—Saco river and Mt. Agamenticus, near the southern coast; New Hampshire—belts or patches in the eastern part of the state and along the southern border, Hinsdale, Winchester, Brookline, Manchester, Hudson; Vermont—western part of the state throughout, not common; abundant at Smoke mountain at an altitude of 1,300 feet, and along the western flank of the Green mountains, at least in Addison county; Massachusetts—eastern sections, Sterling, Lancaster, Russell, Middleboro, rare in Medford and Sudbury, frequent on the Blue hills; Rhode Island—locally common.

IN CONNECTICUT—Occasional near the coast; frequent or common elsewhere.

**WOOD**—Heavy, hard, strong, rather tough, close grained, durable in contact with the soil, largely used for fencing, railroad ties, ranking next to the White Oak for this purpose, and for fuel. The bark is rich in tannin and is consumed in large quantities in tanning leather.

CHESTNUT OAK

# RED OAK
## Quercus rubra L.

**HABIT**—The largest of our New England oaks, 50-85 ft. high, reaching an exceptional height of 150 ft.; with trunk diameter of 2-6 ft.; trunk branching rather higher up than in the White Oak, often continuous into the top of the tree with ascending branches forming a rather narrow, round-topped head or spreading more widely as shown in the specimen photographed becoming even broader than high. The limbs in the main are not so horizontal or declined nor so crooked as in the White Oak and the tree in consequence offers a less gnarled aspect.

**BARK**—On young trees and upper parts of older trees smooth, gray-brown; on trunks of mature trees and on their thicker limbs up to 4 cm. thick, tardily broken by shallow furrows into dark brown, rather regular, elongated, firm, coarse, flat-topped ridges. The flat ridges which are characteristic of the species are often in older trees roughened up toward the base of the trunk so that the distinctive character of the bark must be sought higher up on the trunk or on the larger limbs. Inner bark, light reddish, not bitter.

**TWIGS**—Mediumly stout to slender, reddish to greenish-brown. LENTICELS—pale, often inconspicuous. LEAVES—obovate to oblong, with bristle-pointed lobes, often difficult to distinguish from those of Black Oak. PITH—5-pointed, star-shaped.

**BUDS**—Oval to ovate, 4-8 mm. long, with widest part typically ¼ to ⅓ above base suggesting appearance of a short stalk to the bud; sharp pointed with more or less distinct development of rusty hairs at the extreme apex, otherwise smooth or sometimes slightly pale-woolly on upper half. BUD-SCALES—numerous, light chestnut brown seen to be longitudinally striate with darker lines when viewed toward light with a hand-lens, margins slightly hairy.

**FRUIT**—Maturing in autumn of second season, singly or in pairs, sessile or on a short, thick stalk. NUT—ovate to cylindrical with broad base and narrowed, rounded apex, dark chestnut brown, large, 2-3 cm. long. CUP—flat, shallow, thick, saucer-shaped (rarely somewhat top-shaped), rim somewhat constricted, enclosing about ⅕ of the nut, 2.-3.5 cm. across. Scales thin, reddish-brown, shining, not at all or but slightly hairy, closely overlapping. Meat pale yellow, slightly bitter. Immature acorns generally divergent or but slightly appressed, with basal scales reaching about half way up, giving appearance of 3 rows of scales.

**COMPARISONS**—If the acorns are obtainable the Red Oak is not to be confused with any of our other species, the large flat cup being distinctive. The flat flutings of the bark and the fat, basally constricted, sharp-pointed buds are further characteristic. See Black Oak for comparison with Red and Black and Scarlet Oak, and Chestnut Oak for comparison with latter species.

**DISTRIBUTION**—Woods, widely adapted to various conditions of soil and situation except distinctly wet lands, ranges further north than our other Oaks and is most planted of the American Oaks in Europe. Nova Scotia and New Brunswick to divide west of Lake Superior; south to Tennessee, Virginia, and along mountain ranges to Georgia; reported from Florida; west to Minnesota, Nebraska, Kansas and Texas.

IN NEW ENGLAND—Maine—common, at least south of the central portions; New Hampshire—extending into Coos County, far north of the White Mountains; Vermont, Massachusetts, Rhode Island—common; probably in most parts of New England the most common of the genus; found higher up the slopes of mountains than the White Oak.

IN CONNECTICUT—Frequent throughout.

**WOOD**—Heavy, hard, strong, close-grained, light reddish-brown, with thin lighter colored sapwood; used in construction, for the interior finish of houses, and in furniture. Timber of this species as also of Black and Scarlet Oak is relatively poor but is more used than formerly on account of scarcity of better.

RED OAK

# PIN OAK
## Swamp Oak, Water Oak.
### Quercus palustris Muench.

**HABIT**—A medium sized tree 40-50 ft. high with trunk diameter of 1-2 ft., reaching a maximum height of over 100 ft. in the lower Ohio basin; trunk tall, straight, continuous up through the pyramidal head; limbs numerous, slender; lower limbs short, drooping, upper limbs longer horizontal or ascending, generally studded with short lateral shoots which give rise to the common name. The habit of this tree is very characteristic and is well shown in the two specimens in the illustration. In older trees the head is more open and irregular.

**BARK**—Of young trunks and limbs, smooth, shiny, light brown; on older trunks darker, furrowed with close, narrow, firm, low ridges.

**TWIGS**—Slender, reddish-brown to orange, shining. LENTICELS—pale, scattered, inconspicuous. LEAVES—small, obovate or oblong; lobes bristle-tipped, separated by deep-rounded sinuses, resembling leaves of Scarlet Oak but smaller. PITH—5-pointed, star-shaped.

**BUDS**—Conical to ovate, generally sharp-pointed, small, 2-4 mm. long. BUD-SCALES—light chestnut brown, sometimes slightly hairy on the thin margins.

**FRUIT**—Maturing the second season, abundant, sessile or short-stalked, solitary or in pairs or clusters. NUT—light brown, often striate, nearly hemispherical, 10-15 mm. long, wider than long, and generally wider than the cup. CUP—thin, saucer-shaped, 10-15 mm. across, enclosing only the base of the nut; scales thin, slightly downy, closely overlapping. Meat pale yellow, slightly bitter.

**COMPARISONS**—When young the Pin Oak is one of the most easily recognized of any of our trees in winter from its general habit of growth. Its continuous trunk, fringed with slender branches and its comparatively smooth bark roughened only slightly by narrow, low ridges are alone distinctive. Further characteristics are the small sharp-pointed buds and the small acorns with saucer-shaped cup.

**DISTRIBUTION**—Borders of swamps and river bottoms in deep moist rich soil. Ontario; south to the valley of the lower Potomac in Virginia; west to Minnesota, east Kansas, Missouri, Arkansas, and Indian Territory.

IN NEW ENGLAND—Massachusetts—Amherst; Springfield, south to Connecticut, rare; Rhode Island—southern portions, bordering the great Kingston swamp and on the margin of the Pawcatuck River.

IN CONNECTICUT—Common in the Connecticut river valley and near the coast in southwestern Connecticut; occasional or local elsewhere.

**WOOD**—Heavy, hard, coarse-grained, but liable to warp and check in drying; light brown, with thin rather darker colored sapwood; sometimes used in construction and for shingles and clapboards.

Pin Oak

# SCARLET OAK
### Quercus coccinea Muench.

**HABIT**—A tree of medium size, 30-50 ft. high with trunk diameter of 1-3 ft., larger further south; trunk tends to be continuous into the crown, narrowed and giving off ascending branches above and horizontal, often terminally declined branches below; limbs long and comparatively slender for an Oak, forming a rather narrow, open head.

**BARK**—Of young trunks and limbs smooth, light brown, on older trunks and limbs up to 2.5 cm. thick, divided by shallow furrows into irregular ridges which in general are neither so regularly flat-topped as the ridges of the Red Oak nor so roughly broken up as those of the Black Oak. The bark therefore may be considered as intermediate in character between these two species. Inner bark, reddish not bitter.

**TWIGS**—Mediumly stout to slender, light red to orange red. LENTI-CELS—numerous, minute, pale, inconspicuous. LEAVES—broadly oval or obovate, with bristle-tipped lobes separated by deep rounded sinuses. PITH—5-pointed, star-shaped.

**BUDS**—Broadly oval to ovate, narrowed above to a typically rather blunt apex, widest at or slightly below middle, dark reddish-brown, 4-8 mm. long, pale woolly above middle, lower half mostly free from wool. BUD-SCALES—numerous, free from distinct longitudinal striations.

**FRUIT**—Maturing in autumn of second season, sessile or short-stalked, singly or in pairs. NUT—oval to oblong, variable in shape, 1 to 2.5 cm. long, light reddish-brown, occasionally striate. CUP—thin, top-shaped or cup-shaped, constricted at base, enclosing ⅓ to ½ of nut. Scales, light reddish-brown, thin, closely overlapping, slightly downy, tips of scales at rim typically appressed against the nut—not spreading. Meat pale yellow, slightly bitter. Immature acorns appressed, rather smooth and shiny, light brown, main basal scales generally reaching less than halfway up giving appearance of 2 rows of scales.

**COMPARISONS**—The size and shape of the acorn cup as well as the greater woolliness of the upper part of the buds distinguish this species from the Red Oak. From the Black Oak it is distinguished by the appressed scales of acorn cup, by the fatter buds which are less woolly, and that only above the middle, and by the pale inner bark. See also under Black Oak.

**DISTRIBUTION**—Most common on dry, sandy soil. Ontario; south to the middle states and along the mountains to North Carolina and Tennessee; reported from Florida; west to Minnesota, Nebraska and Missouri.

**IN NEW ENGLAND**—Maine—valley of the Androscoggin, southward; New Hampshire and Vermont—not authoritatively reported by recent observers; Massachusetts—more common in the eastern than western sections, sometimes covering considerable areas; Rhode Island—common.

**IN CONNECTICUT**—Frequent throughout.

**WOOD**—Heavy, hard, strong, coarse-grained, light or reddish-brown, with thick darker colored sapwood, less valuable than wood of Red Oak but used for the same purposes.

SCARLET OAK

# BLACK OAK
## Yellow-barked Oak, Quercitron, Yellow Oak.
### Quercus velutina Lam.
*Q. coccinea,* var. *tinctoria* A.DC.; *Q. tinctoria* Bartr.

**HABIT**—One of our largest oaks 50-75 ft. high with a trunk diameter of 2-4 ft., reaching its greatest development in Ohio basin with a maximum height of 150 ft.; somewhat similar in general habit to the Scarlet Oak; limbs generally somewhat stouter; head may be wide spreading or narrowed oblong.

**BARK**—Dark gray to blackish often lighter near the seashore, up to 4 cm thick, very rough, broken by deep furrows into thick ridges which are further divided by cross fissures giving an appearance of irregular block-like strips. The bark is roughened especially at the base of trunk even in quite young trees. The young bark in beginning to fissure for a time may have flattened ridges resembling those of Red Oak but they are soon transversely roughened. Inner bark orange-yellow, intensely bitter; this with the buds forms the most distinctive character.

**TWIGS**—Stout, reddish-brown or reddish, mottled with gray; tasting bitter if chewed and coloring saliva yellowish. LENTICELS—scattered, generally large, conspicuous. LEAVES—obovate to oblong with broad bristle-pointed lobes sometimes indistinguishable from those of Scarlet Oak. Large, thin-walled, spherical insect galls formed on leaves seem to be most common on the Black Oak. PITH—5-pointed, star-shaped.

**BUDS**—Ovate to conical, large, 6-12 mm. long, narrowed above to a rather sharp point, generally 5-sided, strongly angled, covered except basal row of scales with dense, pale yellowish-gray to dirty-white wool. BUD-SCALES—numerous, not distinctly longitudinally striate.

**FRUIT**—Maturing in autumn of second year, singly or in pairs, sessile or short-stalked, deep cup-shaped to top-shaped. NUT—ovate-oblong, variable in shape, 1.2 cm. long, light reddish-brown, frequently coated with soft down, often striate. CUP—thin, deeply cup to top-shaped, more or less constricted at base; scales of cup thin, light reddish-brown, finely woolly, closely overlapping at base loosely overlapping above with free tips horizontally wrinkled and forming a loose more or less spreading fringe-like border to cup. Meat yellower and more bitter than that of the Scarlet Oak. Immature acorns appressed or recurved toward twig, slightly woolly; main scales extending nearly to the top giving the appearance of a single row of scales.

**COMPARISONS**—The three most common trees of the Black Oak group (the Red, the Black and the Scarlet) are readily distinguished by their bud characters. Those of the Black Oak are densely pale woolly over whole surface, those of Scarlet Oak are less densely pale woolly, and the woolliness is confined to upper half. They are more nearly oval than those of the Black Oak, the widest part being toward the middle. The Red Oak buds are generally free from pale woolliness though having often rusty hairs at extreme apex; in distinction from the Scarlet Oak the widest part is nearer the base. The yellow bitter inner bark and the yellow discoloration of the saliva when the twigs are chewed distinguish the Black Oak from the other two. The Red Oak has flat-topped ridges, these in the Black Oak are broken into rough blocks, while the bark of the Scarlet Oak is intermediate between the two types. The acorns of the Red Oak are large with large shallow saucer-shaped cups, those of the Red and Black are smaller, and have deeper cups. The cup scales of the Black Oak form a loose fringe at the rim and are wrinkled, those of the Scarlet are closely over-lapping and form no fringe. The acorn characters are distinctive for the Red Oak but are not so good quite in separating the Black and Scarlet Oaks from each other, although when typically developed, the acorns of the two trees can be readily distinguished. The bark characters can be used when typically developed in separating the Red from the Black Oak but are not as decisive as bud or inner bark characters.

**DISTRIBUTION**—In poor soils; on dry gravelly plains and ridges. Southern and western Ontario; south to the Gulf states; west to Minnesota, Kansas, Indian Territory, and Texas.

IN NEW ENGLAND—Maine—York county; New Hampshire—valley of the lower Merrimac and eastward, absent on the highlands, reappearing within three or four miles of the Connecticut, ceasing at North Charlestown; Vermont—western and southwestern sections; Massachusetts—abundant eastward; Rhode Island—frequent.

IN CONNECTICUT—Occasional or frequent.

**WOOD**—Heavy, hard, strong though not tough, coarse-grained and liable to check in drying, bright brown tinged with red, with thin lighter colored sapwood; of little value except as fuel. The bark abounds in tannic acid and is largely used in tanning, as a yellow dye and an astringent in medicine.

Black Oak

# BEAR OAK
## Black Scrub Oak.
### Quercus ilicifolia Wang.
*Q. nana* Sarg.; *Q. pumila* Sudw.

**HABIT**—Usually a shrub 3-10 ft. high, though frequently becoming tree-like and reaching a maximum height of 25 ft. with a trunk diameter of ½ to 1 ft.; trunk short; branches stiff, contorted, slender, spreading and forming a wide flat or round-topped head.

**BARK**—Thin, dark brown, smooth, except for small, close, thin scales on older trunks, never however breaking into large, flaky scales.

**TWIGS**—Slender, yellowish-green to reddish-brown, covered with greenish-yellowish to reddish down which often disappears from exposed parts of the twig during the winter but which can generally be found in protected parts at the tips, bases or between the ridges of the season's shoots. LENTICELS—minute, pale, inconspicuous on shoots of season. Leaves often breaking off above place of attachment leaving base of leaf-stalk projecting throughout winter (see illustration). LEAVES—small, obovate, nearly entire or with 3-7 bristle-tipped lobes, downy beneath. PITH—5-pointed, star-shaped.

**BUDS**—Ovate to conical, sharp or blunt pointed, small, generally not over 3 mm. long. BUD-SCALES—dark chestnut brown, generally minutely hairy on the margins.

**FRUIT**—Maturing in second season, produced in great abundance, clustered along the stem, generally in pairs or rarely singly, sessile or generally short stalked. NUT—varying in shape, ovate to spherical, 10-15 mm. long, light brown, shining, generally more or less longitudinally striate. CUP—top-shaped to rather deeply saucer-shaped, more or less constricted at base, thick, enclosing about ½ the nut; scales of cup reddish-brown, slightly downy, thin, closely overlapping with free tips of upper scales forming a fringe-like border to cup.

**COMPARISONS**—The Dwarf Chinquapin Oak is the only one likely to be confused with the Bear Oak. The points of difference between the two species may be found in Comparisons under Dwarf Chinquapin Oak.

**DISTRIBUTION**—Dry sandy or rocky sterile ground. Maine; south to Ohio and the mountain regions of North Carolina and Kentucky; west to the Alleghany mountains.

IN NEW ENGLAND—Maine—frequent in eastern and southern sections and upon Mount Desert Island; New Hampshire—as far north as Conway, more common near the lower Connecticut; Vermont—in the eastern and southern sections as far north as Bellows Falls; Massachusetts and Rhode Island—abundant, forming in favorable situations, dense thickets, sometimes covering several acres.

IN CONNECTICUT—Rare in northwestern part of the state, local, frequent or common elsewhere.

**WOOD**—Too scant to be of any economic value.

BEAR OAK

# SLIPPERY ELM
## Red Elm, Moose Elm.
### Ulmus fulva Michx.
*U. pubescens* Walt.

**HABIT**—A small to medium-sized tree, 40-60 ft. in height with a trunk diameter of 1-2½ ft.; forming a broad open rather flat-topped head, resembling the White Elm but with less drooping branches.

**BARK**—Grayish-brown, more or less deeply furrowed, internally reddish-brown without conspicuously whitish layers (see bark section in plate); inner bark next the wood, whitish, strongly mucilaginous, giving the name Slippery Elm.

**TWIGS**—Light, grayish, hairy, roughened by numerous raised lenticels, strongly and characteristically mucilaginous if chewed.

**LEAF-SCARS**—Alternate, 2-ranked, with generally 3 sunken bundle-scars, resembling those of the White Elm.

**BUDS**—Terminal bud absent; lateral buds about 6 mm. long, dark brown, covered especially at their tips with long rusty hairs; flower buds more or less spherical. BUD-SCALES—in 2 ranks of a nearly uniform color.

**FRUIT**—A flat round entire-winged fruit without hairy fringe, ripening in spring.

**COMPARISONS**—The Slippery Elm is easily distinguished from the common White Elm and the rarer Cork Elm by its rough gray twigs, its dark buds covered with long rusty hairs, and by the strongly mucilaginous character of the inner bark of the trunk and even, though to a somewhat less extent, of the twigs, and further from the White Elm by the absence of distinct white layers in the outer bark.

**DISTRIBUTION**—Rich, low grounds; low, rocky woods and hillsides. Valley of the St. Lawrence, apparently not abundant; south to Florida; west to North Dakota and Texas.

IN NEW ENGLAND—Maine—District of Maine, rare; Waterborough, (York county); New Hampshire—valley of the Connecticut, usually disappearing within ten miles of the river; ranges as far north as the mouth of the Passumpsic; Vermont—frequent; Massachusetts—rare in the eastern sections, frequent westward; Rhode Island—infrequent.

IN CONNECTICUT—Rare to frequent.

**WOOD**—Heavy, hard, strong, very coarse-grained, durable, easy to split, dark brown or red, with thin lighter colored sapwood; largely used for fence posts, railroad ties, the sills of buildings, the hubs of wheels and in agricultural implements. The thick fragrant mucilaginous inner bark is used in medicine as a demulcent and is somewhat nutritious.

SLIPPERY ELM

# ENGLISH ELM
Ulmus campestris L.
*U. glabra* Mill.

**HABIT**—A large tree reaching 100 ft. in height; trunk erect, generally continuous well into the crown, with branches given off at a broad angle and continued horizontally or inclined upward, not drooping at the ends in the graceful curves characteristic of the American White Elm, producing rather an Oak-like appearance with an oblong round-topped head.

**BARK**—Dark, with ridges broken transversely into firm oblong blocks.

**TWIGS**—Similar to the White Elm but generally a darker reddish-brown, usually smooth or somewhat downy.

**LEAF-SCARS**—Similar to the White Elm, bundle-scars frequently more than 3.

**BUDS**—Similar to the White Elm but of a dark smoky brown color or almost black, smooth or more or less hairy.

**FRUIT**—A flat, ovate, smooth, entire-winged fruit, ripening in spring.

**COMPARISONS**—The erect Oak-like habit, the firm blocked ridges of the bark, and the smoky smoothish buds will serve to distinguish the English Elm from its American cousins. There are a number of varieties of the English Elm differing in habit of growth, one form having corky ridges. We have described the most familiar type.

**DISTRIBUTION**—The English Elm is not confined to England but like the English sparrow occurs through Europe. It is not native to America but was considerably planted formerly in the eastern sections especially in Boston and vicinity, where some fine old specimens are to be found. The trees in the plate were taken from Boston Common, the two in the foreground at the right and the one in the background at the left being English Elms while the smaller one, indistinctly outlined in the foreground at the left is an American White Elm. They have all been rather severely pruned on account of insect depredations.

**WOOD**—Heavy, hard, fine-grained, durable in water, not liable to crack when exposed to sun or weather; used in Europe for ships' blocks and other wooden parts of rigging, for the keels of ships, for pumps and water pipes, piles and other construction under water and for the hubs of wheels.

ENGLISH ELM

# WHITE ELM
## American or Water Elm.
### Ulmus americana L.

---

**HABIT**—A large tree 50-110 ft. in height with a trunk diameter of 1-8 ft.; trunk more or less widely buttressed dividing high up into a number of large limbs which grow upward and bend gradually and gracefully outward dividing repeatedly to form a broad round or flat-topped inversely conical head with drooping branchlets. In respect to its general outline various types of the Elm have been distinguished as the "Vase Form" shown in the photograph; the "Umbrella Form" with trunk undivided to near the top with abruptly spreading branches forming a broad shallow arch; the "Plume Form" with a one-sided development of drooping branches from a tall trunk; the "Oak Form" with more tortuous and less arching limbs forming a wide rounded head; the "Feathered Form." a modification of any of the other types with the trunk fringed with short branches.

**BARK**—Dark gray divided by irregular longitudinal fissures into broad flat-topped ridges, rather firm though sometimes in very old trees coming off in flakes; the bark is internally stratified by thick conspicuously whitish layers alternating with layers of a dark brown (see plate for section of a ridge of bark).

**TWIGS**—Slender, smooth or slightly or sometimes densely downy, light reddish-brown, often tinged with yellow, very slightly mucilaginous if chewed. LENTICELS—pale, scattered, more or less inconspicuous.

**LEAF-SCARS**—Alternate, 2-ranked, semi-circular, raised, small but conspicuous because of contrast in color between the light corky surface of the scar and the darker brown of the twig. STIPULE-SCARS—narrow. minute, sometimes indistinct. BUNDLE-SCARS—relatively large, conspicuous. typically 3 in number though often more by compounding of single scars, generally sunken in depressions of the leaf-scar.

**BUDS**—Terminal bud absent; lateral buds small, often placed at one side of leaf-scar, ovate-conical, pointed, about 4 mm. long, slightly flattened and more or less appressed against the twig, light reddish-brown, smooth and shining or slightly pale-downy; flower buds stouter, obovate. appearing as if stalked. BUD-SCALES—about 6-9 to a leaf-bud in 2 ranks increasing in size from without inward, generally with darker and more or less hairy-edged margins.

**FRUIT**—A flat, oval, terminally deeply notched, winged fruit, hairy-fringed on edges, ripening in spring and scarcely to be found in winter.

**COMPARISONS**—The White Elm differs from the Slippery Elm in the whitish layers of the bark, the absence of rusty hairs on the buds and the brownish color of its relatively smooth twigs. From the Cork Elm it may be separated by its habit of growth and by the absence of corky ridges on the twigs. The graceful drooping habit of growth of its branches and the light reddish brown of its buds are sufficient to distinguish the American from the English Elm.

**DISTRIBUTION**—Low, moist ground; thrives especially on rich intervales. Frequently planted as a street and shade tree. From Cape Breton to Saskatchewan, as far north as 54° 30'; south to Florida; west to Dakota, Nebraska, Kansas, and Texas.

IN NEW ENGLAND—Maine—common, most abundant in central and southern portions; New Hampshire—common from the southern base of the White Mountains to the sea; in the remaining New England states—very common, attaining its highest development in the rich alluvium of the Connecticut river valley.

**WOOD**—Heavy, hard, strong, tough, difficult to split, coarse-grained, light brown, with thick somewhat lighter colored sapwood, largely used for the hubs of wheels, saddle-trees, in flooring and cooperage, and in boat and ship building.

WHITE ELM

# CORK ELM
## Rock Elm, Hickory Elm, Northern Cork Elm.
### Ulmus racemosa Thomas.
#### *U. Thomasi* Sarg.

**HABIT**—A large tree 50-75 ft. in height, with a trunk diameter of 2-3 ft., in southern Michigan, reaching 100 ft. in height with a trunk diameter of 5 ft.; trunk slender, erect, generally continuous into the crown, developing numerous slender rigid branches arising at a wide angle, those below generally strongly drooping near the point of origin, forming a narrow, oblong, round-topped head having somewhat the aspect of a Hickory with short twiggy, generally corky-ridged branches in the interior of the tree. A young tree showing corky-ridged branchlets and an old tree showing a more characteristic habit, though with rather long trunk for the open, are shown in the plate.

**BARK**—On young trunks more deeply furrowed than in the White Elm, becoming with age flat-ridged, resembling the latter species.

**TWIGS**—More or less downy, resembling twigs of White Elm but generally developing several irregular thick corky ridges not interrupted at the nodes.

**LEAF-SCARS**—Alternate, 2-ranked, resembling these of White Elm but with bundle-scars generally more than 3 (4-6).

**BUDS**—Terminal bud absent; lateral buds similar to those of White Elm but longer (about 5 mm. long) narrower, sharp-pointed, scarcely flattened, generally downy. BUD-SCALES—with darker and hairy-edged margins.

**FRUIT**—A flat, oval, downy, shallow-notched, winged fruit, with hairy-fringed margins ripening in spring.

**COMPARISONS**—In Hickory-like habit the Cork Elm differs from all our other Elms. The corky ridges on the twigs, moreover, occur on no other native New England Elm. The Winged Elm [*Ulmus alata* Michx.], a native of the south, is rarely cultivated in southern New England but is not hardy north. It has two opposite thin corky ridges which are abruptly interrupted at the nodes. A variety of the English Elm has several corky ridges to the twig which are interrupted at the nodes. The Cork Elm differs further from the White and especially from the Slippery Elm in its narrower buds.

**DISTRIBUTION**—Dry, gravelly soils, rich soils, river banks. Quebec through Ontario; south to Tennessee; west to Minnesota, Iowa, Nebraska, and Missouri. Occasionally planted as an ornamental shade tree.

IN NEW ENGLAND—Maine—not reported; New Hampshire—rare and extremely local; Meriden and one or two other places; Vermont—rare, Bennington, Pownal, Knowlton, Highgate; comparatively abundant in Champlain valley and westward; Massachusetts—rare; Rhode Island—not reported native.

IN CONNECTICUT—Not reported native.

**WOOD**—Heavy, hard, very strong and tough, close-grained and difficult to split, light clear brown, often tinged with red with thick, lighter colored sapwood; largely used in the manufacture of many agricultural implements, for the framework of chairs, hubs of wheels, railroad ties, the sills of buildings and other purposes demanding toughness, solidity and flexibility.

CORK ELM

# HACKBERRY
## Sugar Berry, Nettle Tree, False Elm, Hoop Ash.
### Celtis occidentalis L.

**HABIT**—A small to medium sized tree 20-45 ft. in height with a trunk diameter up to 2 ft., reaching over 100 ft. in height further south; rather variable in habit, generally forming a flattish to round-topped wide-spreading, oblong head with somewhat the aspect of an Elm; branches numerous, horizontal or slightly drooping, more or less zigzag; spray slender; berry-like fruit generally persistent throughout the winter.

**BARK**—Grayish-brown, on trunk and older limbs roughened with narrow projecting ridges which are sometimes reduced to warts or are almost entirely lacking.

**TWIGS**—Slender, somewhat zigzag, brownish, more or less shining, more or less downy; wood of twigs light greenish yellow when moistened. LENTICELS—scattered, raised and more or less elongated longitudinally. PITH—white, finely chambered.

**LEAF SCARS**—Alternate, 2-ranked, small, semi-oval, placed at right angles to the twig on a projecting cushion. STIPULE-SCARS—present, elongated, inconspicuous. BUNDLE-SCARS—appearing as a single confluent scar, evidently 3 in surface section.

**BUDS**—Small, 6 mm. or generally under in length, downy, chestnut brown, ovate, sharp-pointed, flattened, appressed; terminal bud absent. Buds frequently transformed into insect galls (swellings on twig photographed). BUD-SCALES—3-4 visible, closely overlapping in two ranks increasing in size from without inward. longitudinally striate if viewed toward light, generally dark margined.

**FRUIT**—A small, purplish, more or less spherical stone-fruit on long, slender stems. 7-10 mm. in diameter, often remaining on tree throughout winter. Flesh edible, sweet as is also the seed inside the stone.

**COMPARISONS**—The Hackberry is often taken for an Elm. The warts or narrow ridges on its bark, however, and its chambered pith readily distinguish it from the Elm if the berry-like fruit which is generally present fails to be found. The twigs are so frequently disfigured by insect galls that their presence might almost be given as a distinguishing character.

**DISTRIBUTION**—In divers situations and soils; woods, river banks, near salt marshes. Province of Quebec to Lake of the Woods, occasional; south to the Gulf states; west to Minnesota and Missouri.

IN NEW ENGLAND—Maine—not reported; New Hampshire—sparingly along the Connecticut valley, as far as Wells river; Vermont—along Lake Champlain, not common; Norwich and Windsor on the Connecticut; Massachusetts—occasional throughout the state; Rhode Island—common.

IN CONNECTICUT—Occasional to frequent, especially in river valleys and along the coast.

**WOOD**—Heavy, rather soft, not strong, coarse-grained, clear light yellow, with thick lighter colored sapwood; largely used for fencing and in the manufacture of cheap furniture.

HACKBERRY

# RED MULBERRY
## Morus rubra L.

**HABIT**—A small tree 15-25 ft. in height with trunk diameter of 8-15 inches, of larger size in the Ohio and Mississippi basins; trunk short, dividing into a number of stout spreading limbs developing a compact, broad, rounded head with numerous small branches in aspect resembling an apple tree, somewhat less scraggly than the White Mulberry. (The tree photographed had been considerably trimmed).

**BARK**—Dark brown, divided into irregular longitudinal plates which tend to lift at the ends and flake off, sometimes however not conspicuously flaky.

**TWIGS**—Slender though rather stouter than those of the White Mulberry; somewhat zigzag, reddish to greenish-brown, with rather sweetish taste, cut twig showing milky juice. LENTICELS—small, scattered, inconspicuous.

**LEAF-SCARS**—Alternate, 2-ranked, raised, nearly circular, slightly hollowed in the center. STIPULE-SCARS—narrow. BUNDLE-SCARS—raised but generally less distinctly so than in the White Mulberry, forming a closed ring or irregularly scattered in the center.

**BUDS**—Terminal bud absent, lateral buds ovate, pointed, about 6 mm. long, stout but longer than broad, not at all or but slightly flattened, divergent, shining, greenish to chestnut brown. BUD-SCALES—2-ranked, with thin distinctly darker margins, 4-8 scales visible.

**FRUIT**—Red, not to be found in winter.

**COMPARISONS**—The Red is most readily separated from the White Mulberry by its darker twigs, its larger shining, greenish to chestnut brown buds with dark-margined bud-scales.

**DISTRIBUTION**—Banks of rivers, rich woods. Canadian shore of Lake Erie; south to Florida; west to Michigan, South Dakota, and Texas.

**IN NEW ENGLAND**—A rare tree; Maine—doubtfully reported; New Hampshire—Pemigewasset valley, White Mountains; Vermont—northern extremity of Lake Champlain, banks of the Connecticut, Pownal, North Pownal; Massachusetts—rare; Rhode Island—no station reported.

**IN CONNECTICUT**—Rare or occasional; Bristol, Plainville, North Guilford, East Rock and Norwich.

**WOOD**—Light, soft, not strong, rather tough, coarse-grained, very durable, light orange color with thick lighter colored sapwood, used largely for fencing, in cooperage and in ship and boat building.

RED MULBERRY

# WHITE MULBERRY
## Silkworm Mulberry.
### Morus alba L.

**HABIT**—A small tree with a maximum height of 30-40 ft. and with a trunk diameter of less than 3 ft.; branching low with wide spreading limbs forming a low rounded head resembling an apple tree somewhat in habit, but with a characteristic scraggly twigginess to the branchlets.

**BARK**—Deeply furrowed into long more or less wavy light yellowish brown ridges.

**TWIGS**—Slender, yellowish-green to brownish-gray, for the most part smooth, round, more or less shining, generally zigzag, swollen at the nodes, short branches numerous, often arising at right angles to ranks of previous years and producing a characteristic scraggly complex of branchlets. Twigs slightly sweetish if chewed; bark exuding a white milk if cut on warm days or after being brought into a warm room. LENTICELS—scattered, similar in color to the twigs and hence inconspicuous. PITH—light, rounded in cross-section.

**LEAF-SCARS**—Alternate, in 2 ranks, small, projecting, oval to depressed circular. STIPULE-SCARS—narrow, inconspicuous. BUNDLE-SCARS—conspicuous, 3-10 projecting above leaf-scar; irregularly scattered. If leaf-scar is surface-sectioned leaf traces are reduced to 3 in number.

**BUDS**—Terminal bud absent; lateral buds small, about 3 mm. long, bright reddish-brown, roundish, generally about as broad as long, sharp or blunt pointed, somewhat flattened against twigs, often set oblique to the leaf-scar, 1 to 2 small collateral accessory buds sometimes present. BUD-SCALES—in 2 ranks, about 5 scales visible, increasing in size from below upward, margins somewhat finely hairy.

**FRUIT**—A white, juicy, multiple fruit not to be found in winter.

**COMPARISONS**—The projecting bundle-scars are characteristic of the Mulberries; for points of distinction from the Red Mulberry see under this species.

**DISTRIBUTION**—Probably a native of China where its leaves have from time immemorial furnished food for silkworms, introduced into the United States and Canada from Ontario to Florida and naturalized more or less throughout New England appearing by roadsides or along fences and in waste places, being spread by birds which are very fond of its fruit.

**IN CONNECTICUT**—Occasional; early in last century extensively planted to furnish food for silkworms and many large trees remain about farm houses.

**WOOD**—Moderately hard, close-grained, light yellowish-brown.

WHITE MULBERRY

# CUCUMBER TREE
## Mountain Magnolia.
### Magnolia acuminata L.

**HABIT**—When fully developed a tall tree up to 90 ft. in height with a trunk diameter of 3-4 ft. with comparatively slender branches widely spreading at the base, ascending above, forming a broadly conical head; when young having somewhat the aspect of a Pear Tree.

**BARK**—Grayish-brown ridged and flaky.

**TWIGS**—Slender, brown, shining, smooth or at times slightly downy, aromatic. LENTICELS—scattered, inconspicuous, orange colored. PITH —white.

**LEAF-SCARS**—Alternate, more than 2-ranked, crescent to U-shaped, elevated. STIPULE-SCARS—distinct, arising from upper margins of leaf-scar and encircling twig. BUNDLE-SCARS—large, few to numerous. scattered in an imperfectly double row, more or less raised.

**BUDS**—Thickly covered with pale silky hairs; lateral buds blunt, nearly surrounded by leaf-scars, about ⅓ the size of terminal bud; terminal bud oblong, blunt, 10-20 mm. long. BUD-SCALES—valvate and adhering in pairs, with rudimentary leaf-scar and decurrent ridge at side of bud.

**FRUIT**—An ovate to oblong cone, often curved, generally under 6 cm. long; in the young condition supposedly resembling a cucumber; seed flattish about 1 cm. in diameter.

**COMPARISONS**—The Cucumber Tree belongs to the same genus as the Umbrella Tree but differs from it in its smaller, blunt, downy buds, its narrow leaf-scars and its scaly ridged bark; from the Large-leaved Magnolia by the smaller size of its buds, its narrow leaf-scars and its scaly ridged bark; from the Sweet Bay by its larger size, the color of its twigs and the character of its bark. The Chinese Magnolia [*Magnolia conspicua* Salisb.] is often cultivated and has downy buds resembling those of the Cucumber Tree. The buds, however, are stouter, the bark is smooth and the species is more shrubby than tree-like.

**DISTRIBUTION**—Not native to New England; the hardiest of the Magnolias and extensively planted as an ornamental shade tree. It grows wild from western New York to southern Illinois and southward along the Appalachian mountains to southern Alabama.

**WOOD**—Light, soft, not strong, close-grained and durable, light yellow-brown, with thin lighter colored often nearly white sapwood of usually 25-30 layers of annual growth; occasionally manufactured into lumber used for flooring and cabinet making.

CUCUMBER TREE

# UMBRELLA TREE
## Elkwood.
### Magnolia tripetala L.
*M. Umbrella* Lam.

---

**HABIT**—A small tree with a maximum height of about 40 ft. and a trunk diameter of 1½ ft., in New England generally much smaller; trunk erect or inclined with wide-spreading branches which generally bend up at their tips forming a wide spreading irregular open head; at times with several stems springing from near the base of the trunk, forming a bushy growth around the main stem.

**BARK**—Light gray, smooth, marked with small excrescences, frequently wrinkled and lumpy at the scars of branches.

**TWIGS**—Stout, reddish to greenish-brown, shining, swollen at the base of each year's growth, aromatic. LENTICELS—conspicuous, scattered pale dots. PITH—white, with minute pink dots.

**LEAF-SCARS**—Alternate, more than 2-ranked, large, conspicuous, oval, slightly raised, mainly clustered at swellings along the twig. STIPULE-SCARS—distinct, arising from the side of leaf-scar and encircling twig. BUNDLE-SCARS—numerous, irregularly scattered, often slightly raised.

**BUDS**—Lateral buds at best small, conical, divergent, frequently undeveloped or showing as mere bulges of the bark; terminal buds large up to 5 cm. long, conical, with curved pointed apex, purple, with a bloom, with minute pale dots, smooth with patch of rusty hairs at base of leaf-ridge. BUD-SCALES—valvate and adhering in pairs corresponding to stipules, each pair enclosing in succession an erect folded downy leaf, the stalk of which is united with the next inner pair of scales; the leaf connected with the outer pair of scales falls off before maturing, leaving a rudimentary scar on the bud with a decurrent ridge corresponding to its leaf-stalk.

**FRUIT**—Ovate to oblong cone, 6-10 cm. long, made up of numerous follicles which split open in the fall and let out the red flattish seeds which are about 1 cm. in diameter.

**COMPARISONS**—For comparisons with the Tulip Tree see this species. The Umbrella Tree differs from the Cucumber Tree, the Large-leaved Magnolia and the Chinese Magnolia by its smooth buds and from the Sweet Bay by the size and color of its twigs and buds.

**DISTRIBUTION**—Not native to New England but extensively cultivated as an ornamental tree. It grows wild in the Appalachian mountain region from the valley of the Susquéhanna river, Pennsylvania to southern Alabama.

**WOOD**—Light, soft, close-grained, not strong, light brown, with creamy white sapwood of 35-40 layers of annual growth.

UMBRELLA TREE

# TULIP TREE
## Whitewood, Yellow Poplar.
### Liriodendron Tulipifera L.

**HABIT**—A good sized tree 50-70 ft. in height with a trunk diameter of 2-3 ft., in the Ohio basin reaching an exceptional height of nearly 200 ft.; trunk tall, straight, continuous into the crown and giving off comparatively short, horizontal, declined or slightly ascending branches with upcurved tips, forming in young trees a pyramidal and in older trees an oblong head. Light yellow fruiting cones or at least their axes conspicuous at ends of twigs.

**BARK**—Somewhat resembling bark of White Ash but ridges are longer and the furrows are shallower and more rounded and less inclined to form diamond-shaped patches; inner bark bitter; young bark ashy-gray and smooth, becoming dark with light colored seams.

**TWIGS**—Slender to somewhat stout, reddish-brown, smooth and shining with more or less evident bloom, with an agreeable aromatic smell when broken but with an intensely bitter taste, not mucilaginous; on vigorous shoots often branching the first season. LENTICELS—conspicuous pale dots. PITH—white with rather inconspicuous transverse woody partitions through the ground-mass.

**LEAF-SCARS**—Alternate, more than 2-ranked, large, conspicuous, elevated, circular or slightly flattened at the top. STIPULE-SCARS—conspicuous, arising from top of leaf-scar, encircling twig. BUNDLE-SCARS—small, numerous, scattered like perforations in a sieve.

**BUDS**—Dark reddish-brown, covered with a bloom, white-dotted, blunt, flattish; lateral buds small, on vigorous twigs superposed accessory buds sometimes present which may be stalked or develop into branches the first season; terminal buds large 5-20 mm. long, oblong, blunt. BUD-SCALES—spoon-shaped, smooth, valvate in pairs corresponding to stipules, each pair enclosing in succession a long-stalked, smooth, reflexed and folded leaf with its 2 scale-like stipules; leaf-stalk attached only at its base, hence scar of rudimentary leaf when present located at base of bud.

**FRUIT**—A light brown cone made up of winged seed-like portions, 20-40 mm. long which remain aggregated together into the winter but which are gradually dropped leaving the persistent terminal axis.

**COMPARISONS**—The Magnolias to which the Tulip Tree is botanically related have likewise aromatic twigs with circular stipule-scars. Their leaf-scars, however, are not circular; their buds are pointed or hairy and the scar of the rudimentary leaf is considerably above base of bud. The light brown fruiting cones from which the winged seed-like bodies have partially fallen are generally to be found on the Tulip Tree and are distinctive for this species.

**DISTRIBUTION**—Prefers a rich, loamy, moist soil. Is sometimes planted as an ornamental tree. From New England south to the Gulf states; west to Wisconsin; occasional in the eastern sections of Missouri and Arkansas.

IN NEW ENGLAND—Vermont—valley of the Hoosac River in the southwestern corner of the state; Massachusetts—frequent in the Connecticut river valley and westward; reported as far east as Douglas, southeastern corner of Worcester county; Rhode Island—frequent.

IN CONNECTICUT—Occasional, local or frequent.

**WOOD**—Light, soft, brittle not strong, easily worked, light yellow or brown, with thin creamy white sapwood; largely manufactured into lumber generally under the name of "Whitewood"; used in construction, the interior finish of houses, boat building and for shingles, brooms and woodenware. The intensely acrid bitter inner bark, especially of the root, is used domestically as a tonic and stimulant and hydrochlorate of tulipiferine, an alkaloid, separated from the bark, possesses the property of stimulating the heart.

TULIP TREE

# SASSAFRAS

Sassafras variifolium (Salisb.) Kuntze.

*S. officinale* Nees & Eberm. ; *S. Sassafras* Karst.

---

**HABIT**—A small tree at times reaching 40-50 ft. in height, with a trunk diameter of 2-4 ft.; at the north smaller and often shrubby; in the southern states reaching a height of 100 ft.; branches numerous, stout, more or less contorted, often distinctly in yearly whorls, horizontal or forming a broad angle with the trunk, subdividing to produce a bushy spray and forming a flat-topped or slightly rounded oblong head. Limbs brittle and frequently lost through ice storms or other injuries, giving the tree a battered appearance as shown in photograph. The tree sprouts abundantly from the roots often surrounding itself with a thicket of saplings (see those at right in picture).

**BARK**—Reddish-brown, deeply furrowed even in comparatively young trees into broad flat ridges with narrow horizontal cracks running part way around the trunk and dividing the ridges into short blocks.

**TWIGS**—Slender to stout, bright yellowish-green, often reddish where exposed to light, smooth and shining or somewhat downy; internodes very unequal; rapidly grown shoots freely branching the first season, the branches exceeding the main axis; twigs spicy-aromatic to both smell and taste, mucilaginous if chewed. LENTICELS—scattered, very inconspicuous.

**LEAF-SCARS**—Alternate, more than 2-ranked, small, raised, semi-elliptical, with elevated margins. STIPULE-SCARS—absent. BUNDLE-SCARS—single, forming horizontal line.

**BUDS**—Green, more or less tinged with red toward tip; lateral buds small, divergent; terminal buds large. 5-10 mm. long, ovate, pointed; flower buds terminal. BUD-SCALES—with thickened veins; generally 3, narrower, thicker, shorter scales surrounding terminal bud.

**COMPARISONS**—Its bright green aromatic mucilaginous twigs which form branches the first season surpassing the main axis, its single bundle-scar and the transverse cracking of the ridges of the bark render the Sassafras one of the most interesting of our native trees in winter. It is scarcely to be confused with any other form.

**DISTRIBUTION**—In various soils and situations; sandy or rich woods, along the borders of peaty swamps, thickets and fence-rows. Provinces of Quebec and Ontario; south to Florida; west to Michigan, Iowa, Kansas, and Texas.

IN NEW ENGLAND—Maine—this tree grows not beyond Black Point (Scarboro, Cumberland county) eastward; (Josselyn's New England Rarities, 1672); not reported again by botanists for more than two hundred years; rediscovered at Wells in 1895 and North Berwick in 1896; New Hampshire—lower Merrimac valley, eastward to the coast and along the Connecticut valley to Bellows Falls; Vermont—occasional south of the center; Pownal; Hartland and Brattleboro; Vernon; Massachusetts—common especially in the eastern sections; Rhode Island—common.

IN CONNECTICUT—Frequent.

**WOOD**—Soft, weak, brittle, coarse-grained, very durable in the soil, aromatic, dull orange-brown, with thin light yellow sapwood of 7-8 layers of annual growth; largely used for fence-posts and rails and in the construction of light boats, ox-yokes, and in cooperage. The roots and especially their bark are a mild aromatic stimulant, and oil of sassafras used to perfume soaps, flavor candy, etc. and as an ingredient in liniment is distilled from them.

SASSAFRAS

# WITCH HAZEL
## Hamamelis virginiana L.

**HABIT**—A large shrub or small tree occasionally 25-30 ft. in height with a trunk diameter of 10-14 inches, with short trunk, spreading crooked branches with conspicuous persistent fruiting capsules, forming a broad open head.

**BARK**—Light brown, more or less mottled, generally smooth or minutely scaly.

**TWIGS**—Rather slender, light orange brown, smooth and shining, or downy especially toward apex, more or less zigzag. LENTICELS—few, scattered, whitish dots.

**LEAF-SCARS**—Alternate, 2-ranked, small, inversely triangular. STIPULE-SCARS—distinct, narrow, oblong, somewhat separate from leaf-scar. BUNDLE-SCARS—whitish in conspicuous contrast to dark brown surface of leaf-scar, generally 3 and separate or these may be compounded or more or less confluent.

**BUDS**—Stalked, flattish, slightly curved, densely downy with short fine light to dark olive brown hairs; terminal bud larger than laterals, 5-12 mm. long. BUD-SCALES—an outer pair of relatively thin scales corresponding to stipules and often represented by only a scar accompanying the outermost thick downy laterally folded undeveloped leaf, which with smaller leaves within serves the function of bud-scales. The bud is therefore essentially naked.

**FRUIT**—Produced in abundance, a downy 2-chambered capsule about 15 mm. long, surrounded by the persistent calyx, discharging in autumn 4 shining, brown, oblong seeds and remaining widely gaping on the tree throughout winter (see lower part of twig picture). The plant produces flowers in the autumn at the same time with the ripening of the fruit, and the remains of the flowers, showing the 4 downy sepals with their enclosing bracts, are to be found in clusters on the recent twigs (upper part of twig picture).

**COMPARISONS**—In habitat and in its stalked buds the Witch Hazel resembles the Alders. The buds of the latter however are essentially smooth or at most fine-downy, not hairy and their fruit is a woody cone not a capsule.

**DISTRIBUTION**—In moist or wet often rocky places. Nova Scotia to Ontario and Minnesota; south to Florida and Texas; west to eastern Nebraska.

IN NEW ENGLAND—Common throughout.

**WOOD**—Heavy, hard, very close-grained, light brown tinged with red, with thick nearly white sapwood of 30-40 layers of annual growth. The bark is slightly astringent and though not known to have essential properties is largely used in the form of fluid extracts and decoctions as a popular application for sprains and bruises, Pond's Extract being made by distilling the bark in dilute alcohol. Probably equally efficacious is the use of the twigs as divining rods to locate water and minerals.

WITCH HAZEL

# SWEET GUM
## Bilsted, Red Gum, Alligator-wood, Liquidambar.
### Liquidambar Styraciflua L.

**HABIT**—A tree 40-60 ft. in height with a trunk diameter up to 2 ft., reaching 150 ft. in height and a trunk diameter of 3-5 ft. in the Mississippi and Ohio valleys; branches slender, regular and spreading, forming a very symmetrical tree, when young (right hand tree in plate) narrowly oblong-conical, with age (left hand tree in plate) becoming broader and rounded ovate, generally showing persistent stalked spherical fruits.

**BARK**—Grayish brown, deeply furrowed into broad more or less flaky ridges.

**TWIGS**—Mediumly stout to slender, light to dark reddish to yellowish-brown, rounded or often somewhat angled, smooth and shiny or seldom slightly hairy; generally developing the second season 3-4 parallel corky ridges on the upper side of horizontal branchlets and on all sides of vertical branchlets (lower twig figure). LENTICELS—scattered, dark. PITH—wide, 5-pointed, star-shaped.

**LEAF-SCARS**—Alternate, more than 2-ranked, broadly crescent-shaped to inversely triangular, raised. STIPULE-SCARS—absent. BUNDLE-SCARS—3, each a circular white ring with dark center conspicuous against the dark surface of leaf-scar.

**BUDS**—Ovate to conical, pointed, shiny, reddish-brown, more or less fragrant when crushed, lateral buds divergent, on rapidly grown shoots sometimes stalked or developing into branches the first season and then frequently with a pair of collateral accessory buds at a node; terminal bud exceeding the laterals, 5-10 mm. long. BUD-SCALES—ovate, fine-downy on the margins, rounded on the back, generally with a short abrupt point at the apex.

**FRUIT**—A long stalked spherical spiny aggregate of ovaries, 2-4 cm. in diameter, hanging on the tree through the winter; the mature seeds falling in autumn leaving many minute abortive seeds in the ovaries.

**COMPARISONS**—The corky ridges on the twigs of the Sweet Gum are striking distinctive characters which are found also in the Cork Elm and the Bur Oak. The Elm, however, has 2-ranked leaf-scars and the buds of the Oak are bunched at the twig ends; neither are shiny reddish-brown between the ridges. The corky ridges may be but sparingly developed upon some trees and may even fail entirely. The spiny fruits which persist through winter form the best single distinctive character.

**DISTRIBUTION**—Low, wet soils, swamps, moist woods, somewhat cultivated as an ornamental tree. Connecticut; south to Florida; west to Missouri and Texas.

IN NEW ENGLAND—Growing native only in Connecticut.

IN CONNECTICUT—South Norwalk and occasional or frequent westward near the shores of the Sound.

**WOOD**—Heavy, hard, straight, close-grained, not strong, bright brown tinged with red, with thin almost white sapwood of 60-70 layers of annual growth, inclined to warp and shrink badly; used for the outside finish of houses, in cabinet making, for street pavement, wooden dishes and fruit boxes. The resinous exudation from the stems (liquidambar) which is more marked in trees grown in the south, is used in the preparation of chewing gum.

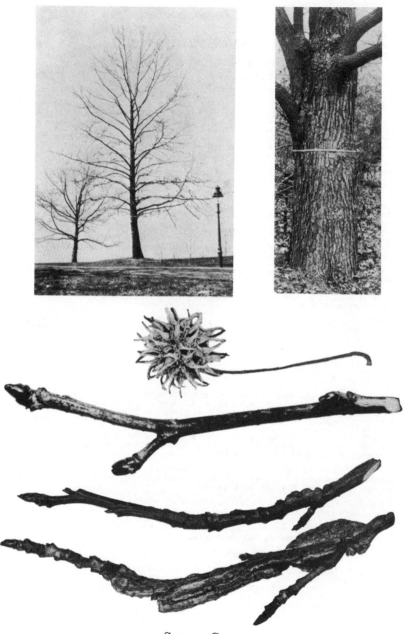

SWEET GUM

# SYCAMORE
## Buttonwood, Buttonball, Plane Tree.
### Platanus occidentalis L.

**HABIT**—A large tree 50-100 ft. in height with a trunk diameter of 3-8 ft., in the bottom lands of the lower Ohio and Mississippi valleys reaching occasionally a height of 170 ft. with a trunk diameter of 10-11 ft., the largest tree of the New England forest; with an erect or often declined trunk very gradually tapering and continuous into the top (see habit picture) or branched near the base into two or three secondary trunks (see bark picture) forming an open, irregular or rounded wide-spreading head; branchlets scraggly, often in tufts with dead twigs not infrequent. (See low cross-branch in bark picture).

**BARK**—Dark brown, at the base of older trunks shallowly furrowed into broad ridges which are broken into small oblong thick plate-like scales; higher up on the trunk peeling off in large thin plates, exposing conspicuous areas of the whitish, yellowish or greenish inner bark.

**TWIGS**—Slender, rather shiny, smooth, yellowish-brown, generally zigzag, swollen at the nodes, rounded or with decurrent ridges from the bundle-scars; medulary rays conspicuous in sectioned twig. LENTICELS—pale, minute. PITH—thick.

**LEAF-SCARS**—Alternate, generally 2-ranked, sometimes appearing more ranked; narrow, projecting, nearly surrounding the bud, more or less swollen at the bundle-scars. STIPULE-SCARS—encircling twig. BUNDLE-SCARS—conspicuous, dark, generally raised, 5-10 or more in single curved line.

**BUDS**—Terminal bud absent; lateral buds large, conical, 5-10 mm. long, blunt-pointed, smooth, shiny, dark reddish-brown, divergent. BUD-SCALES—a single scale visible, forming a cap to the bud, second scale green, gummy, innermost scale covered with long rusty hairs.

**FRUIT**—Spherical heads 2.5-4 cm. in diameter, on long stalks mostly solitary or seldom in 2's composed of small hairy 1-seeded nutlets. The heads hang on the tree till spring.

**COMPARISONS**—The native Sycamore [*Platanus occidentalis*] is closely related to the Oriental Sycamore [*Platanus orientalis* L.] which is extensively planted as an ornamental tree. It bears its fruiting heads singly or rarely in 2's, while the Oriental Sycamore has its fruiting heads in clusters of 2-4. The whitewashed appearance of the upper limbs, the single cap-like scale of its bud, which is nearly surrounded by the leaf-scar, present characters which prevent the Sycamores from being confused with any other trees.

**DISTRIBUTION**—Near streams, river bottoms, and low, damp woods; sometimes in dryer places. Ontario; south to Florida; west to Minnesota, Nebraska, Kansas and Texas.

IN NEW ENGLAND—Maine—apparently restricted to York county; New Hampshire—Merrimac valley towards the coast; along the Connecticut as far as Walpole; Vermont—scattering along the river shores, quite abundant along the Hoosac in Pownal; Massachusetts—occasional; Rhode Island—rather common.

IN CONNECTICUT—Frequent.

**WOOD**—Reddish-brown with light somewhat yellowish sapwood, heavy, tough, hard, not very strong, coarse-grained, difficult to split and work; is used in manufacture of tobacco boxes, crates, butchers' blocks, ox-yokes and when cut quartering is used for inside finishing of buildings and for furniture.

SYCAMORE

# PEAR
### Pyrus communis L.

**HABIT**—A tree sometimes 75 ft. in height with a trunk diameter of 2 ft. or more; trunk erect, more or less continuous into the head, with ascending branches and numerous stubby branchlets forming an upright pyramidal head.

**BARK**—Grayish-brown, on young trunks and branches smooth becoming with age longitudinally fissured into flat-topped ridges which are further broken by transverse fissures into oblong scales.

**TWIGS**—Stout, smooth or but slightly downy, yellowish-green or sometimes with tinge of brown, without characteristic taste; short sharp-pointed branches not infrequently present; stubby, branched slow-growing fruit spurs abundant, with prominent fruit scars. **LENTICELS**—scattered, pale, more or less conspicuous.

**LEAF-SCARS**—Alternate, more than 2-ranked, narrow, crescent-shaped, raised. **STIPULE-SCARS**—absent. **BUNDLE-SCARS**—3, often indistinct.

**BUDS**—Conical, sharp-pointed, smooth or but slightly hairy; terminal bud about 8 mm. or less in length, lateral buds smaller, generally divergent and not flattened or at times on vigorous shoots both flattened and appressed. **BUD-SCALES**—ovate, generally with conspicuous grayish skin on surface, generally 4 or more visible scales to lateral buds, more to terminal bud.

**FRUIT**—A large fleshy pome.

**COMPARISONS**—The Pear Tree may be distinguished from the Apple by its erect habit of growth. The twig characters vary somewhat among the different varieties but in general the twigs of the Pear differ from those of the Apple in being smooth, generally of a yellowish-green color, devoid of a licorice-like taste and in having pointed, mostly divergent buds the scales of which are more or less covered with a grayish skin.

**DISTRIBUTION**—A native of the Old World cultivated in this country for its fruit and escaped from cultivation in waste places.

**WOOD**—Hard, close-grained, reddish-brown; used for drawing instruments, for tools, in imitation of ebony and by the wood engraver.

PEAR

# APPLE
## Pyrus Malus L.
*Malus Malus* (L.) Britton.

---

**HABIT**—A tree reaching 30-50 ft. in height and a trunk diameter of 2-3 ft.; trunk short with wide spreading limbs forming a broad round-topped head of familiar and very characteristic habit.

**BARK**—Grayish-brown, scaling off in thin, brittle, flaky plates.

**TWIGS**—Stout, pale-woolly, at least toward the apex, mostly reddish-brown, rarely yellowish, shining where free from wool, with character-istically slightly bitter and licorice-like taste when chewed; short, stubby, contorted fruit-spurs abundantly present. LENTICELS—scattered, pale, more or less conspicuous. PITH—white.

**LEAF-SCARS**—Alternate, more than 2-ranked, narrow, crescent-shaped, raised. STIPULE-SCARS—absent. BUNDLE-SCARS—3, often indistinct.

**BUDS**—Ovate, blunt, bright reddish-brown, more or less densely covered with pale wool; terminal bud 8 mm. or less long, lateral buds smaller, often triangular, flattened and appressed against twig. BUD-SCALES—ovate, about 3 scales visible to lateral bud, more to terminal bud.

**FRUIT**—A large fleshy pome.

**COMPARISONS**—The Apple Tree resembles the Pear but is readily distinguished from this species by its low spreading habit of growth. The numerous varieties differ somewhat in the twig characters, some with twigs and buds nearly smooth, others with yellowish rather than reddish-brown twigs. The licorice-like taste of the twigs seems to be a constant character for the Apple. Among its distinguishing characters which in the main hold good, may be mentioned the pale wool on the twigs and buds, the flat appressed lateral buds and the reddish-brown color of the twigs.

**DISTRIBUTION**—A native of the Old World, cultivated in this country for its fruit and frequently escaped from cultivation in waste places when it assumes a bushier habit of growth with smaller twigs frequently beset with short sharp-pointed thorn-like branches.

**WOOD**—Hard, tough, close-grained, reddish-brown, used for tool handles, shoe makers' lasts, by the cabinet maker and esteemed as a fuel in open grate fires.

APPLE

# AMERICAN MOUNTAIN ASH
## Rowan or Service Tree.
### Pyrus americana (Marsh.) DC.
*Sorbus americana* Marsh.

**HABIT**—A shrub or small tree 15-20 ft. high or in northern New England reaching a height of 25-30 ft. with a trunk diameter of 12-15 inches; with slender spreading branches forming a rather narrow round-topped head.

**BARK**—Grayish-brown, smooth or on older trees somewhat roughish.

**TWIGS**—Stout, smooth, reddish to grayish-brown. LENTICELS—conspicuous, large, pale, oblong, remotely scattered. PITH—broad, slightly reddish-brown.

**LEAF-SCARS**—Alternate, more than 2-ranked, large, crescent to broadly U or V-shaped, raised on a projection darker than the twig. STIPULE-SCARS—absent. BUNDLE-SCARS—regularly 5, often raised, arranged in a single curved line.

**BUDS**—Terminal buds large, about 13 mm. long, ovate to broadly conical with a curved pointed apex, dark purplish-red, gummy and smooth or with few hairs on the surface, densely woolly within; lateral buds smaller, flattened and appressed. BUD-SCALES—2-3 visible to terminal bud; 1-2 to lateral bud.

**FRUIT**—Berry-like, bright red, strongly acid, round, about the size of a pea, in flat-topped clusters persistent through the winter.

**COMPARISONS**—A larger fruited form, the Western Mountain Ash [*Pyrus sitchensis* (Roem.) Piper], is considered by some a distinct species but by others only a variety of the type described. It is more northerly and westerly in its distribution. The European Mountain Ash [*Pyrus Aucuparia* (L.) Ehrh.] with many horticultural forms is more frequently cultivated than the American species and has escaped from cultivation in some places. It may be distinguished by the white hairy down present especially on the upper half of the terminal bud and by the larger fruits (about 10 mm. broad) arranged in a rather round-topped cluster. The habit, bark, fruit and lower twig photographs are of the European species.

**DISTRIBUTION**—River banks, cool woods, swamps, and mountains. Newfoundland to Manitoba; south, in cold swamps and along the mountains to North Carolina; west to Michigan and Minnesota.

IN NEW ENGLAND—Maine—common; New Hampshire—common along the watersheds of the Connecticut and Merrimac rivers and on the slopes of the White Mountains; Vermont—abundant far up the slopes of the Green mountains; Massachusetts—Graylock, Wachusett, Watatic, and other mountainous regions; rare eastward; Rhode Island—occasional in the northern sections.

IN CONNECTICUT—Rare or local. Swamps and about ponds or sometimes on dry ledges or in rocky woods; Stafford, Durham and Meriden, Granby, Winchester, Norfolk, Canaan, Salisbury, Kent.

The variety *(Pyrus sitchensis)* the Western Mountain Ash, has the following distribution—Mountain slopes, cool woods, along the shores of rivers and ponds, often associated with *Pyrus americana*, but climbing higher up the mountains. From Labrador and Nova Scotia west to the Rocky mountains, then northward along the mountain ranges to Alaska. In New England, confined to Maine, New Hampshire and Vermont.

**WOOD**—Close-grained, light, soft and weak, pale brown with lighter colored sapwood of 15-20 layers of annual growth; of little economic value. The very astringent bark and berries are employed medicinally.

MOUNTAIN ASH

# QUINCE

### Cydonia vulgaris Pers.

*Pyrus Cydonia L.*

**HABIT**—A low bushy straggling rounded shrub or small tree rarely exceeding 15 ft. in height with crooked distorted branches.

**BARK**—Dark gray, finely streaked, becoming with age more or less roughened with large flaky scales.

**TWIGS**—Slender, dark reddish-brown, often with tinge of green; in protected places and especially toward the tip of the twig generally more or less densely covered with pale wool, bright-shining where smooth; mostly tasteless. LENTICELS—small, numerous, becoming conspicuous brownish dots on older growth. PITH—narrow, greenish.

**LEAF-SCARS**—Alternate, more than 2-ranked, small, crescent-shaped to inversely triangular, raised on a somewhat shrivelled projection slightly darker than the twig and containing at its outer edges the roundish, rather inconspicuous stipule-scars at either side of the leaf-scar. BUNDLE-SCARS—3.

**BUDS**—Terminal bud absent; lateral buds minute, about 3 mm. or often less in length, ovate, blunt, flattened and appressed against twig; smoothish or somewhat hairy at base, with dense pale-rusty hairs within showing through at apex. BUD-SCALES—not easily distinguished, about 2 visible, reddish-brown to light reddish, breaking away at the tip.

**FRUIT**—A large, firm, fleshy, downy pome.

**COMPARISONS**—The twigs and buds of the Quince resemble somewhat those of the Apple but the twigs are much more slender and the buds show a distinctive tuft of rusty hairs. The bushy habit of growth further will distinguish the Quince from the other cultivated fruit trees.

**DISTRIBUTION**—A tree native of Europe, cultivated for the fruit and escaped to a slight extent in some localities.

**WOOD**—The wood is of no commercial importance. The fruit is valued for preserving. The raw fruit and mucilaginous seed are used in domestic medicinal practice.

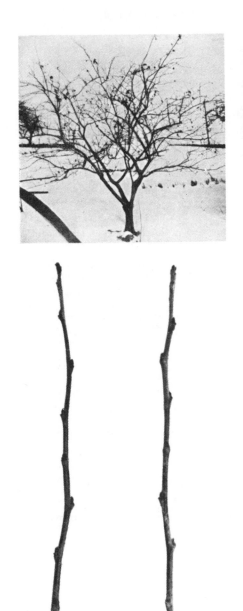

QUINCE

## SHAD BUSH
### Service Berry, Shadblow, Juneberry.
Amelanchier canadensis (L.) Medic.

**HABIT**—A shrub or small tree 10-25 ft. in height with a trunk diameter of 6-10 inches, sometimes reaching a height of 40 ft. with a trunk diameter of 1½ ft.; of variable habit, at times a shrub with many stems in a clump (see plate, picture at right) or again a symmetrical tree with a single trunk with many small limbs and fine branchlets forming an oblong or rather widespreading round-topped head (see plate.)

**BARK**—Essentially smooth, grayish-brown, older trunks with narrow longitudinal fissures separating off shallow flat ridges which are somewhat scaly at base of trunk; younger trunks and branches smooth, often characteristically streaked with darker longitudinal lines (see plate).

**TWIGS**—Slender, grayish, olive-green to reddish-brown covered with a gray skin, generally smooth, with slight taste of bitter almonds. LENTICELS—scattered or numerous, pale, minute dots. PITH—greenish with irregular edges.

**LEAF-SCARS**—Alternate, 2-ranked or at times appearing more than 2-ranked, a raised very narrow flattened V-shaped line swollen at the bundle-scars, often with short somewhat decurrent ridges at outer edges. STIPULE-SCARS—absent. BUNDLE-SCARS—3, rather large.

**BUDS**—Terminal buds present, long, narrow, 7-12 mm. long and 3-4 times as long as broad, narrowly ovate to conical, sharp-pointed, greenish-yellowish more or less tinged with reddish-purple, smooth or with white silky hairs at apex and edges of scales, mostly appressed; lateral buds on rapidly grown shoots normal, on slowly grown spurs, undeveloped or rudimentary; generally a small lateral bud just below terminal bud. BUD-SCALES—increasing from below upward, the two lowest about ¼ length of the bud more or less keeled and 3-nerved, dark, margined and with a single short dark spiny tip, lower scales often 3-tipped, edges from slightly downy on outermost scales to densely silky-hairy on inner scales; on terminal buds about 5 scales visible. more or less imperfectly 2-ranked; lateral buds on vigorous shoots often with pair of extra lateral scales basally united giving short-stalked appearance to bud.

**FRUIT**—Berry-like, sometimes if infected by a rust fungus remaining dried on the tree through the winter.

**COMPARISONS**—The long narrow buds of the Shad Bush bear a superficial resemblance to those of the Beech. The Beech buds, however, are divergent, narrower, with 10-20 scales regularly arranged in four rows and have stipule-scars nearly encircling the twig. The Shad Bush is subject to the attacks of a fungus [*Dimerosporium Collinsii*] which blackens the leaves and causes a profuse branching at the point of infection. The "witches' brooms" thus formed with the persistent blackened leaves often enables the tree to be recognized at a distance.

**DISTRIBUTION**—Dry, open woods, hillsides. Newfoundland and Nova Scotia to Lake Superior; south to the Gulf of Mexico; west to Minnesota, Kansas, and Louisiana.

IN NEW ENGLAND—Throughout.

IN CONNECTICUT—Frequent.

**WOOD**—Heavy, exceedingly hard, strong, close-grained, dark brown often tinged with red, with thick lighter colored sapwood of 40-50 layers of annual growth; occasionally used for the handles of tools and other small implements; under the name of "Lancewood" it is used in the manufacture of fish rods.

SHAD BUSH

# THE HAWTHORNS

## Thorns, Haws, Thorn Apples, White Thorns.

### Crataegus L.

**NOTE**—The Hawthorns form one of the most complexing genera among flowering plants. Some 600 species have been described and Sargent in his Manual gives descriptions of 132 tree-like forms for North America. The distinctions used are based largely upon flower and fruit characters. They are at best often difficult of application and entirely unavailable in the winter. It seems, therefore, most advisable to give a description which will hold good for the whole group rather than a detailed account of any single species. The twig photographed was taken from the Cockspur Thorn [*Crataegus Crus-galli* L.]; the habit photograph from an undetermined specimen belonging to the *Pruinosa* group growing in a deserted pasture.

**HABIT**—Generally low wide spreading trees or shrubs.

**BARK**—Generally dark, scaly.

**TWIGS**—Rigid, round in section, more or less zigzag, rarely unarmed, generally armed with axillary thorns which are almost always unbranched—not infrequently branched when arising from the trunk and larger branches—generally similar in color to branches from which they grow; thorns generally absent from many of the nodes. LENTICELS—oblong, generally pale.

**LEAF-SCARS**—Alternate, more than 2-ranked, small, narrow, crescent-shaped, slightly raised. STIPULE-SCARS—absent. BUNDLE-SCARS—3.

**BUDS**—Small, spherical or nearly so; terminal bud generally present, scarcely larger than lateral buds; a lateral accessory bud on each side of the axillary thorn, frequently only one of the two developed. BUD-SCALES--numerous, overlapping, thick, rounded, blunt, bright chestnut brown, shining.

**FRUIT**—Berry-like, botanically a small drupe-like pome with 1-5 nutlets.

**COMPARISONS**—The Hawthorns may be distinguished from other genera by the unbranched axillary thorns usually present on their twigs and by the bright, shining, chestnut brown, generally spherical buds. The thorns of the Honey Locust are branched and situated some distance above the axillary buds. The Osage Orange [*Maclura pomifera* (Raf.) Schneider], sometimes grown in hedges, has unbranched thorns generally present at all the nodes, decreasing regularly toward the tip of the greenish-gray twig, with buds lateral to the thorns and a single more or less ring-shaped bundle-scar to the broad leaf-scar.

**DISTRIBUTION**—The Hawthorns are most abundant in eastern North America occurring here from Newfoundland to the mountains of northern Mexico. A few species occur in the Rocky mountains and Pacific coast regions and in China, Japan, Siberia, central and southern Asia and in Europe.

**WOOD**—Heavy, hard, tough, close-grained, reddish-brown, with thick lighter colored usually pale sapwood; useful for the handles of tools, mallets and other small articles.

HAWTHORN

# WILD BLACK CHERRY
## Rum, Cabinet or Black Cherry.
### Prunus serotina Ehrh.
*Padus serotina* (Ehrh.) Agardh.

**HABIT**—A medium sized tree 30-50 ft. in height with a trunk diameter from 8 or 10 inches to 2 feet, becoming much larger in the middle and southern states; branches spreading often more or less zigzag forming an irregular oblong head.

**BARK**—On young trunks and branches smooth reddish-brown with conspicuous oblong whitish horizontal lenticels, easily peeled off in thin dark papery layers exposing the bright green bark below, becoming with age very much roughened by irregular, close, dark, scaly plates with upturned edges.

**TWIGS**—Rather slender, smooth, reddish-brown, more or less covered with a grayish skin easily rubbed off; crushed twigs with odor and taste of bitter almonds. LENTICELS—numerous, pale, minute, rounded dots, becoming horizontally elongated and more conspicuous on later growth. PITH—of recent growth, generally whitish.

**LEAF-SCARS**—Alternate, more than 2-ranked, small, semi-oval to inversely triangular, raised. STIPULE-SCARS—inconspicuous or apparently absent. BUNDLE-SCARS—3, often inconspicuous.

**BUDS**—Medium sized, ovate, blunt to sharp-pointed, about 4 mm. long, smooth, bright reddish-brown, divergent or sometimes somewhat flattened and appressed; terminal bud slightly larger than lateral buds. BUD-SCALES—about 4 visible, broadly ovate, more or less rounded and keeled on the back, of nearly uniform color or with darker edges, sometimes partially covered with a grayish skin, similar to that usual on the twigs.

**FRUIT**—A drupe about the size of a pea, ripening in summer in drooping elongated clusters.

**COMPARISONS**—The Wild Black Cherry in its young growth resembles the Choke Cherry but grows to be a good sized tree and develops a very rough scaly bark. Further the lenticels tend to be whitish and elongate horizontally with age, the buds are smaller and redder and their scales are not white-margined. From the cultivated Sweet and Sour Cherries the Black Cherry is distinguished by absence of fruiting spurs, by smaller buds and by the character of its bark.

**DISTRIBUTION**—In all sorts of soils and exposures; open places and rich woods. Nova Scotia to Lake Superior; south to Florida; west to North Dakota, Kansas, and Texas, extending through Mexico, along the Pacific coast of Central America to Peru.

IN NEW ENGLAND—Maine—not reported north of Oldtown (Penobscot county); frequent throughout the other New England states.

**WOOD**—Light, strong, rather hard, close straight-grained, with a satiny surface, light brown or red, with thin yellow sapwood of 10-12 layers of annual growth; largely used in cabinet-making and the interior finish of houses. The bark, especially that of the branches and roots, yields hydrocyanic acid used in medicine as a tonic and sedative. The ripe fruit is used to flavor alcoholic liquors whence one of the common names.

WILD BLACK CHERRY

# CHOKE CHERRY
### Prunus virginiana L.
*Padus virginiana* (L.) Roemer.

**HABIT**—Generally a tall shrub or a small tree rarely reaching 20-30 ft. in height with a trunk diameter of 6-8 inches.

**BARK**—Dull grayish-brown, smoothish but slightly roughened with raised buff-orange rounded dots formed by the enlarged lenticels, not becoming rough-scaly with age; on young trunks and branches easily peeled off in thin, dark papery layers exposing the bright green bark below.

**TWIGS**—Slender to rather stout, averaging stouter than those of the Wild Black Cherry, smooth, reddish to grayish-brown, without grayish skin easily rubbed off, crushed twigs with a rank odor and taste in addition to that of bitter almonds. LENTICELS—numerous, rather conspicuous, buff-orange dots, slightly elongated longitudinally the first year and not becoming distinctly elongated horizontally on later growth. PITH—of recent growth white.

**LEAF-SCARS**—Alternate, more than 2-ranked, elliptical, raised. STIPULE-SCARS—inconspicuous or absent. BUNDLE-SCARS—3, frequently sunken.

**BUDS**—Rather large, narrow, ovate to conical, about 6 mm. or more long, smooth, pale brown, sharp-pointed, generally divergent with more or less strongly curved apex; terminal bud frequently slightly smaller than lateral buds. BUD-SCALES—a half dozen or more scales visible, broadly ovate, more or less rounded and keeled on the back, with thin grayish margins.

**FRUIT**—A drupe about the size of a pea, ripening in summer in drooping elongated clusters.

**COMPARISONS**—The Choke Cherry may be distinguished from the Wild Black Cherry with which it is frequently confused by its smaller size, smoothish bark even in old age, its buff colored lenticels which do not elongate horizontally, the rank odor of its twigs and by its larger and paler buds with whitish-margined bud-scales. From the cultivated Sweet and Sour Cherries the Choke Cherry is distinguished by the absence of short fruit spurs and by its gray-margined bud-scales. The lower twig in the plate is infected by a fungus disease—Black Knot *(Plowrightia morbosa)* which occurs also upon the Wild Black and Wild Red Cherries and upon our cultivated Cherries and also upon the Plums.

**DISTRIBUTION**—In varying soils; along river banks, on dry plains, in woods, common along walls and often in thickets. From Newfoundland across the continent, as far north on the Mackenzie river as 62 degrees; south to Georgia; west to Minnesota and Texas.

**IN NEW ENGLAND**—Common throughout; at an altitude of 4,500 feet upon Mt. Katahdin.

**IN CONNECTICUT**—Rare near the coast in the southeastern part of the state but frequent or common elsewhere.

**WOOD**—Hard, close-grained, weak, light brown; of insufficient size to be of value commercially.

CHOKE CHERRY

# WILD RED CHERRY
## Bird, Fire, Pin or Pigeon Cherry.
### Prunus pennsylvanica L. f.

**HABIT**—A shrub or small tree generally under 30 ft. in height with trunk diameter of 8-10 inches; trunk erect generally continuous into crown with slender branches arising at a rather sharp angle, forming a rather narrow oblong open head. The trees growing in the open about Storrs have in general a narrower outline than the tree photographed.

**BARK**—Reddish-brown, for the most part smooth, often slightly peeling in transverse strips especially toward the base of the trunk and in old trees somewhat roughened; inner bark on young branches bright green. LENTICELS—conspicuous, horizontally elongated, lens-shaped, orange colored and powdery on the surface.

**TWIGS**—Slender, generally less than 2 mm. thick, often less than 1.5 mm. thick, smooth, bright red and shining, more or less covered with a gray skin easily rubbed off; bitter aromatic. LENTICELS—scattered, pale to bright orange colored, becoming slightly elongated horizontally and more conspicuous on older growth. PITH—brown, narrow.

**LEAF-SCARS**—Alternate, more than 2-ranked, semi-oval, raised. STIPULE-SCARS—back of leaf-scars, generally indistinct or absent. BUNDLE-SCARS—3, the central larger one often alone distinct.

**BUDS**—Minute, generally under 3 mm. long, blunt-pointed, ovate, reddish-brown, smooth, often partially covered with a grayish skin, divergent, on rapidly grown shoots characteristically clustered at the tips as well as scattered, with the terminal bud present but generally smaller than those in the cluster around it; also clustered buds at ends of short fruiting spurs; collateral accessory buds sometimes present. BUD-SCALES—ovate, often notched and short-pointed, not readily distinguished as separate scales with the naked eye.

**FRUIT**—A drupe about the size of a pea, ripening in summer in short clusters or with stalks arising from a common point on the stem.

**COMPARISONS**—The appearance of the bark and the taste of the twigs shows the Wild Red Cherry to belong to the Cherry group. It differs from the other Cherries in its very slender twigs and small buds which are constantly clustered at the tips even of rapidly grown shoots. The Wild Black Cherry when tree-like is further distinguished by its scaly bark. The powdery bright reddish-orange lenticels on young and even old trunks form a striking character but a similar color may occur in the lenticels of the other Cherries especially if the outer surface is rubbed off.

**DISTRIBUTION**—Roadsides, clearings, burnt lands, hill slopes, occasional in rather low grounds. From Labrador to the Rocky mountains, through British Columbia to the Coast Range; south to North Carolina; west to Minnesota and Missouri.

IN NEW ENGLAND—Throughout; very common in the northern portions, as high up as 4,500 ft. upon Katahdin, less common southward and near the seacoast.

IN CONNECTICUT—Occasional. Found in various soils and situations, but especially in rocky woods and clearings.

**WOOD**—Light, soft, close-grained, light brown, with thin yellow sapwood of little commercial importance.

WILD RED CHERRY

# SWEET CHERRY
## Mazzard Cherry, European Bird Cherry.
### Prunus avium L.

**HABIT**—A good sized tree reaching 50-75 ft. in height with a trunk diameter of 2-3 ft.; trunk erect continuous into the crown with slender ascending branches forming a narrow pyramidal head; with age becoming broad-spreading.

**BARK**—Characteristically reddish-brown with horizontally elongated buff colored lenticels, tardily peeling off in transverse strips which curl back and expose the lighter bark below which on very old trunks may be roughened by scaly ridges; on young branches bark easily peeled off in a thin dark papery layer exposing the bright green bark below.

**TWIGS**—Stout, bright reddish-brown, smooth and shining, more or less covered with a grayish skin easily rubbed off; crushed twigs with bitter taste. In addition to long rapidly grown shoots, stubby slowly grown fruit spurs with terminally clustered buds are abundant. LEN-TICELS—rather numerous, pale, becoming horizontally elongated. PITH—brown.

**LEAF-SCARS**—Alternate, more than 2-ranked, rather broad, semi-oval to inversely triangular. raised. STIPULE-SCARS—slightly behind leaf-scars, oblique, often indistinct or absent. BUNDLE-SCARS—3.

**BUDS**—Clustered at ends of fruiting spurs or scattered on rapidly grown shoots; terminal bud scarcely larger than lateral buds; lateral buds divergent, stout, ovate, pointed, constricted at base, about 7 mm. long, reddish-brown, smooth, often partially covered with a grayish skin. BUD-SCALES—broadly ovate, with edges often lighter colored and more or less frayed and ragged.

**FRUIT**—A drupe with edible flesh, generally sweet though in some varieties tart, with hard stone or pit enclosing the seed. ripening in summer, with stalks generally several in a cluster arising from a common point on the stem.

**COMPARISONS**—The two types of cultivated cherries, the Sweet and the Sour are to be distinguished chiefly by habit of growth and relative size of twigs and buds, the Sweet Cherry having a pyramidal outline generally with a central leader and with relatively stout twigs and larger buds. These differences are well shown in the plates. (See Comparisons under Sour Cherry).

**DISTRIBUTION**—A native of Europe, in this country cultivated for its fruit in several improved varieties such as the Black Tartarian, May Duke, Windsor, Napoleon, etc. and in some places escaped from cultivation.

**WOOD**—Strong, rather soft, close-grained, yellowish-red, taking a fine polish; largely used in Europe for fine furniture, inside finishing and for musical and other instruments.

SWEET CHERRY

# SOUR CHERRY
## Pie or Morello Cherry.
### Prunus Cerasus L.

**HABIT**—A small tree 20-30 ft. or less in height with a trunk diameter of 10 or 12 inches; with stout spreading branches and more or less drooping branchlets forming a broad. low, rounded head.

**BARK**—Similar to that of the Sweet Cherry, but the outer smooth bark sooner peeling back and exposing the roughened inner bark.

**TWIGS**—Slender, otherwise resembling twigs of Sweet Cherry.

**LEAF-SCARS**—Similar to those of the Sweet Cherry.

**BUDS**—Similar to those of the Sweet Cherry but smaller and apparently more frequently clustered toward the ends of long shoots. Compare the twig photographs of the two species.

**FRUIT**—Similar to that of Sweet Cherry but flesh tart.

**COMPARISONS**—The Sour Cherry differs from the Sweet Cherry in its spreading habit of growth, its more slender twigs and smaller buds. Compare plates of the two species. From the native Wild Black and Choke Cherries the cultivated Sweet and Sour Cherries are distinguished by the short fruit spurs; from the Wild Red Cherry by their stouter twigs and buds and absence of a bud cluster at the tip of long shoots.

**DISTRIBUTION**—A native of Europe, in this country cultivated for its fruit in several improved varieties such as the Amarelles, Early Richmond, Montmorency, etc. and the Morellos, Louis Philippe, etc. and in some places escaped from cultivation.

**WOOD**—Similar in appearance and uses to that of the Sweet Cherry from which it is not distinguished by wood workers.

SOUR CHERRY

# CANADA PLUM
## Red, Horse or Wild Plum.
### Prunus nigra Ait.
### P. americana, var. nigra Waugh.

**HABIT**—A shrub or small tree 20-25 ft. in height with a trunk diameter of 5-8 inches; with contorted branches and more or less zigzag branchlets forming a low spreading head. It tends to sucker freely forming low thickets.

**BARK**—On young trunks and branches dark brown with prominent raised lenticels which are horizontally slightly elongated; at first smooth but soon splitting and curling back in thick grayish-brown layered plates exposing the rough scaly bark below.

**TWIGS**—Slender, smooth, reddish-brown, often more or less covered with a grayish skin, bitter aromatic, lateral spiny spurs generally present. LENTICELS—scattered, large and rather conspicuous pale dots.

**LEAF-SCARS**—Alternate, more than 2-ranked, broadly crescent-shaped. STIPULE-SCARS—indistinct or absent. BUNDLE-SCARS—3, often inconspicuous.

**BUDS**—Terminal bud absent, lateral buds about 4-8 mm. long, conical, narrow-pointed, grayish-brown; collateral buds sometimes present. BUD-SCALES—triangular, pale and thin on the margins, generally hairy at the apex.

**FRUIT**—A smooth-skinned drupe with smooth stone.

**COMPARISONS**—The Plums are distinguished from the other members of the genus Prunus by the absence of a terminal bud. The Canada Plum so far as one can judge from the material investigated is distinguishable by its larger buds from the American Plum, of which it is considered by some only as a variety.

**DISTRIBUTION**—Native along streams and in thickets, often spontaneous around dwellings and along fences. From Newfoundland through the valley of the St. Lawrence to Lake Manitoba; rare south of New England; west to Wisconsin. Has given rise to some valuable fruit-bearing varieties in cultivation.

**IN NEW ENGLAND**—Maine—abundant in the northern sections and common throughout; New Hampshire and Vermont—frequent, especially in the northern sections; Massachusetts—occasional; Rhode Island—not reported.

**IN CONNECTICUT**—Rare. Norfolk, a few trees about an abandoned garden; Oxford.

**WOOD**—Heavy, hard, strong, close-grained, rich bright reddish-brown with thin lighter colored sapwood.

CANADA PLUM

## CULTIVATED PLUMS

NOTE—The Cultivated Plums are either improved forms of originally wild species or have been derived by hybridization from a number of such forms. The types most cultivated in the United States are the American (derived from *Prunus americana),* the European (derived from *Prunus domestica)* and the Japanese (derived from *Prunus triflora).* Although the varieties of a given type differ considerably so that without further study it does not seem desirable to try to offer a detailed winter classification of the cultivated plums, still the general characteristics of the unmixed types are recognizable in winter. Certain varieties, the Gold, the Lombard and the Red June have been chosen for the photographs to illustrate respectively the American, the European and the Japanese types.

## THE AMERICAN PLUM.  VARIETY—GOLD
### Prunus americana Marsh.
Illustrations on page 509.

The American cultivated type of Plum has very slender grayish-brown twigs and branches which have a decidedly drooping habit of growth. The bark is brown; on young trunks and branches smooth, shining, with prominent, light-colored, horizontally elongated lenticels (see upper part of bark picture). The habit photograph was taken from a specimen of the native form, grown in the Arnold Aboretum. The American Plum, as growing wild, closely resembles the Canada Plum and by some this latter species is considered merely a variety of the former. The material examined shows smaller twigs than the Canada Plum with buds generally under 4 mm. long. The most northern station has been reported to be along the slopes of Graylock, Mass. In Connecticut it is reported as rare in the southern district, becoming occasional northward.

## THE EUROPEAN PLUM.  VARIETY—LOMBARD
### Prunus domestica L.
Illustrations on page 510.

The European Plum has a lighter bark than the other two types without conspicuous horizontal lenticels, with stout, upright, long shoots and an upright habit of growth.

## THE JAPANESE PLUM.  VARIETY—RED JUNE.
### Prunus triflora Roxbg.
Illustrations on page 511.

The Japanese Plum has a very dark deeply ridged bark without conspicuous lenticels. The long shoots are rather slender and bright colored and stout fruit spurs are numerous.

AMERICAN PLUM

EUROPEAN PLUM

JAPANESE PLUM

# PEACH
## Prunus Persica (L.) Stokes.
### *Amygdalus Persica* L.

**HABIT**—A small tree generally under 20 ft. in height with a trunk diameter of about 6 inches; trunk low with spreading limbs and ascending branchlets forming a low broad rounded head.

**BARK**—Dark reddish-brown, smooth, with prominent horizontally elongated lenticels, becoming roughened and scaly at base.

**TWIGS**—Of medium thickness, smooth and very shiny, greenish to bright reddish-purple, often green below and red above toward the light, becoming redder as spring approaches; on rapidly grown shoots branches sometimes produced the same season; crushed twigs with odor and taste of bitter almonds. LENTICELS—very numerous and very minute pale dots, in reality stomata, best seen with hand-lens and on reddish portions of twigs, only part of them elongating with age. PITH—rather wide, often somewhat 5-pointed, whitish or tinged with brown.

**LEAF-SCARS**—Alternate, more than 2-ranked, elliptical to semi-oval, strongly raised, often more or less decurrent. STIPULE-SCARS—behind and above leaf-scars or raised on persistent bases of stipules, often indistinct and readily confused with broken bud-scales; often a small raised leaf-scar above and on either side of the main leaf-scar in connection with the collateral buds when these are present. BUNDLE-SCARS—3, often inconspicuous.

**BUDS**—Ovate, rounded at apex or blunt-pointed, generally under 5 mm. long, densely pale-woolly at least toward apex and within, more or less appressed, 1 or 2 collateral buds often present at a node—these generally stout flower buds in sharp contrast to the narrower leaf bud between (in the group of three buds on twig in plate all are flower buds); terminal bud present often with one or more lateral buds adjacent. BUD-SCALES—reddish-brown, often with ragged edges and generally indistinct and covered with grayish wool.

**FRUIT**—A large downy drupe with an irregularly pitted stone.

**COMPARISONS**—The dense woolliness of its stout buds and the very numerous and extremely minute pale dots on its highly colored and polished twigs readily distinguish the Peach from its near relatives.

**DISTRIBUTION**—A native of Asia, cultivated in this country for its fruit, naturalized throughout the greater portion of the southern states and spontaneous in waste places and on road-sides in the northern states.

**WOOD**—Rather soft, close-grained and light brown. The seeds develop considerable hydrocyanic acid and are used in the manufacture of a substitute for oil of bitter almonds.

PEACH

# KENTUCKY COFFEE TREE
## Coffee Nut, Coffee Bean, Nicker Tree, Mahogany.
### Gymnocladus dioica (L.) Koch.
#### *G. canadensis* Lam.

---

**HABIT**—A medium sized tree 30-60 ft. in height, trunk generally soon dividing into 3 or 4 slightly spreading limbs or less frequently with a continuous trunk, forming a narrow obovate head with thick branchlets devoid of spray; the large stout pods often remaining on tree throughout the winter.

**BARK**—Dark brown, characteristically roughened with thin tortuous recurved scale-like ridges which are distinct even upon comparatively young branches.

**TWIGS**—Very stout, more or less contorted, blunt, brown or slightly greenish, generally white-crusted, smooth or often velvety-downy. LENTICELS—rather numerous, large, generally more conspicuous on second year's growth. PITH—wide, salmon-pink to brown.

**LEAF-SCARS**—Alternate, more than 2-ranked, large, pale, raised, broadly heart-shaped. STIPULE-SCARS—absent. BUNDLE-SCARS—large, raised, generally 3-5.

**BUDS**—Terminal bud absent, lateral buds small, bronze, silky pubescent, partially sunken, scarcely projecting beyond the surface of the twig, surrounded by an incurved downy rim of the bark; axillary bud in the depression at top of leaf-scar, one or sometimes 2 superposed buds present. BUD-SCALES—sometimes 2 lateral scales visible.

**FRUIT**—A reddish-brown, large, broad, flat, oblong, abruptly pointed pod, 4-10 inches long by 1½-2 inches wide, frequently remaining unopened on tree during winter, generally somewhat larger than shown in the photograph. Seed, dark brown, flattish.

**COMPARISONS**—A superficial glance at the habit of the Kentucky Coffee Tree might lead one to mistake its stout branchlets for those of the Ailanthus. Its curious narrow ridged bark, however, should at once prevent any confusion between the two trees. The silky bronze superposed buds partially sunken in downy dimples of the bark in connection with the stout twigs and salmon-colored pith are sufficient characters to distinguish this tree from all other forms.

**DISTRIBUTION**—Not native in New England but frequently cultivated as an ornamental tree; grows wild in rich deep soil from central New York and southern Minnesota southward to Tennessee and the Indian Territory.

**WOOD**—Heavy, though not hard, strong, coarse-grained, very durable in contact with soil, rich light brown tinged with red, with thin lighter colored sapwood of 5-6 layers of annual growth; it takes a fine polish and is occasionally used in cabinet-making and for fence-posts, rails and in construction. Its seeds were formerly used as a substitute for coffee.

KENTUCKY COFFEE TREE

# HONEY LOCUST

## Three-thorned Acacia, Honey Shucks, Sweet Locust, Thorn Tree.

### Gleditsia triacanthus L. (Sometimes called Gleditschia.)

**HABIT**—A medium sized tree 40-60 ft. in height with a trunk diameter of 1-3 ft.; trunk commonly short dividing into a number of slightly spreading limbs, with somewhat drooping lateral branches, forming a broad rounded obovate or flat-topped head. Seen against the sky the smaller branches appear zigzag with characteristic swellings at the nodes often surmounted with thorns and rudimentary branchlets developed from the extra buds. (See branches at side of trunk in bark picture).

**BARK**—Grayish-brown darkening with age, on young trunks and branches smooth, on older trunks more or less roughened into broad ridges with firm persistent recurved edges. Some trunks have bark practically smooth except for a few deep fissures; some trunks are thickly fringed with dense masses of long branched spines, while others are free from them.

**TWIGS**—Slender, shining, smooth, reddish to greenish-brown, often light mottled or streaked, zigzag with enlarged nodes; a large branched thorn with pale reddish-brown pith, discontinuous with that of the stem, generally present above node. LENTICELS—minute, scattered, becoming conspicuous brown raised dots on older growth. PITH—thick, whitish.

**LEAF-SCARS**—Alternate, generally more than 2-ranked, V-shaped with upper margins and apex generally swollen. STIPULE-SCARS —absent or inconspicuous. BUNDLE-SCARS—3, rather inconspicuous.

**BUDS**—Terminal bud absent, the lateral buds small, generally about 5 more or less distinct at a node, separated one above the other, decreasing in size from above downward, the uppermost a superposed smooth scaly bud breaking through the bark, the next also scaly covered by or breaking through the leaf-scar, the lower buds without scales, covered by bark and seen as minute green dots in a longitudinal section of twig; buds often continue to be produced at the nodes for several years especially when the twigs are trimmed as in hedges and give rise to a bunch of more or less rudimentary branches.

**FRUIT**—A long, flat, reddish-brown, more or less twisted, indehiscent pod 10 to 18 inches long, containing numerous flat oval seeds about 10 mm. long. The photograph of the fruit is reduced to about ⅓ natural size.

**COMPARISONS**—The Honey Locust is at once distinguished from the various other thorny species such as the Hawthorn and Common Locust by its large branched thorns situated above the leaf-scar. When the thorns are absent as is sometimes the case the vertical row of separated smooth buds, the upper scaly and superposed, the lower hidden by the bark, are sufficient points of distinction.

**DISTRIBUTION**—In its native habitat growing in a variety of soils; rich woods, mountain sides, sterile plains. Southern Ontario; spreading by seed southward; indigenous along the western slopes of the Alleghanies in Pennsylvania; south to Georgia and Alabama; west from western New York through southern Ontario and Michigan to Nebraska, Kansas, Indian Territory, and Texas.

IN NEW ENGLAND—Not native, but frequently planted as an ornamental tree or for hedges and escaped from cultivation: Maine—young trees in the southern sections said to have been produced from self-sown seed; New Hampshire and Vermont—introduced; Massachusetts—occasional; Rhode Island—introduced and fully at home. Probably sparingly naturalized in many other places in New England.

IN CONNECTICUT—Rare, occasional or local.

**WOOD**—Hard, strong, coarse-grained, very durable in contact with soils, red or bright red-brown, with thin, pale sapwood of 10-12 layers of annual growth; largely used for fence posts and rails, for the hubs of wheels and in construction.

HONEY LOCUST

# REDBUD
## Judas Tree.
### Cercis canadensis L.

**HABIT**—A small tree up to 40 ft. in height though generally smaller, developing an upright or a low, broad, irregular head.

**BARK**—Reddish-brown to almost black, somewhat ridged and scaly.

**TWIGS**—Slender, dark reddish-brown, smooth, more or less zigzag. LENTICELS—very numerous, minute. PITH—especially of older growth, generally with reddish longitudinal streaks.

**LEAF-SCARS**—Alternate, 2-ranked, small, slightly raised, inversely triangular, with short, decurrent, spreading, more or less evident ridge from outer edges.    STIPULE-SCARS—absent.    BUNDLE-SCARS—3, large.

**BUDS**—Terminal bud absent, lateral buds small, 3 mm. long, or generally much smaller, blunt, dark purplish-red, somewhat flattened and appressed, one or more superposed buds often present the uppermost the largest; flower buds conspicuously present on older wood often at the base of a branch (see plate) or even on the trunk itself. BUD-SCALES—overlapping, somewhat hairy on the edges, about 2 visible to a leaf bud, several to a flower bud.

**FRUIT**—A flat pod about 3 inches long, with small compressed seeds.

**COMPARISONS**—The stout purplish flower buds below the insertion of the branches on the old wood will serve to identify this small tree. The reddish streaks in the older pith seem to be a constant character so far as investigated and if so will be a useful mark of distinction.

**DISTRIBUTION**—Not native to New England but frequently planted as an ornamental tree. It grows native along the borders of streams and rich bottom land from Ontario to New Jersey south to Florida and west to Minnesota and Arkansas.

**WOOD**—Heavy, hard, not strong, close-grained, rich dark brown tinged with red, with thin lighter colored sapwood of 8-10 layers of annual growth; of little commercial importance.

Redbud

# YELLOW WOOD
## Virgilia, Gopher Wood.
### Cladrastis lutea (Mx. f.) Koch.

**HABIT**—A small tree under 50 ft. in height with trunk diameter of 1-2 ft.; trunk generally dividing low down into several slightly spreading limbs with numerous slender more or less zigzag branches, the lower often strongly declined, forming a broad rounded head.

**BARK**—Thin, gray to light brown, in general smooth, resembling bark of the Beech with slight protuberances or ridges and horizontal wrinkles.

**TWIGS**—Rather slender, more or less zigzag, brittle, smooth bright reddish-brown, covered often by a grayish skin, odor and taste resembling that of a raw dried pea or bean. LENTICELS—pale, scattered, generally conspicuous. PITH—wide, white, round in section.

**LEAF-SCARS**—Alternate, 2-ranked, or more than 2-ranked, raised, pale yellow, forming a V-shaped collar of almost uniform diameter nearly encircling the bud. STIPULE-SCARS—absent. BUNDLE-SCARS—typically 5 (4-9) generally regularly spaced and raised or at times some of the five indistinct or lacking.

**BUDS**—Terminal bud absent, lateral buds naked, superposed, 3-4, the uppermost the largest and generally alone developing, flattened, closely packed together to form a pointed bud-like hairy cone generally under 5 mm. long, nearly surrounded by the leaf-scar. BUD-SCALES—absent, their place taken by the densely hairy immature leaves.

**FRUIT**—A smooth flat margined pod 5-10 cm. long, containing a few small oblong compressed seeds.

**COMPARISONS**—The Yellow Wood is well characterized by its beech-like bark, its slender twigs, and its superposed hairy buds closely clustered into a bud-like cone and practically surrounded by the leaf-scar and is therefore scarcely to be confused with any other tree.

**DISTRIBUTION**—In rich soil, limestone ridges and often along mountain streams, rare and local. Western North Carolina, Kentucky, Tennessee, Alabama, Missouri; often cultivated in New England as an ornamental tree.

**WOOD**—Heavy, very hard, strong and close-grained, with a smooth, satiny surface, bright clear yellow changing to light brown on exposure, with thin nearly white sapwood; used for fuel, occasionally for gun stocks and yielding a clear yellow dye.

YELLOW WOOD

# COMMON LOCUST
## Black, Yellow or White Locust, Locust, Acacia.
### Robinia Pseudo-Acacia L.

**HABIT**—Generally a small tree 20-35 ft. or occasionally 50-75 ft. in height with a trunk diameter of eight inches to 2½ ft.; trunk erect or inclined, frequently dividing into a number of ascending limbs with slender scraggly branches forming a narrow oblong open head; often spreading by underground stems and forming thickets of small trees. A rapidly growing tree but short lived and subject to the attacks of borers.

**BARK**—Rough even on young trunks, dark reddish to yellowish-brown, becoming deeply furrowed into rounded ridges, not flaky.

**TWIGS**—Rather slender, brittle, often zigzag, light reddish to greenish-brown, smooth or nearly so, more or less angled with decurrent ridges from base and outer angles of leaf-scars, generally spiny with paired stipular prickles at nodes. LENTICELS—pale, scattered. PITH—wide, more or less angled.

**LEAF-SCARS**—Alternate, more than 2-ranked, generally large and conspicuous, inversely triangular to pentagonal, raised, covering the buds. STIPULES—in the form of prickles, sometimes poorly developed or entirely lacking. BUNDLE-SCARS—3.

**BUDS**—Terminal bud absent; lateral buds minute, rusty-downy, 3-4 superposed, generally close together, enclosed in a rusty-downy cavity below the leaf-scar which cracks between the bundle-scars at the development of a branch usually from the uppermost bud exposing the long rusty hairs attached to under side of the three persistent lobes of the leaf-scar; on rapidly grown shoots, the uppermost bud often develops into a branch the first season, which may be rudimentary and deciduous, leaving a small scar above leaf-scar.

**FRUIT**—A dark brown, flat pod, 5-10 cm. long, containing 4-8 small brown mottled flatish seeds, persistent on the tree throughout the winter.

**COMPARISONS**—The paired prickles at the nodes form the most striking character of the Common Locust but since they are absent on some twigs and entirely lacking on certain varieties, the hidden closely-packed downy buds must be taken as the chief distinguishing features. They separate the Common Locust from the Honey Locust when the characteristic branched thorns are not present on the latter species. The Clammy Locust [*Robinia viscosa* Vent.] is a small southern tree frequently cultivated and established at many points throughout New England. It has the general characters of the Common Locust but the stipular prickles are less well developed and its twigs are covered with a sticky glandular coating. The Bristly Locust [*Robinia hispida* L.] is a mere shrub with twigs beset with bristly hairs but without stipular prickles. The Prickly Ash or Toothache Tree [*Zanthoxylon americanum* L.], a shrub occurring throughout New England, resembles the Locust in its stipular prickles (lower twig in plate). It is readily distinguished from the Locusts, however, by the red downy exposed clustered buds, the presence of a terminal bud and the pungent flavor of its twigs.

**DISTRIBUTION**—In its native habitat growing upon mountain slopes, along the borders of forests, in rich soils. Naturalized from Nova Scotia to Ontario. Native from southern Pennsylvania along the mountains to Georgia; west to Iowa and southward. Formerly much planted as an ornamental and timber tree; more cultivated in Europe than any other American tree.

IN NEW ENGLAND—Maine—thoroughly at home, forming wooded banks along streams; New Hampshire—abundant enough to be reckoned among the valuable timber trees; Vermont—escaped from cultivation in many places; Massachusetts, Rhode Island—common in patches and thickets and along the roadsides and fences.

IN CONNECTICUT—Frequent as an escape from cultivation.

**WOOD**—Heavy, exceedingly hard and strong, close-grained, very durable in contact with the soil, brown or rarely light green, with pale yellow sapwood of two or three layers of annual growth; extensively used in shipbuilding for all sorts of posts, in construction and turnery; preferred for tree nails and valued as fuel.

COMMON LOCUST
PRICKLY ASH (lower twig only)

# AILANTHUS
## Tree of Heaven, Chinese Sumach.
### Ailanthus glandulosa Desf.

**HABIT**—A small to good sized tree 50-75 ft. in height with a trunk diameter of 2-3 ft.; forming a wide flat-topped head with stout branch-lets devoid of spray; freely sprouting from the roots; the female trees which are more frequently planted than the male often retaining the clusters of winged fruit throughout the winter.

**BARK**—Grayish, slightly roughened with fine light colored longitu-dinal streaks in striking contrast to the darker background.

**TWIGS**—Stout, yellowish to reddish-brown covered with very short fine velvety down, or smooth, rather rank-smelling when crushed, older twigs often shedding the down in the form of a thin skin and exposing very fine light longitudinal striations below. LENTICELS—scattered, pale, somewhat longitudinally elongated becoming on older growth con-spicuous more or less diamond-shaped cracks. PITH—wide, chocolate brown.

**LEAF-SCARS**—Alternate, more than 2-ranked, large, conspicuous, heart-shaped. STIPULE-SCARS—absent. BUNDLE-SCARS—conspicuous, often compound or curved, generally under a dozen in number, forming a curved line.

**BUDS**—Terminal bud absent, lateral buds relatively small generally under 4 mm. long, half-spherical, reddish-brown, downy. BUD-SCALES—thick, the 2 opposite lateral scales generally alone showing.

**FRUIT**—About 4 cm. long, winged, spirally twisted, the seed in the center, borne in conspicuous clusters which frequently remain on tree during winter. The species is dioecious, there being male trees bear-ing only staminate flowers and hence producing no fruit and female trees bearing only pistillate flowers and producing fruit. Owing to the vile smelling character of the staminate flowers, the male trees are now seldom planted.

**COMPARISONS**—The Ailanthus in its stout twigs resembles somewhat the Kentucky Coffee Tree but its buds are solitary and not sunken, its pith is brown rather than salmon-colored and its bark is not ridged as is the bark of the Kentucky Coffee Tree. From the stout-twigged Black Walnut and Butternut it is distinguished by its solitary buds and continuous pith; from the Staghorn and Smooth Sumachs by its broad leaf-scars.

**DISTRIBUTION**—A native of China sparsely and locally naturalized in southern Ontario, New England and southward; a very rapid grower, thriving under the most unfavorable conditions of city existence.

**WOOD**—Light brownish-yellow, with lighter sapwood, soft, weak, rather open-grained; in Europe used in the manufacture of woodenware and charcoal, little used in this country.

AILANTHUS

# STAGHORN SUMACH

Rhus typhina L.

*R. hirta* (L.) Sudw.

(Lefthand twig and lower habit picture in plate)

**HABIT**—A shrub or small tree rarely over 25 ft. in height with a trunk diameter less than a foot; making a straggling growth with forked branching forming a flat head with conspicuous red fruit clusters generally present and stout velvety branchlets; sprouting abundantly from the roots and thus forming broad thickets.

**BARK**—Thin, dark brown, smooth or in older trees more or less rough-scaly.

**TWIGS**—Stout, conspicuously covered with long velvety olive brown to almost black hairs. whence the common name from resemblance to a stag's antlers in the "velvet"; the tips often killed back several inches by the frost; cut twig exuding a copious white milky juice. LENTICELS—conspicuous except as covered by the hairs, orange colored, becoming laterally enlarged rough dots on older growth. PITH —wide, yellowish-brown.

**LEAF-SCARS**—Alternate, more than 2-ranked, deeply V-shaped, almost encircling the bud. STIPULE-SCARS—absent. BUNDLE-SCARS —scattered or frequently arranged in 3 groups, generally not conspicuous.

**BUDS**—Terminal buds absent, lateral buds conical, densely coated with long rusty hairs.

**FRUIT**—In rather compact, erect, cone-like clusters; individual fruits, drupes about 4 mm. in diameter coated with acid-tasting red hairs and enclosing a small bony-covered seed. The conspicuous red fruiting clusters are persistent throughout the winter but, since the species tends to be dioecious, are not borne by all trees.

**COMPARISONS**—A somewhat smaller form, the Smooth Sumach [*Rhus glabra* L.], closely resembles the Staghorn Sumach in habit, twig and fruit characters but the twigs are smooth (except the fruit stalks which may be downy) and generally are covered with a bloom. (See twig on right and upper habit picture in plate.) The Dwarf Sumach, [*Rhus copallina* L.], is generally smaller in New England than the other Sumachs. It has red fruit clusters like the Smooth and the Staghorn Sumachs but is distinguished from these two forms by the watery instead of white milky juice, by the leaf-scars which do not surround the bud and by the turpentine flavor to the young twigs. For comparison with the Poison Sumach see latter species.

**DISTRIBUTION**—In widely varying soils and localities, river banks, rocky slopes to an altitude of 2,000 ft., cellar holes and waste places generally, often forming copses. From Nova Scotia to Lake Huron; south to Georgia; west to Minnesota and Missouri.

IN NEW ENGLAND—Common throughout.

**WOOD**—Light, brittle, soft, coarse-grained, orange-colored, streaked with green, with thick nearly white sapwood. Pipes for drawing the sap of the Sugar Maple are made from the young shoots. The bark especially of the roots is rich in tannin.

STAGHORN AND SMOOTH SUMACH

# POISON SUMACH
## Poison Dogwood, Poison Elder, Swamp Sumach.
### Rhus Vernix L.
*R. venenata* DC.

---

**HABIT**—A shrub or small tree 5-20 ft. in height with a trunk diameter reaching 8-10 inches; trunk generally forking near the ground producing an open, rounded, bushy head.

**BARK**—Thin, light gray, smooth or slightly roughened with more or less conspicuous horizontally elongated lenticels.

**TWIGS**—Stout, brown to orange brown, older growth light gray, smooth, with watery resinous juice turning black on exposure. LENTICELS—numerous, minute, raised dots. PITH—yellowish-brown.

**LEAF-SCARS**—Alternate, more than 2-ranked, comparatively large, conspicuous, inversely triangular, raised, upper margin straight, slightly depressed or elevated, pointed and projecting. STIPULE-SCARS —absent. BUNDLE-SCARS—conspicuous, irregularly scattered in a closed ring or a single curved line.

**BUDS**—Terminal buds present, small but larger than laterals; short-conical, 3-20 mm. long, purplish. BUD-SCALES—finely downy on the back and margins.

**FRUIT**—A globular, slightly compressed, striate drupe about 5 mm. in diameter, very shiny, ivory white or yellowish-white, generally persistent through the winter in long pendant clusters. The species is dioecious, however, and therefore some trees do not fruit.

**COMPARISONS**—From the other Sumachs the Poison Sumach is distinguished by the presence of a terminal bud, its broad leaf-scars not encircling the bud, with conspicuous generally scattered bundle-scars. The loose clusters of white fruit are distinctive when present. The Poison Sumach is almost entirely confined to swamps or wet places while the other Sumachs grow for the most part in dryer situations. The Poison Sumach resembles its climbing relative the Poison Ivy [*Rhus Toxicodendron* L.] in that all parts of the plant at all times of the year contain an oil poisonous to the touch, only more actively so. Some individuals are more and others less susceptible. A preventive against the poison is thoroughly to wash as soon as possible in strong alcohol or strong soap suds the parts of the body that have come in contact with the plant.

**DISTRIBUTION**—Low grounds and swamps; occasional on the moist slopes of hills. Infrequent in Ontario; south to northern Florida; west to Minnesota and Louisiana.

IN NEW ENGLAND—Maine—local and apparently restricted to the southwestern sections; as far north as Chesterville, Franklin county; Vermont—infrequent; common throughout the other New England states, especially near the seacoast.

IN CONNECTICUT—Occasional in most districts, becoming frequent near the coast.

**WOOD**—Light, soft, coarse-grained, light yellow, streaked with brown, with lighter colored sapwood. The juice can be used as a black lustrous durable varnish.

POISON SUMACH

# HOLLY
## American Holly, White Holly.
### Ilex opaca Ait.

**HABIT**—A shrub or small tree rarely reaching 30 ft. in height, with a trunk diameter of 15-18 inches; larger south and west; with slender horizontal drooping or slightly ascending branches forming a compact conical head with spiny evergreen leaves.

**BARK**—Light gray, smooth becoming somewhat roughened with age.

**TWIGS**—Rather slender, grayish to yellowish brown, smooth or more or less downy. LENTICELS—inconspicuous.

**LEAF-SCARS**—Alternate, more than 2-ranked, semi-oval. BUNDLE-SCARS—solitary.

**LEAVES**—Thick, evergreen, elliptical to obovate, spiny-tipped and with few spiny teeth or rarely entire, dull yellowish-green above, pale and yellower beneath; midrib prominent beneath, with short, stout, slightly fine-downy leaf-stalks, grooved above. STIPULES—minute, awl-shaped, persistent.

**BUDS**—Short, blunt, roundish, more or less downy, terminal bud pointed.

**FRUIT**—Persistent through the winter, about the size of a pea, dull red or rarely yellow, berry-like, with four ribbed nutlets. Some trees bear only sterile flowers and therefore never produce fruit.

**COMPARISONS**—The American Holly closely resembles the cultivated European Holly [*Ilex Aquifolium* L.] but the leaves of this latter species are described as glossier, of a deeper green color, more wavy-margined with whitish translucent edges, and the berries as of a deeper red color.

**DISTRIBUTION**—Generally found in somewhat sheltered situations in sandy loam or in low, moist soil in the vicinity of water. Massachusetts, southward to Florida; westward to Missouri and the bottom-lands of eastern Texas.

IN NEW ENGLAND—Maine—reported on the authority of Gray's Manual, sixth edition, in various botanical works but no station is known; New Hampshire and Vermont—no station reported; Massachusetts—occasional from Quincy southward upon the mainland and the island of Naushon; rare in the peat swamps of Nantucket; Rhode Island —common in South Kingston and Little Compton and sparingly found upon Prudence and Conanicut islands in Narragansett Bay.

IN CONNECTICUT—Rare; roadsides and thickets; escaped from cultivation or possibly native.

**WOOD**—Light, tough, not strong, close-grained, nearly white when first cut, turning brown with age and exposure, with thick rather lighter colored sapwood, valued and much used in cabinet making, in the interior finish of houses and in turnery; the branches are much used in Christmas decorations.

HOLLY

# STRIPED MAPLE
## Moosewood, Whistlewood.
### Acer pennsylvanicum L.

**HABIT**—A shrub or small tree 15-30 ft. high with a short trunk 5-10 inches in diameter and slender straight branches, forming in northern New England a large part of the underbrush and a favorite food of moose and deer whence the name of Moosewood.

**BARK**—Rather thin, reddish-brown or dark green, conspicuously streaked longitudinally with narrow white lines, at length dark gray, often transversely warty.

**TWIGS**—Stout, smooth, red or green; year's growth marked by two circles formed by scars of the two outer pairs of bud-scales. LENTICELS—inconspicuous. PITH—brown.

**LEAF-SCARS**—Opposite; wide, broadly V-shaped; their adjacent edges nearly meeting and forming a pair of short stubby teeth separated by a more or less well developed decurrent ridge. BUNDLE-SCARS—3, generally more or less compounded forming often 5 to 7 separate bundle-scars.

**BUDS**—Distinctly stalked, 6-10 mm. long exclusive of the rather long stalk, tapering to a blunt tip, red, shining, more or less 4-sided; terminal bud larger than appressed lateral buds. BUD-SCALES—the thick, red, single, outer pair only visible, enclosing an inner pair of thick pale-hairy scales, within which are enclosed one or more pairs of thin green scales.

**FRUIT**—In long drooping terminal racemes with thin widely spreading wings; 2-2.5 cm. long, seed-like portion rather long with a pit-like depression on one side; the elongated racemes from which the fruit has fallen often remaining on tree throughout winter.

**COMPARISONS**—Easily distinguishable at all times from all other Maples by the striking white streaks in the young bark which appear often as early as the second year (see photograph of twig) and persist even on comparatively old trunks. The large stalked buds are also characteristic. The brown pith of the twig and the one-sided pitting of the seed-like portion of the fruit are characters which distinguish the Bush Maples (i.e. the Mountain and the Striped) from our other species of the genus. Forms of the genus Viburnum, which are for the most part shrubs, resemble somewhat the Bush Maples but, aside from having drupe-like fruits, may generally be easily distinguished by bud characters:—some having naked, others scurfy buds, some with the first pair of scales shorter than the bud and some with the second pair of scales smooth.

**DISTRIBUTION**—Cool, rocky or sandy woods, usually in the shade of other trees. Nova Scotia to Lake Superior; south on shaded mountain slopes and in deep ravines to Georgia; west to Minnesota.

IN NEW ENGLAND—Maine—abundant, especially northward in the forests; New Hampshire and Vermont—common in highland woods; Massachusetts—common in the western and central sections, rare towards the coast; Rhode Island—frequent northward.

IN CONNECTICUT—Rocky woods in rich soil; occasional in the north western part of the state, becoming rare eastward and southward, reaching Ashford, East Haddam, Huntington and Redding.

**WOOD**—Light, soft, close-grained, light brown with thick lighter colored sapwood of 30-40 layers of annual growth.

STRIPED MAPLE

# MOUNTAIN MAPLE
### Acer spicatum Lam.

**HABIT**—Shrub or small bushy tree up to 25 ft. in height with a trunk diameter of 6-8 inches; trunk short, straight, with slender upright branches.

**BARK**—Very thin, reddish-brown to dingy-gray, smooth or slightly furrowed.

**TWIGS**—Slender, bright red to purple on upper side where exposed to the light, yellowish to greenish on shaded under side, color persisting for several years; covered especially toward tip with short appressed grayish hairs, which may persist in scant amount for several years toward upper part of each year's growth. Year's growth marked by 2-3 circles formed by scars of bud-scales. LENTICELS—few, inconspicuous. PITH—brown.

**LEAF-SCARS**—Opposite, narrow, V-shaped, margined by a lighter colored and more or less raised rim, nearly meeting. BUNDLE-SCARS—3, undivided.

**BUDS**—Stalked, small, slender, pointed; generally under 6 mm. in length including stalk, red or greenish, covered, especially the terminal buds, with short appressed grayish hairs; terminal bud larger than appressed lateral buds. BUD-SCALES—thick, 2-3 pairs, one or at most 2 pairs visible, the second pair hairy.

**FRUIT**—In drooping racemes with wide more or less spreading wings about 2 cm. or less long, seed-like portion short, with pit-like depression on one side.

**COMPARISONS**—Resembles the Striped Maple (which see) in habit, distribution, color of twigs and few scales to the stalked buds. It differs from the Striped Maple in absence of white streaks on young bark and by pale down on twigs and especially on the smaller buds.

**DISTRIBUTION**—Moist rocky hillsides usually in the shade of other trees. From Nova Scotia and Newfoundland to Saskatchewan, along mountain ranges to Georgia.

IN NEW ENGLAND—Maine—common, especially northward in the forests; New Hampshire and Vermont—common; Massachusetts—rather common in western and central sections, occasional eastward; Rhode Island—occasional northward.

IN CONNECTICUT—Occasional in the northern part of the state, becoming rare southward, reaching East Haddam, Guilford at Bluff Head, Meriden and Redding.

**WOOD**—Light, soft, close-grained, light brown tinged with red, with thick lighter colored sapwood.

MOUNTAIN MAPLE

# SUGAR MAPLE
## Rock Maple, Hard Maple.
### Acer saccharum Marsh.
*A. saccharinum* Wang., not L.; *A. barbatum* Michx.

**HABIT**—A large tree 50-90 ft. in height, with trunk diameter of 2-5 ft.; trunk more or less continuous, in the open developing at 8-10 ft. from the ground stout, erect branches which form in young trees a broad or narrow egg-shaped head, becoming frequently a broad, round-topped head when older. Leaves sometimes persistent into winter especially on lower branches of young trees.

**BARK**—On young trunks and limbs dark gray, with tinge of buff, close and firm, smooth or slightly fissured, becoming deeply furrowed into long, thick, irregular plates which often curve back along one edge, giving ploughed appearance to the trunk. Some trees are to be found with yellowish-gray, more or less flaky bark. (See upper bark picture).

**TWIGS**—Slender, shining, reddish-brown to buff tinged with orange, smooth. LENTICELS—numerous, pale, conspicuous. PITH—white.

**LEAF-SCARS**—Opposite, narrow V-shaped; outer margins of a pair nearly meeting; often pale downiness within leaf-scar. BUNDLE-SCARS—3, sometimes compound.

**BUDS**—Conical to ovate, sharp-pointed, reddish-brown, rather downy especially toward tip; terminal bud 4-6 mm. long, about twice as long as appressed lateral buds. BUD-SCALES—overlapping, 4-8 pairs visible, their margins finely hairy.

**FRUIT**—3-5 cm. long, in short terminal clusters, wings broad, parallel or slightly spreading.

**COMPARISONS**—The Sugar Maple is readily distinguished from other maples by its narrow, conical, sharp-pointed, brown buds and by the large number of scales to the bud. The fruit clusters of the Sugar Maple are from terminal buds, those of the Red and the Silver Maple are from lateral buds. The fruiting of the Sugar Maple in consequence causes a noticeable forking of the twigs while it does not interrupt the growth in the Red and the Silver Maple. Further, fruit stalks and sometimes even the fruits themselves are persistent into winter on the Sugar Maple and are not persistent on the Red and the Silver. The Black Maple [*Acer saccharum*, var. *nigrum* (Michx. f.) Britton] is found in the northern part of New England but is too closely related to the Sugar Maple to be considered a distinct species. It has darker buds and bark than the type form.

**DISTRIBUTION**—Rich woods and rocky slopes, frequently planted by roadsides. Nova Scotia and Newfoundland; westward to Lake of the Woods; south to the Gulf States; west to Minnesota, Nebraska, Kansas and Texas.

IN NEW ENGLAND—Abundant, distributed throughout the woods, often forming in the northern portions extensive upland forests; attaining great size in the mountainous portions of New Hampshire and Vermont, and in the Connecticut river valley; less frequent toward the seacoast.

IN CONNECTICUT—Frequent or common in northern districts, becoming rare near the coast, except as an escape from cultivation.

**WOOD**—Heavy, hard, strong, close-grained, tough, with a fine satiny surface susceptible of receiving a good polish, light brown tinged with red, with thin sapwood of 30-40 layers of annual growth; largely used for the interior finish of buildings, especially for floors, in the manufacture of furniture and in turnery, in shipbuilding, shoe-lasts and pegs and largely as fuel. Accidental forms with the grain curled and contorted, known as Curly Maple and Bird's Eye Maple, are common and highly prized in cabinet making. Maple sugar is principally made from the sap of this tree.

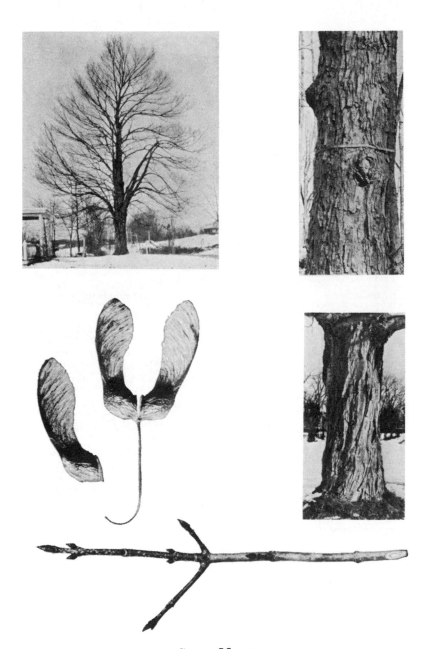

SUGAR MAPLE

# SILVER MAPLE
## White, River, or Soft Maple.
### Acer saccharinum L.
#### *A. dasycarpum* Ehrh.

**HABIT**—A good sized tree 50-60 ft. high with trunk diameter of 2-5 ft.; dividing near the ground into several slightly spreading limbs which branch further up, forming a very wide, broad-topped head. Lateral branchlets strongly tend to grow downward and then curve sharply upward at their tips.

**BARK**—Smooth, gray, with reddish tinge on young trunks and branches; on older trunks reddish-brown more or less furrowed; the surface separating into long thin flakes which become free at the ends and flake off exposing the redder inner layers.

**TWIGS**—Similar to those of Red Maple but with a distinct rank odor when freshly cut or broken.

**LEAF-SCARS**—Similar to those of Red Maple.

**BUDS**—Similar to those of the Red Maple but generally somewhat larger, the flower buds more densely clustered with a larger number of buds in a cluster.

**FRUIT**—Large, 4-7 cm. long, wings spreading, in lateral clusters, ripening in early spring and therefore difficult to find in winter.

**COMPARISONS**—The Silver Maple closely resembles the Red Maple in twig characters but can be readily distinguished from the latter by the rank odor of the fresh twigs when broken. The flakiness of the bark of the Silver Maple is also distinctive. The bending down of the branchlets with a sharp upward curve at their tips while much more marked in the Silver Maple occurs to a certain extent in the Red and therefore cannot be depended upon alone as a distinctive character. If the flower buds be dissected out and examined with a hand-lens the immature flowers of the Silver Maple will be found to be surrounded by a cup-like calyx which in the Red Maple is made up of separate divisions. See under Red Maple for Comparisons with other species.

**DISTRIBUTION**—Along river banks and in moist deep-soiled woods, not typically in swamps; often planted for ornament under the name of White Maple. Infrequent from New Brunswick to Ottawa, abundant from Ottawa throughout Ontario; south to the Gulf states; west to Dakota, Nebraska, Kansas, and Indian Territory; attaining its maximum size in the basins of the Ohio and its tributaries; rare towards the seacoast throughout the whole range.

IN NEW ENGLAND—Occasional throughout; most common and best developed upon the banks of rivers and lakes at low altitudes.

IN CONNECTICUT—Frequent inland along the larger streams, rare elsewhere.

**WOOD**—Hard, strong, close-grained, easily worked, rather brittle, pale brown with thick sapwood of 40-50 layers of annual growth; now sometimes used for flooring and in the manufacture of furniture. Sugar is occasionally made from the sap.

SILVER MAPLE

# RED MAPLE
## Swamp, Soft or White Maple.
### Acer rubrum L.

**HABIT**—A medium sized tree, 40-50 ft. high, occasionally in swamps reaching 75 ft. in height, with trunk diameter of 2-4 ft; branching low down and forming an oblong, rather compact head, frequently largest at the top but sometimes broad at the base. Branches slender as well as branchlets, the latter showing slight tendency to turn up at their tips; upper branches appearing decidedly gray and often resembling those of the Beech if viewed with the light.

**BARK**—Smooth, light gray on young trunks and branches; on older trunks very dark gray, roughened into long ridges, sometimes somewhat shaggy and separating in long plates. (See right hand bark photograph).

**TWIGS**—Rather slender, bright or dark red, shining; odorless when cut. LENTICELS—numerous, conspicuous. PITH—pinkish toward upper part at least of each year's growth beyond the second.

**LEAF-SCARS**—Broad, U to V-shaped, adjacent edges not meeting. BUNDLE-SCARS—3.

**BUDS**—Red, blunt-pointed, broadly oval-ovate to spherical in flower buds, generally under 5 mm. long, short-stalked; flower buds numerous, stout, collateral (one on either side of smaller axillary bud). BUD-SCALES—4 pairs or generally fewer visible with pale hairs on margins, outer pair of scales not over half covering the bud.

**FRUIT**—Small, generally under 3 cm. long, wings spreading, in lateral clusters, ripening in spring and therefore difficult to find in winter.

**COMPARISONS**—The Red Maple closely resembles the Silver Maple in the winter condition. See Silver Maple under Comparisons for differences. The Red and the Silver Maple are distinguishable from our other Maples except the Box Elder by presence of collateral buds, and the numerous clusters of these flower buds give a characteristic beaded appearance to the twigs against the sky; from the Striped and Mountain Maples by the larger number of scales exposed in the bud; from the Striped and the Norway and Sycamore Maples by much smaller buds; from the Mountain Maple and the Box Elder by their smooth outer bud-scales; from the Sugar Maple by their red twigs and by their red, blunt buds with few scales. See under Sugar Maple.

**DISTRIBUTION**—Borders of streams, in low lands, wet woods and swamps or sometimes in dry ground, of rapid growth and a favorite for park planting but usually not adapted to city streets. Nova Scotia to the Lake of the Woods; south to southern Florida; west to Dakota, Nebraska and Texas.

IN NEW ENGLAND—Common throughout from the sea to an altitude of 3,000 ft. on Katahdin.

IN CONNECTICUT—Common.

**WOOD**—Very heavy, close-grained, not strong, light brown often slightly tinged with red, with thick, rather lighter colored sapwood; used in large quantities in the manufacture of chairs and other furniture, in turnery, for wooden-ware and gun-stocks.

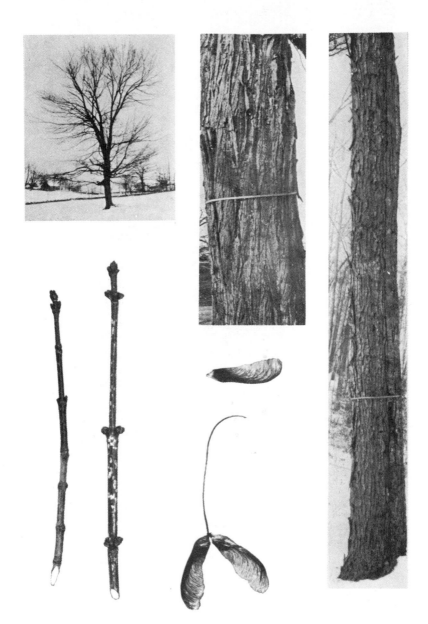

RED MAPLE

# NORWAY MAPLE
## Acer platanoides L.

**HABIT**—A mediumly large tree reaching in Europe 100 ft. in height, with round spreading head.

**BARK**—Dark, broken into firm, close, narrow ridges which run together and enclose small diamond-shaped spaces, somewhat resembling bark of White Ash but the ridges and diamond-shaped spaces are finer.

**TWIGS**—Stout, smooth, shining, brown to greenish or yellowish-brown, branchlets of two or more years growth and even vigorous season's shoots plainly streaked with fine, irregular, longitudinal cracks in bark.

**LEAF-SCARS**—Opposite, narrow V-shaped, half encircling the twig, the adjacent edges of opposite leaf-scars meeting and continued upward into a short tooth. BUNDLE-SCARS—3.

**BUDS**—Completely red or yellowish-green toward the base, sometimes whole bud strongly tinged with yellowish-green; terminal bud larger than lateral buds, 5-8 mm. long, more than ½ as broad as long, oval to ovate; generally with a pair of comparatively large lateral buds below terminal bud; lateral buds small, appressed. BUD-SCALES—thick, more or less keeled, margin very finely hairy; scales to terminal bud generally 5 pairs—2, or at most 3 pairs only showing smooth but enclosing 2 pairs which are thickly covered with dark rusty-brown hairs; in small buds sometimes 4 pairs smooth and 1 pair hairy.

**FRUIT**—Generally over 5 cm. long, seed-like portion flattish, with wings diverging in a straight line.

**COMPARISONS**—The Norway Maple is easily distinguished from the Sycamore Maple by the redness of its buds, the brown hairiness of the inner scales, the ridging of the bark and the divergence of the wings of the fruit; from the native Maples by the large buds and the characteristically ridged bark.

**DISTRIBUTION**—A European form extensively cultivated as a shade tree being more tolerant of unfavorable city conditions than most other forms. Its low head, however, is a disadvantage for city street planting.

**WOOD**—Moderately heavy, hard, close-grained, white or yellowish-white, fairly durable under cover but of short duration in the open; used in Europe by joiners, for finer wheelwrights' work, for carving, for mathematical instruments and for various other purposes.

NORWAY MAPLE

# SYCAMORE MAPLE
## Acer Pseudo-Platanus L.

**HABIT**—A rather large tree of vigorous growth, reaching in Europe 120 ft. in height, with large spreading head.

**BARK**—Dark reddish-brown, flaking off in squarish or short oblong scales.

**TWIGS**—Stout, smooth, shining, yellowish-greenish to brown.

**LEAF-SCARS**—Opposite, shallow, V-shaped; adjacent edges of opposite leaf-scars not meeting. BUNDLE-SCARS—3 elongated lengthwise with the leaf-scar or compound.

**BUDS**—Green, sometimes slightly reddish, terminal bud larger than lateral buds, 7-12 mm. long, broadly oval to ovate to nearly spherical, much more than ½ as wide as long; lateral buds divergent. BUD-SCALES—more or less keeled, with dark brown edging, dark pointed apex and finely hairy margin; scales to terminal bud, 6-7 pairs, 3 pairs at least generally visible, the outer scales smooth, the 2 inner scales thickly covered with silvery white hairs.

**FRUIT**—Generally less than 5 cm. long, seed-like portion nearly spherical, wings making about a right angle resembling fruit of the Sugar Maple.

**COMPARISONS**—Distinguished from the Norway Maple by the green buds, having outer scales with dark margins and white-hairy inner scales and by the flaky bark; from the native Maples by the larger buds and the peculiar bark.

**DISTRIBUTION**—A European form, cultivated in the United States as a shade tree but less extensively than the Norway Maple.

**WOOD**—Similar in character to that of the Norway Maple and used for the same purposes.

SYCAMORE MAPLE

# BOX ELDER
## Ash-leaved Maple.
### Acer Negundo L.
*Negundo aceroides* Moench   *Negundo Negundo* Karst.

**HABIT**—A medium sized tree 40-50 ft. high with a trunk diameter of 1-2 ft.; dividing low down, sometimes only a few feet from the ground into a number of stout spreading branches, forming a wide head.

**BARK**—Pale gray or light brown, broken by rather shallow furrows into narrow, firm, close, irregular flat-topped ridges which are further cracked horizontally; bark of young trunks and branches smooth, with raised buff lenticels, which are horizontally more or less elongated.

**TWIGS**—Stout, reddish-purple or green, smooth, polished or often with a whitish bloom which readily rubs off. LENTICELS—conspicuous, forming somewhat longitudinally elongated, scattered, raised buff dots.

**LEAF-SCARS**—Opposite, narrow V-shaped, margined by a lighter colored outer rim. half encircling the twig, the adjacent edges of opposite leaf-scars meeting and prolonged upward into a conspicuous narrow tooth, the inner margin often hairy. BUNDLE-SCARS—large, 3 in number, generally undivided.

**BUDS**—Short-stalked, red, more or less white-woolly, the terminal buds 6 mm. or less long, rather longer than the appressed lateral buds. BUD-SCALES—outer pair less densely woolly than inner pairs. grown together at base, entirely enclosing the bud or slightly gaping and exposing next inner pair; outer scales of lateral buds often distended by formation in their axils of stout collateral buds.

**FRUIT**—3.5-5 cm. long in drooping racemes, wings spreading at a sharp angle, seed-like portion long; flattish; fruit stalks remaining on tree throughout winter. The Box Elder is strictly dioecious, therefore fruit is not borne by all individuals.

**COMPARISONS**—The stout brightly colored red or green twigs and branchlets often covered with a bloom the first year and the downy buds with generally collateral buds present on some of the twigs, as well as the narrow tooth formed at the junction of adjacent deeply V-shaped leaf-scars render the Box Elder easily distinguishable in the winter condition.

**DISTRIBUTION**—Banks of streams, lakes and borders of swamps; a rapid grower and often planted as a shade tree, thrives best in moist soil but is tolerant of dry situations. Infrequent from eastern Ontario to Lake of the Woods; abundant from Manitoba westward to the Rocky mountains south of 55 degrees north latitude; south to Florida; west to the Rocky and Wahsatch mountains, reaching its greatest size in the river bottoms of the Ohio and its tributaries.

**IN NEW ENGLAND**—Maine—along the St. John and its tributaries, especially in the French villages, the commonest roadside tree, brought in from the wild state according to the people there; thoroughly established young trees, originating from planted specimens, in various parts of the state; New Hampshire—occasional along the Connecticut, abundant at Walpole; extending northward as far as South Charlestown; Vermont—shores of the Winooski river and of Lake Champlain.

**IN CONNECTICUT**—Rare or local; apparently native along the Housatonic river from Oxford to Salisbury; escaped from cultivation at Putnam, Groton, Southington, Wethersfield and Norwalk.

**WOOD**—Light, soft, close-grained, not strong, creamy white with thick hardly distinguishable sapwood; occasionally manufactured into cheap furniture and sometimes used for the interior finish of houses, for wooden ware, cooperage and paper pulp. Small quantities of maple sugar are occasionally made from this tree.

Box Elder

# HORSE-CHESTNUT
## Aesculus Hippocastanum L.

**HABIT**—A good sized tree reaching 70 ft. in height with a trunk diameter of 2-3 ft.; sometimes with trunk continuous into top of tree but more frequently dividing soon into a number of large slightly spreading limbs forming an oblong or broadly conical head, in old age with drooping lower branches with upturned tips; spray stiff and coarse with conspicuous terminal buds.

**BARK**—Dull brown becoming shallowly fissured into irregular plate-like scales somewhat resembling bark of Apple Tree.

**TWIGS**—Stout, reddish-yellowish to grayish-brown, smooth or slightly fine-downy. SCALE-SCARS—marking annual growth, distinct. LENTICELS—large, conspicuous, scattered. PITH—wide.

**LEAF-SCARS**—Opposite, large, inversely triangular. STIPULE-SCARS—absent. BUNDLE-SCARS—3-9, generally 7, large, conspicuous, in a single curved line.

**BUDS**—Large, dark reddish-brown, varnished with sticky gum; terminal buds often flower buds, larger than laterals, 1.5 to 3 cm. long; when a flower bud, a terminal scar is left and the twig forks from growth of bud pair below. BUD-SCALES—opposite in 4 rows, about 5 pairs visible in terminal bud, thick with thin margins, the lower pairs more or less keeled and often with abrupt sharp points.

**FRUIT**—A weak-spined bur, containing the large seeds marked with a large conspicuous scar; not remaining on the tree during winter.

**COMPARISONS**—Two western trees with buds free from resinous coating i. e. the Fetid or Ohio Buckeye [*Aesculus glabra* Willd.] and the Sweet Buckeye [*Aesculus octandra* Marsh.] are sometimes planted in New England. They belong with the Horse-chestnut to the genus *Aesculus* which is readily distinguished from other New England genera by the large size of the twigs, buds, opposite leaf-scars and bundle-scars.

**DISTRIBUTION**—A native of southern Asia much planted as an ornamental shade tree in this country and in Europe and naturalized in many places.

**WOOD**—Light, soft, very close-grained, whitish, slightly tinged with yellow; in Europe used by carvers and turners.

HORSE-CHESTNUT

# LINDEN
## Basswood, Lime  Whitewood, Beetree.
### Tilia americana L.

---

**HABIT**—A large tree 50-75 ft., to 100 ft. in height in the upper valley of the Connecticut river, with a trunk diameter of 2-4 ft.; with a straight trunk generally continuous into the top, beset with numerous slender branches, those at the base often strongly drooping, forming a narrow pyramidal head as shown in habit picture or more commonly becoming broadly ovate or round-topped and oblong. [Habit picture is taken from the European Linden, which resembles the American species in habit.]

**BARK**—Dark gray, firm but easily cut, in young stems smooth (upper part of smaller trunk in photograph), becoming fissured into long rather narrow flat-topped ridges, divided by characteristically transverse cracks into short blocks (lower bark picture), becoming with age deeply furrowed with broader more rounded ridges (older trunk).

**TWIGS**—Rather slender, smooth, shining, bright red or greenish or covered with a gray skin; generally zizag, somewhat mucilaginous; fibres in inner bark long, tough, appearing as blunt conical masses in cross-section of older twig, and in surface sections of the bark as whitish wavy lines enclosing lens-shaped darker masses which show externally as wrinkled depressions of the bark. LENTICELS—scattered, dark, oblong.

**LEAF-SCARS**—Alternate, 2-ranked; large, elevated, semi-oval to elliptical.  STIPULE-SCARS—narrow, often showing bundle-scars. BUNDLE-SCARS—few to many, scattered or in a ring or forming a single curved line, showing as 3 in deep surface section.

**BUDS**—Terminal bud absent; lateral buds large to medium, ovate, 3-10 mm. long, somewhat flattened, often lopsided, divergent, dark red or sometimes green, smooth or slightly downy at apex.  BUD-SCALES—rarely more than 2-3 visible, thick, rounded at the back, not 2-ranked nor in pairs.

**FRUIT**—About the size of a pea, woody, spherical, singly or in clusters of several with a common stalk attached midway to a leafy bract, sometimes remaining on the tree into the winter.

**COMPARISONS**—The American Linden, more commonly known among lumbermen as Basswood differs but slightly in winter or summer condition from the European species [*Tilia vulgaris* Hayne] which is much cultivated as a street tree. Another Basswood [*Tilia Michauxii* Nutt.] has been reported in New England only from Connecticut, but is rare in this state. The Lindens are sometimes confused with the Elms, but aside from the different habit of growth the Linden has larger, bright colored buds with 2-3 scales only showing, while the Elms have many scales visible and their bundle-scars are depressed.

**DISTRIBUTION**—In rich woods and loamy soils and often cultivated. Southern Canada from New Brunswick to Lake Winnipeg; south along the mountains to Georgia; west to Kansas, Nebraska and Texas.

IN NEW ENGLAND—Throughout, frequent from the sea coast to altitudes of 1,000 ft., rare from 1,000 to 2,000 ft.

IN CONNECTICUT—Occasional.

**WOOD**—Soft, straight-grained, light brown faintly tinged with red, with thick hardly distinguishable sapwood of 55-65 layers of annual growth, employed in the manufacture of paper-pulp; under the name of Whitewood largely used for woodenware, cheap furniture, the panels of carriages, and for inner soles of shoes. The tough inner bark furnishes fibres for mats, cordage, etc.

LINDEN

# FLOWERING DOGWOOD
## Boxwood, Dogwood, Flowering Cornel.
### Cornus florida L.

**HABIT**—A small tree 15-30 ft. in height, with a trunk diameter of 6-10 inches; developing a low spreading bushy head with slender upright or spreading branches and divergent sinuously curved branchlets turning upward near the end and bearing on their upper sides clusters of fruiting twigs terminated by large conspicuous erect flower buds.

**BARK**—Dark brown to blackish, ridged and broken into small 4-sided or rounded plate-like scales, resembling alligator leather in appearance.

**TWIGS**—Slender, bright red or yellowish-green, smooth or generally appearing more or less mealy from minute closely appressed gray hairs; with bitter taste. LENTICELS—inconspicuous. PITH—gritty, granular.

**LEAF-SCARS**—Opposite, on twigs of the season raised on bases of leaf-stalks with deep V-shaped notch between, on older growth practically encircling twig. STIPULE-SCARS—absent. BUNDLE-SCARS—3, in leaf-scars of the season often confluent and first seen in section through persistent base of leaf-stalk.

**BUDS**—Lateral buds minute, covered by persistent bases of leaf-stalks; terminal leaf-buds flattened-conical, red, generally downy at least at apex, covered by a single pair of opposite pointed scales rounded at back and joined below for ⅓ their length; flowering buds very abundant, terminal, large, spherical to inverted flat turnip-shaped, 4-8 mm. broad, covered by two opposite pairs of bud-scales, the first 2-3 pairs of leaves below the flower buds generally reduced to narrow-pointed scales.

**FRUIT**—Scarlet, oblong, about 1.5 cm. long, fleshy, with a grooved stone, clustered, ripening in October and generally not remaining on the tree during winter.

**COMPARISONS**—The Flowering Dogwood differs from its relative the Alternate-leaved Dogwood [*Cornus alternifolia* L.] by its opposite leaf-scars, from the Bush Maples,—the Striped and the Mountain—which it somewhat resembles in twig characters, by its alligator bark, the presence of but a single pair of scales to terminal leaf-bud, by the persistent bases of leaf-stalks covering the lateral buds and by the abundant large flower buds.

**DISTRIBUTION**—Woodlands, rocky hillsides, moist, gravelly ridges, frequently cultivated as an ornamental tree. Provinces of Quebec and Ontario; south to Florida; west to Minnesota and Texas.

IN NEW ENGLAND—Maine—Fayette Ridge, Kennebec county; New Hampshire—along the Atlantic coast, and very near the Connecticut river, rarely farther north than its junction with the West river; Vermont—southern and southwestern sections, rare; Massachusetts—occasional throughout the state, common in the Connecticut river valley, frequent eastward; Rhode Island—common.

IN CONNECTICUT—Occasional, local or frequent.

**WOOD**—Heavy, hard, strong, close-grained, brown sometimes changing to shades of green and red, with lighter colored sapwood of 30-40 layers of annual growth; largely used in turnery, for the bearings of machinery, the hubs of small wheels, barrel hoops, the handles of tools and occasionally for engravers' blocks.

FLOWERING DOGWOOD

# TUPELO
## Pepperidge, Sour or Black Gum.
### Nyssa sylvatica Marsh.
#### *N. multiflora* Wang.

---

**HABIT**—A tree 20-50 ft. in height with trunk diameter of 1-2 ft. or in the forest 60-80 ft. high, reaching greater dimensions further south; generally easily recognized from the manner of branching alone, though extremely variable in outline. The trunk is erect, generally continuous well into the top, lower branches developed low down on trunk, horizontal or declined often to the ground, upper branches horizontal or slightly ascending, with numerous lateral branches and stubby branchlets forming horizontal layers. The branches are slender and exceedingly numerous, more so than in any other of our trees. The head may be short, cylindrical and flat-topped, or low and broader than tall, (see plate lower habit picture) or more commonly as when crowded in the forest, narrow, pyramidal or conical (see plate upper habit picture) or inversely conical and broad and flat at top.

**BARK**—On young tree, grayish, flaky, on older trunks darker with deeper furrows and ridges broken into somewhat regular hexagonal blocks.

**TWIGS**—Slender, smooth or nearly so, grayish to light reddish-brown, producing numerous short slow growing spurs crowded with leaf-scars on the sides of more rapidly grown shoots. LENTICELS—scattered, inconspicuous. PITH—with thin transverse woody partitions through the ground-mass, best seen with aid of a hand-lens.

**LEAF-SCARS**—Alternate, generally more than 2-ranked, distinct, broadly crescent-shaped. STIPULE-SCARS—absent. BUNDLE-SCARS—conspicuous, 3, simple or slightly compound but in 3 distinct groups, generally depressed, whitish in contrast to reddish-brown of leaf-scar.

**BUDS**—Ovate, dark reddish-brown, smooth or slightly downy at tip, the lateral buds generally blunt-pointed, divergent, on vigorous shoots slightly raised on a cushion of the bark, sometimes on vigorous shoots developing a superposed accessory bud larger than the axillary one; terminal bud slightly larger than laterals, about 5 mm. long, generally sharper pointed, with slightly curved apex. BUD-SCALES—3-4 visible, broadly ovate, rounded, terminally somewhat keeled and pointed.

**FRUIT**—A small bluish drupe ripening in autumn.

**COMPARISONS**—Although the outline of the crown differs widely, the numerous slender horizontally layered branches generally render the Tupelo distinguishable at a distance. Its 3 conspicuous bundle-scars in connection with the woody partitions in the pith will prevent its being confused with any other tree.

**DISTRIBUTION**—In rich, moist soil, in swamps and on the borders of rivers and ponds. Ontario; south to Florida; west to Michigan, Missouri, and Texas.

IN NEW ENGLAND—Maine—Waterville on the Kennebec, the most northern station yet reported; New Hampshire—most common in the Merrimac valley, seldom seen north of the White Mountains; Vermont—occasional; Massachusetts and Rhode Island—rather common.

IN CONNECTICUT—Frequent.

**WOOD**—Heavy, soft, strong, fine-grained, very tough, difficult to split, not durable, light yellow or nearly white, with thick lighter colored sapwood of 80-100 layers of annual growth; used for the hubs of wheels, rollers in glass factories, ox-yokes, wharf piles and sometimes for the soles of shoes.

TUPELO

# WHITE ASH
## Fraxinus americana L.

**HABIT**—In the forests a large tree with straight, tall trunk, free from branches to near the narrow crown, 50-75 ft. in height with trunk diameter of 2-3 ft., reaching over 100 ft. in height in the Ohio basin; in the open a broader tree with ovate, round-topped or pyramidal to oblong outline, the trunk at times continuous into the crown but generally dividing comparatively low down into a number of slightly spreading limbs with slender spreading branches, the lower more or less drooping and recurved. The coarse twigs are formed at a broad angle approaching a right angle with the branch and this cross-shaped branching seen against the sky is an easy means of identification.

**BARK**—Grayish-brown, characteristically furrowed with narrow, flat-topped, firm, irregular, longitudinal ridges which are transversely broken, more or less confluent and enclosing diamond-shaped hollows; old trunks becoming smoother by scaling off of the ridges.

**TWIGS**—Stout, smooth and shining, grayish or greenish-brown often with a slight bloom, very brittle, flattened at nodes at right angles to leaf-scars. LENTICELS—large, pale, scattered dots.

**LEAF-SCARS**—Opposite, large, conspicuous, raised, crescent-shaped to nearly semi-circular but always notched at the top. STIPULE-SCARS—absent. BUNDLE-SCARS—numerous, minute, in a curved line, often indistinct, sometimes more or less confluent.

**BUDS**—Stout, semi-spherical to broadly ovate, scurfy, and more or less slightly downy, rusty to dark brown to sometimes almost black; on rapidly growing shoots, superposed buds often present; terminal bud larger than the laterals, about 5 mm. or less long, blunt, generally decidedly broader than long. A pair of lateral buds generally present at end of twig nearly on level with terminal bud, their leaf-scars causing terminal swelling of twig. BUD-SCALES—generally broadly ovate, opposite in pairs, 2-3 pairs visible, those of terminal bud with sharp, abrupt, sometimes deciduous points.

**FRUIT**—Winged, 2-5 cm. long, the seed-bearing portion round in section, marginless below with much longer wing dilating from near the tip, hanging on the tree in clusters into the winter. The Ash is dioecious and consequently only the female trees ever bear fruit. Since further these do not bear every season, the fruit does not form a very usable winter character for any of the Ashes. The staminate flowers on the male trees are frequently infected by mites and persist through the winter in blackish distorted clusters.

**COMPARISONS**—The White Ash is hardly to be confused with the few other genera of trees that have opposite leaf-scars. It is distinguished from the other Ashes figured here in that its leaf-scar is generally narrow and deeply concave, further from the Black Ash by its rough ridged bark and generally rusty and blunter bud-scales and from the Red Ash by its smooth, generally shiny twigs.

**DISTRIBUTION**—Rich or moist woods, fields and pastures near streams. Newfoundland and Nova Scotia to Ontario; south to Florida; west to Minnesota, Nebraska, Kansas and Texas.

IN NEW ENGLAND—Maine—very common, often forming large forest areas; in the other New England states, widely distributed, but seldom occurring in large masses.

IN CONNECTICUT—Frequent.

**WOOD**—Heavy, hard, strong, close-grained, tough and brown with thick lighter colored sapwood; used in large quantity in the manufacture of agricultural implements for the handles of tools, in carriage building, for oars and furniture, and in the interior finish of buildings; the most valuable of the American species as a timber tree.

WHITE ASH

# RED ASH

## Brown, or River Ash.

### Fraxinus pennsylvanica Marsh.

*F. pubescens* Lam. ; *F. Darlingtonii* Britton.

---

**HABIT**—A medium to large-sized tree, 30-70 ft. in height with a trunk diameter of 1-3 ft.; in general appearance resembling the White Ash.

**BARK**—Similar to that of White Ash but with somewhat shallower furrows.

**TWIGS**—More slender than those of White Ash, densely velvety-downy in typical condition but often without down especially in the Green Ash [*Fraxinus pennsylvanica*, var. *lanceolata* (Bork.) Sarg.].

**LEAF-SCARS**—Semicircular, upper margin rarely somewhat depressed.

**BUDS**—Dark rusty brown smaller and narrower than those of the White Ash, about 2 pairs of scales visible to terminal bud.

**FRUIT**—Seed-bearing portion round in section, marginless below with wing extending down its sides.

**COMPARISONS**—The Red Ash is not distinguished by most people from the White Ash which it closely resembles. The downiness of its twigs which is considered its chief specific character is not constant. The shape of its leaf-scar, in general semi-circular with upper margin not concave, is perhaps its best distinguishing character. Further its terminal buds are narrower, showing fewer scales and the twigs are more slender. The smooth-twigged Green Ash [*Fraxinus pennsylvanica*, var. *lanceolata* (Bork.) Sarg.] is considered by the best authorities only a variety of the Red. The Black Ash is best separated by its characteristic scaly bark and generally black buds.

The European Ash [*Fraxinus excelsior* L.] is frequently cultivated. It has a bark resembling that of the White Ash and has a pair of lateral buds nearly on level with terminal buds; but its leaf-scars are semicircular and its buds jet black.

**DISTRIBUTION**—River banks, swampy lowlands, margins of streams and ponds. New Brunswick to Manitoba; south to Florida and Alabama; west to Dakota, Nebraska, Kansas, and Missouri.

IN NEW ENGLAND—Maine—infrequent; New Hampshire—occasional, extending as far north as Boscawen in the Merrimac valley; Vermont—common along Lake Champlain and its tributaries; occasional in other sections; Massachusetts and Rhode Island—sparingly scattered throughout.

IN CONNECTICUT—Frequent.

**WOOD**—Heavy, hard, rather strong, brittle, coarse-grained, light brown with thick lighter brown sapwood streaked with yellow; sometimes confounded commercially with the more valuable wood of the White Ash.

RED ASH

# BLACK ASH

## Hoop, Swamp, Basket or Brown Ash.

### Fraxinus nigra Marsh.

#### *F. sambucifolia* Lam.

---

**HABIT**—A tall tree 60-80 ft. in height with trunk diameter of 1-2 ft., larger further south; in swamps in company with other trees with tall slender trunk of nearly uniform diameter to point of branching supporting a narrow head; in the open, where it is seldom found, said to have a habit similar to that of the White Ash.

**BARK**—Ash-gray, slightly tinged with buff, without deep ridges, forming thin scales smoothish on the outside and edges, easily rubbed off and exposing a surface rather soft to the touch suggesting somewhat the feel of asbestos or talcum powder; trunk frequently with knobby excrescences.

**TWIGS**—Very stout, similar to those of White Ash but lighter gray and not shiny.

**LEAF-SCARS**—Opposite, large, conspicuous, circular to semi-circular; the upper margin not concave, often extending upward as a thin flap partially hiding the bud; otherwise resembling the White Ash.

**BUDS**—Resembling those of White Ash but generally decidedly black though occasionally rusty, terminal bud ovate, pointed, as long as or longer than broad, more or less flattened at right angles to outer pair of scales, last pair of lateral buds generally at some distance from the end giving terminal bud a stalked appearance.   BUD-SCALES—of terminal bud broadly keeled and narrower than in White Ash, generally only 1-2 pairs visible.

**FRUIT**—With broad wing, distinctly notched at apex, surrounding the flattened seed-bearing portion.

**COMPARISONS**—The Black Ash is easily distinguished from the White by its soft, scaly bark, the even or raised upper margin of its leaf-scars, its narrower and generally black buds, and the stalked appearance of its terminal bud.   When growing in the swamps beside the White Ash its twigs can be seen to be much stouter and fewer than those of the latter species.

**DISTRIBUTION**—Wet woods, river bottoms, and swamps.   Anticosti through Ontario; south to Delaware and Virginia; west to Arkansas and Missouri.

IN NEW ENGLAND—Maine—common; New Hampshire—south of the White Mountains; Vermont—common; Massachusetts—more common in central and western sections; Rhode Island—infrequent.

IN CONNECTICUT—Occasional.

**WOOD**—Heavy, rather soft, not strong, tough, coarse-grained, durable, easily separable into thin layers, dark brown with thin light brown often nearly white sapwood; largely used for the interior finish of houses and cabinet-making, and for fences, barrel hoops and in the manufacture of baskets.

BLACK ASH

# HARDY CATALPA
## Cigar Tree, Indian Bean, Western Catalpa.
### Catalpa speciosa Warder.

**HABIT**—A tall tree reaching 100 ft. in height and 4 ft. in trunk diamenter in the Ohio basin, of smaller dimensions in New England with slender branches, forming a comparatively narrow round-topped head.

**BARK**—Reddish to grayish brown, with longitudinal scaly ridges.

**TWIGS**—Stout, smooth or slightly short-downy, reddish to yellowish-brown, the tips of twigs generally winter killed. LENTICELS—conspicuous, rather large and numerous. PITH—white, wide, occasionally chambered at the nodes.

**LEAF-SCARS**—Opposite or more frequently 3 at a node, large and conspicuous, round to elliptical, with depressed center. STIPULE-SCARS—absent. BUNDLE-SCARS—conspicuous, often raised, forming a closed ring.

**BUDS**—Terminal bud absent, lateral buds small, semi-spherical, generally under 2 mm. high. BUD-SCALES—brown, loosely overlapping, about 5 or 6 visible.

**FRUIT**—A long cylindrical capsule, 8-20 inches in length, with numerous flattened, winged, white-hairy, fringed seeds, persistent on the tree through winter. The photograph of the capsule is reduced to about ⅖ natural size.

**COMPARISONS**—The 3 large circular leaf-scars at a node with complete ring of bundle-scars renders the Catalpa twig easily recognizable. The long cigar-like fruits that hang on the tree supply a distinctive habit character. A very closely related southern and less hardy species the Common Catalpa [*Catalpa bignonioides* Walt.] was formerly more planted than the Hardy Catalpa. It is a smaller tree with a rather more spreading habit but is most readily distinguished from the western species at the time of flowering.

**DISTRIBUTION**—Not native in New England but planted as an ornamental shade tree and for timber. It grows native along borders of streams and ponds and rich often inundated bottom-land; southern Indiana, Illinois, and Missouri south into Kentucky, Tennessee and Arkansas.

**WOOD**—Light, soft, not strong, coarse-grained, very durable in contact with the soil, light brown with thin nearly white sapwood of 1 or 2 layers of annual growth; largely used for railroad ties, fence posts and rails and occasionally for furniture and the interior finish of houses.

HARDY CATALPA

# GLOSSARY.

*Accessory buds.* Buds at or near the nodes but not in the axil. Of two kinds, collateral and superposed.

*Acorn.* The complete fruit of an Oak consisting of a nut partially enclosed by an involucrate cup.

*Alternate.* Scattered along the stem; said of leaves and scales in distinction from opposite.

*Apex.* The top, as the tip of the bud.

*Appressed.* Lying close against the twig, as the buds of the Shad Bush (p.493).

*Awl-shaped.* Small and tapering to a slender point.

*Axil.* The angle formed at the upper side of the attachment of the leaf to the stem.

*Axillary.* In an axil. An axillary bud is the first bud above the leaf or leaf-scar.

*Bark.* The outer covering of the trunk or branch. Unless otherwise specified, the heading "Bark" in the descriptions refers to the bark of the trunk.

*Berry.* A fruit fleshy throughout.

*Bloom.* The powdery waxy substance easily rubbed off, as the bloom on the twigs of the Box Elder (p.547).

*Bract.* A more or less modified leaf.

*Branch.* A secondary division of a trunk.

*Branchlet.* A small branch.

*Bud.* An undeveloped branch or fruit cluster with or without a protective covering of scales.

*Bud-scales.* Reduced leaves covering a bud.

*Bundle-scars.* Scars of the fibro-vascular bundles which ran up through the leaf-stalk and connected with the veins of the leaf, seen as dots in the leaf-scar (fig.4).

*Bur.* A spiny fruit, as the bur of the Chestnut (p.431).

*Buttressed.* Said of the trunk when enlarged at the base as frequently is the case in the White Elm (p.461).

*Calyx.* The outer portion of a flower consisting of a circle of modified leaves usually green in color.

*Capsule.* A dry fruit which splits at maturity to let out the seeds.

*Catkin.* A unisexual, elongated, compact cluster of flowers with scaly bracts usually falling away in one piece, as in the Alders (p.427), Birches (p.415-425), etc.

*Cell.* One of the chambers of the ovary. One of the microscopic structural elements out of which plant tissues are built up.

*Chambered.* Said of the pith when interrupted by hollow spaces, as in the Butternut (fig.6).

*Collateral buds.* Accessory buds at the side of the axillary bud as in the Red Maple (fig.7).

*Cone.* A fruit such as of the Pines with woody closely overlapping scales.

*Confluent.* Said of bundle-scars, when the separate scars are so close together that they appear to form a single scar.

*Conical.*  Cone-shaped, largest at the base and tapering to the apex.

*Crown.*  The upper mass of branches.

*Cup-shaped.*  Shaped like a cup; deeper than saucer-shaped.

*Deciduous.*  Falling away; said of trees that drop their leaves before winter.

*Decurrent.*  Said of ridges that run down from the leaf-scar.

*Deliquescent.*  Said of a tree with broad spreading habit as the Apple (p.487).

*Dioecious.*  Said of plants such as the Willows and Poplars that have separate male and female individuals.

*Divergent.*  Said of buds that point away from the twig as in the Carolina Poplar (fig.5).

*Downy.*  Covered with fine hairs.

*Drupe.*  A stone-fruit as in the Cherries with the seed enclosed in a stone or pit which is surrounded by a fleshy portion.

*Egg-shaped.*  Shaped like an egg with the broadest part below the middle.

*Elliptical.*  Oblong with regularly rounded ends.

*Entire.*  Margin without indentations.

*Epidermis.*  The outermost layer of cells.

*Escape.*  A plant originally cultivated but now growing like a wild plant.

*Evergreen.*  With green leaves in winter, as the Pines and Holly.

*Excurrent.*  Said of a tree of erect habit of growth, such as the Spruce (p.359) or Poplar (p.395).

*Fan-shaped.*  Shaped like an expanded fan.

*Fibro-vascular bundles.*  The strands containing the elements for the transportation of fluids through the plant. They ultimately connect with the veins of the leaves.

*Flaky* (bark).  With loose scales easily rubbed off.

*Flower bud.*  A bud containing an undeveloped flower or flower cluster.

*Fluted.*  With rounded ridges.

*Fruit.*  The part of a plant containing the seeds.

*Gland.*  A small protuberance, as on the leaves of the Arbor Vitae (p.377).

*Habit.*  The general appearance of the tree as seen at a distance.

*Habitat.*  The place where the tree naturally grows, such as swamps, sandy plains, etc.

*Hairy.*  With long hairs.

*Head.*  The upper portion of a tree.

*Heartwood.*  The dead central portion of the trunk.

*Hoary.*  Grayish-white with a fine close down.

*Hybrid.*  A cross between two species or varieties.

*Internode.*  The portion of the stem between two nodes.

*Inversely triangular.*  Inverted triangular with the apex below.

*Involucre.*  The bracts surrounding the flower cluster.

*Juvenile.*  Youthful, said of the leaves formed in the early stages of development.

*Keeled.* With a central ridge like the keel of a boat.

*Key.* A winged fruit.

*Lanceolate.* Lance-shaped; similar to ovate but narrower with outline tapering gradually to the apex.

*Lateral bud.* A bud produced on the side of a twig.

*Leaf bud.* A bud containing undeveloped leaves but not flowers.

*Leaf-scar.* The scar left by the fall of the leaf (fig.4).

*Leaf-stalk.* The stem of a leaf.

*Lenticels.* Corky spots on the surface which admit air to the interior of the twig.

*Limbs.* The larger branches.

*Linear.* Long and narrow, several times as long as broad with parallel edges, as the leaves of the Pines.

*Lobed.* With rounded indentations running ⅓ to ⅔ the way from the margin inward.

*Longitudinal.* Lengthwise.

*Medullary rays.* Rays of tissue extending from the pith toward the bark, best seen in cross section.

*Midrib.* The central vein of a leaf.

*Naked bud.* A bud without bud-scales.

*Needle.* A narrow leaf as in the Pines.

*Node.* The place on the twig at which one or more leaves were produced (fig.4).

*Nut.* A large hard fruit as in the Hickory, Oak and Chestnut.

*Nutlet.* A small nut.

*Oblanceolate.* Inverted lanceolate.

*Oblong.* Two or three times longer than broad with about uniform diameter.

*Obovate.* Inverted ovate.

*Opposite* (leaves and leaf-scars). With two leaves or leaf-scars opposed at a node.

*Oval.* Broadly elliptical.

*Ovary.* The part of the pistil producing the seeds.

*Ovate.* Egg-shaped, with the broadest part below the middle.

*Persistent.* Remaining on the tree.

*Pistil.* The seed-bearing portion of the flower.

*Pith.* The softer central portion of a twig.

*Pod.* A dry fruit which splits open at maturity.

*Pome.* A fruit like the Apple or Pear.

*Pungent.* Sharp to the taste.

*Pyramidal.* Shaped like a pyramid with broadest portion at the base.

*Raceme.* A simple cluster of stalked flowers arranged along an elongated axis.

*Resin-duct.* A tube for the conduction of resin seen in the leaves of the Pines.

*Sapwood.* The young living wood outside the heartwood.

*Saucer-shaped.* Shaped like a saucer, shallower than cup-shaped.

*Scale.* A small modified leaf seen in buds and cones. One of the flakes into which the outer bark often divides.

*Scurfy.* Covered with small bran-like scales.

*Sepal.* One of the divisions of the calyx.

*Sessile.* Without a stalk.

*Shrub.* A low woody growth, smaller than a tree and generally branching near the base.

*Smooth.* Not rough nor hairy.

*Spray.* The aggregate of smaller branches and branchlets.

*Spur.* A short, slowly-grown branchlet.

*Stamens.* The pollen-bearing portions of a flower.

*Staminate.* Having stamens ; said of trees bearing only male flowers.

*Sterile.* Not producing seed.

*Stipular.* Similar in form or position to stipules.

*Stipules.* Two small leaf-like bodies located at the base of the leaf-stalk in some species.

*Stipule-scar.* The scar left by the fall of a stipule (fig.5).

*Stomata.* Breathing pores in leaves.

*Stone-fruit.* A fruit like that of the Cherry. The same as drupe.

*Strengthening cells.* Thick walled cells present in the leaves of some of the Pines.

*Striate.* Longitudinally streaked.

*Submerged.* Covered, as by the bark.

*Sucker.* A shoot arising from below ground.

*Superposed buds.* Accessory buds above the auxillary bud, as in the Butternut (fig.6).

*Surface-sectioned.* Cut parallel to and near the surface.

*Teeth.*—Small projections along the margin.

*Terminal bud.* The bud formed at the tip of a twig.

*Thorn.* A stiff woody sharp-pointed projection.

*Top-shaped.* Shaped like a top with the broadest part above.

*Tree.* A woody plant, larger than a shrub, from which it cannot always be distinguished. Usually defined as a woody growth, unbranched near the base and reaching a height of at least fifteen feet.

*Triangular.* Shaped like a triangle with the base below.

*Trunk.* The main stem of a tree.

*Twig.* A young shoot. Unless otherwise specified, used in the descriptions to denote the growth of the past season only.

*Valvate.* Said of buds in which the scales meet without overlapping.

*Whorl.* A cluster of three or more leaves or leaf-scars at a single node.

*Wing.* A thin flat appendage.

*Woolly.* Covered with tangled or matted hairs resembling wool.

# INDEX

Where the species receives its most extended description, the page number appears in boldface type. Where the species is otherwise mentioned, the page number is printed in ordinary type. Synonyms of both common and scientific names are printed in italics and their page numbers in ordinary type.

*Abele* ......................386
Abies balsamea ............**370**
*Acacia* ...................**522**
  *Three-thorned* ...........516
Acer ......................**342**
  *barbatum* ...............536
  *dasycarpum* ............538
  Key to Species ..........342
  Negundo ...............**546**
  pennsylvanicum .........**532**
  platanoides .............**542**
  Pseudo-Platanus ........**544**
  rubrum ................**540**
  *saccharinum* ............536
  saccharinum ...........**538**
  saccharum .............**536**
    var. nigrum ...........**536**
  spicatum ..............**534**
Aesculus:
  glabra ................**548**
  Hippocastanum .........**548**
  octandra ..............**548**
Ailanthus .............514, **524**
  glandulosa .............**524**
Alder .................426, 478
  European Black .........**426**
  *Hoary* ..................426
  Smooth ................**426**
  Speckled ..............**426**
*Alligator-wood* ............480
Alternate-leaved Dogwood ...**552**
Amelanchier canadensis ....**492**
Alnus:
  incana ................**426**
  rugosa ................**426**
  vulgaris ...............**426**
*American Aspen* ...........388
  *Beech* ................428
  *Elm* .................460
  *Holly* ................530
  Hornbeam ...318, 325, 410, **412**
  *Larch* ................356
  Mountain Ash ..........**488**
  Plum .............506, **508**
    var. Gold .............**508**
*Amygdalus Persica* .........512
Apple ...................316
  321, 466, 468, 484, **486**, 490, 548

*Apple, Thorn* ..............**494**
Arbor, Vitae ..............**376**
Ash ......325, 327, 328, **343**, 556
  American Mountain .......**488**
  *Basket* ................560
  Black ...... 322, 556, 558, **560**
  *Brown* ..............558, 560
  European ..............**558**
  European Mountain .......**488**
  Green .................**558**
  *Hoop* ...............464, 560
  Key to Species ..........343
  Mountain ..............**488**
  Prickly ...............**522**
  Red ..................**558**
  *River* ................558
  *Swamp* ...............560
  Western Mountain .......**488**
  White ...........319, 322, 327
  328, 406, 474, 542, **556**, 558, 560
*Ash-leaved Maple* ..........546
*Aspen* ..................388
  *American* ..............388
  Large-toothed ....386, 388, **390**
  *Quaking* ..............388
  Small-toothed ............
  .........324, 386, **388**, 390, 392
Austrian Pine ..............**352**
*Balm of Gilead* ............392
  *Fir* ..................370
*Balsam* ...............370, 392
  Fir .............368, **370**, 372
  Poplar ..........388, 390, **392**
*Basket Ash* ...............560
Basswood .................550
*Bay:*
  *Swamp* ...............341
  Sweet ..........**341,** 470, 472
*Bean, Indian* .............562
Bear Oak ............442, **454**
*Beaver Tree* ..............341
Beech ...................318
  321, 412, **428**, 492, 520, 540
  *American* ..............428
  *Blue* .................412
  European ..............**428**
  *Water* ................412
*Beetree* .................550

Betula ..................... 337
  alba ...................... 424
    var. papyrifera ......... 422
    Key to Species .......... 337
    lenta ................... 414
    lutea ................... 416
    nigra ................... 418
    papyrifera .............. 422
    populifolia ............. 420
Big Bud Hickory............. 404
Bilsted .................... 480
Birch .........318, 319, 322, 337
  Black 317, 318, 321, 414, 416, 418
  Canoe ................... 422
  Cherry .................. 414
  European Paper .......... 424
  European White ......... 424
  Gray ................... 416
  Gray .................420, 422
  Key to Species ......... 337
  Old Field .............. 420
  Paper ...318, 416, 420, 422, 424
  Poplar ................. 420
  Poverty ................ 420
  Red .................416, 418
  River .................. 418
  Silver ................. 416
  Small White ............ 420
  Sweet .................. 414
  White ...............420, 422
  Yellow ..318, 414, 416, 418, 422
Bird Cherry ................ 500
Bird's Eye Maple ........... 536
Bitternut ...........398, 400, 408
Black Ash ....322, 556, 558, 560
  Birch 317, 318, 321, 414, 416, 418
  Cherry ................. 496
  Gum .................... 554
  Knot ................... 498
  Larch .................. 356
  Locust ................. 522
  Maple .................. 536
  Oak .........318, 446, 450, 452
  Oak Group ....319, 325, 338, 452
  Pine ................... 352
  Scrub Oak............... 454
  Spruce ................. 350
          356, 358, 360, 362, 370, 376
  Walnut ...........398, 400, 524
  Willow ................. 384
Blue Beech ................. 412
  Oak .................... 438
  Spruce ...........358, 360, 364
Bog Spruce ................. 362
Box Elder .............540, 546
Box White Oak ............. 434
Boxwood .................... 552
Bristly Locust ............. 522

Broom Hickory .............. 406
Brown Ash .............558, 560
Buckeye:
  Fetid .................. 548
  Ohio ................... 548
  Sweet .................. 548
Bur Oak ..............436, 480
Bush Maple ............532, 552
Butternut .................. 322
          323, 324, 398, 400, 408, 524
Buttonball ................. 482
Buttonwood ................. 482
Cabinet Cherry ............. 496
Canada Plum ...........506, 508
Canoe Birch ................ 422
Carolina Popular ........... 321
          323, 324, 388, 390, 394, 396
Carpinus caroliniana ....... 412
Carya ...................... 336
  alba ................... 402
  alba ................... 404
  amara .................. 408
  cordiformis ............ 408
  glabra ................. 406
  Key to Species ......... 336
  microcarpa ............. 406
  ovata .................. 402
  porcina ................ 406
  tomentosa .............. 404
Castanea:
  dentata ................ 430
  sativa, var. americana...... 430
  vesca, var. americana....... 430
Cat Spruce ................. 358
Catalpa ...............309, 562
  bignonioides ........... 562
  Common ................. 562
  Hardy .................. 562
  speciosa ............... 562
  Western ................ 562
Cedar .............374, 376, 380
  Coast White 326, 374, 376, 380
  Red .............374, 378, 380
  White ...............374, 376
Celtis occidentalis ........ 464
Cercis canadensis .......... 518
Chamaecyparis:
  sphaeroidea ............ 374
  thyoides ............... 374
Cherry ....318, 319, 321, 341, 414
  Amarelles .............. 504
  Birch .................. 414
  Bird ................... 500
  Black .................. 496
  Black Tartarian ........ 502
  Cabinet ................ 496
  Choke ...........496, 498, 504
  Early Richmond ......... 504

**Cherry (Continued)**
European Bird .............502
Fire ...................500
Key to Species ...........341
Louis Philippe ...........504
May Duke ...............502
Mazzard ................502
Montmorency ............504
Morello ................504
Napoleon ...............502
Pie ...................504
Pin ...................500
Pigeon ................500
Rum ..................496
Sour ....316, 496, 498, 502, **504**
Sweet 316, 317, 496, 498 **502,** 504
Wild Black **496,** 498, 500, 504
Wild Red ........498, **500,** 504
Windsor ................502

**Chestnut** ....................
......309, 319, 322, 328, **430,** 440
Oak .................**440**
Oak .........440, 442, **444,** 446
Chinese Magnolia ......**470,** 472
Sumach ................524
Chinquapin Oak ....432, **440,** 442
Chinquapin Oak ..........442
Choke Cherry ......496, 498, 504
Cigar Tree ...............562
Cladrastis lutea ...........**520**
Clammy Locust ...........**522**
Coast White Cedar .........
...............326, **374,** 376, 380
Cockspur Thorn ...........**494**
Coffee Bean ..............514
Nut ..................514
Coffee Tree, Kentucky 322, **514,** 524
Colorado Blue Spruce........364
Common Catalpa ..........**562**
Juniper .............**378,** 380
Locust .........324, 516, **522**
Cork Elm ......456, 460, **462,** 480
Cornel, Flowering ...........552
**Cornus:**
alternifolia ...........**552**
florida ...............**552**
Cottonwood ..............394
Crataegus ...............**494**
Crus-galli .............**494**
pruinosa ..............**494**
Cucumber Tree .........**470,** 472
Large-leaved ............340
Cultivated Plums ..........**508**
Cupressus, thyoides .........**374**
Curly Maple .............**536**
Cydonia vulgaris ...........**490**
Deerwood ...............410
Dimerosporium Collinsii ......492

Dogwood ..................552
Alternate-leaved .........**552**
Flowering ...............**552**
Poison .................528
Double Spruce .............362
Douglas Fir ...........**368,** 370
Spruce ................368
Downy Poplar ............**336**
Dwarf Chinquapin Oak ........
...............432, 440, **442,** 454
Juniper ...............378
Sumach ................**526**
**Elder:**
Box ..................**546**
Poison ................528
Elkwood .................472
Elm ........322, **340,** 438, 464, 550
American ..............460
Cork ........456, 460, **462,** 480
English ......316, **458,** 460, 462
False .................464
Hickory ...............462
Key to Species ..........340
Moose .................456
Northern Cork ...........462
Red ..................456
Rock .................462
Slippery .........**456,** 460, 462
Water ................460
White ...316, 456, 458, **460,** 462
Winged ...............**462**
English Elm ..316, **458,** 460, 462
European Ash ..............**558**
Beech .................**428**
Bird Cherry ............502
Black Alder ............**426**
Holly .................**530**
Larch .................**356**
Linden ................**550**
Mountain Ash ...........**488**
Paper Birch ............424
Plum .................508
var. Lombard ...........508
Weeping Willow .........**384**
White Birch .............**424**
White Willow ...........**384**
Evergreens .........316, 321, 329
**Fagus:**
americana .............428
atropunicea ............428
ferruginia .............428
grandifolia ............**428**
sylvatica ..............428
False Elm ...............464
Fetid Buckeye ............**548**
Fir ...................370
Balm of Gilead ..........370
Balsam .........368, **370,** 372
Douglas .............**368,** 370
Red ..................368

Fir (Continued)
Scotch ................... 354
Fire Cherry ............... 500
Flowering Cornel ........... 552
Dogwood ................. 552
Fraxinus ................. 343
americana ........... 328, 556
Darlingtonii ............. 558
excelsior ............... 558
Key to Species ........... 343
nigra .................. 560
pennsylvanica ........... 558
var. lanceolata ......... 558
pubescens ............... 558
sambucifolia ............. 560
Ginkgo ................... 382
biloba .................. 382
Gleditschia ............... 516
Gleditsia triacanthus ....... 516
Golden Osier .............. 384
Gopher Wood .............. 520
Gray Birch ............ 420, 422
Birch .................. 416
Pine ................... 348
Green Ash ............... 558
Gum:
Black .................. 554
Red .................... 480
Sour ................... 554
Sweet .................. 480
Gymnocladus:
canadensis ............. 514
dioica ................. 514
Hackberry ............ 322, 464
Hackmatack ............. 356
Hamamelis virginiana ...... 478
Hard Maple ............. 536
Pine ................... 346
Hardy Catalpa ............ 562
Haw .................... 494
Hawthorn ............ 494, 516
Hazel, Witch ............. 478
Hemlock ............ 370, 372
Spruce ................. 372
Hickoria:
alba ................... 404
glabra ................. 406
minima ................ 408
ovata .................. 402
Hickory .............. 336, 462
Big Bud ............... 404
Broom ................. 406
Elm ................... 462
Key to Species .......... 336
Pignut ................. 406
Shag-bark ...319, 402, 404, 406
Shell-bark .............. 402
Small-fruited ........... 406

Hickory (Continued)
Swamp .................. 408
White-heart ............. 404
Hoary Alder .............. 426
Holly .................... 530
American ............... 530
European ............... 530
White .................. 530
Honey Locust ..309, 494, 516, 522
Shucks ................. 516
Hoop Ash ............ 464, 560
Hop Hornbeam .....325, 410, 412
Hornbeam ................ 412
American ....318, 325, 410, 412
Hop ............325, 410, 412
Horse Plum ............... 506
Horse-chestnut ............
..........319, 320, 321, 322, 548
Ilex:
Aquifolium ............. 530
opaca .................. 530
Indian Bean ............. 562
Iron Oak ............... 434
Ironwood ............ 410, 412
Ivy, Poison ............. 528
Jack Pine ............ 326, 348
Japanese Plum ........... 508
var. Red June .......... 508
Judas Tree .............. 518
Juglans:
cinerea ................ 398
nigra .................. 400
Juneberry ............... 492
Juniper ................. 356
Common ............378, 380
Dwarf ................. 378
Red ................... 380
Juniperus:
communis .............. 378
var. alpina ........... 378
var. canadensis ....... 378
var. depressa ......... 378
nana .................. 378
virginiana ............. 380
Kentucky Coffee Tree 322, 514, 524
Key to Genera and Species ...329
Labrador Spruce ........... 358
Lancewood ............... 492
Larch ..............335, 382
American ............... 356
Black .................. 356
European ............... 356
Key to Species ......... 335
Large-leaved Magnolia .........
..................340, 470, 472
Cucumber Tree ........... 340
Umbrella Tree .......... 340
Large-toothed Aspen 386, 388, 390
Larix ................... 335
americana .............. 356

Larix (Continued)
  decidua ....................356
  *europaea* .................356
  Key to Species ............335
  laricina ..................356
*Laurel Magnolia* ...........341
*Leverwood* .................410
*Lime* ......................550
Linden .................430, 550
  European .................550
*Liquidambar* ...............480
  Styraciflua ..............480
Liriodendron Tulipifera .....**474**
*Locust* ....................522
  *Black* ...................522
  Bristly ..................**522**
  Clammy ...................**522**
  Common ..........324, 516, **522**
  Honey ......309, 494, **516,** 522
  *Sweet* ...................516
  *White* ...................522
  *Yellow* ..................522
Lombardy Poplar 388, 390, 394, **396**
Maclura pomifera ...........**494**
Magnolia ..............**340,** 474
  acuminata ...............**470**
  Chinese .............**470,** 472
  conspicua ...............**470**
  *glauca* .................341
  Key to Species ..........340
  *Laurel* .................341
  Large-leaved .....**340,** 470, 472
  macrophylla .............**340**
  *Mountain* ..............**470**
  tripetala ...............**472**
  *Umbrella* ..............**472**
  virginiana ..............**341**
*Mahogany* ................**514**
*Maidenhair Tree* .........382
*Malus Malus* .............486
Maple .....................**342**
  *Ash-leaved* ............546
  Bird's Eye ..............**536**
  Black ...................**536**
  Bush ...............532, 552
  Curly ...................**536**
  *Hard* ..................536
  Key to Species ..........342
  Mountain ....532, **534,** 540, 552
  Norway .........540, **542,** 544
  Red 323, 324, 325, 536, 538, **540**
  *River* .................538
  *Rock* ..................536
  Silver ........325, 536, **538,** 540
  *Soft* ..................538 540
  Striped ......**532,** 534, 540, 552
  Sugar .......526, **536,** 540, 544
  *Swamp* .................540
  Sycamore ........540, 542, **544**

Maple (Continued)
  White .................538, 540
  *Mazzard Cherry* ...........502
  Mockernut .........402, **404,** 406
  *Moose Elm* ...............456
  *Moosewood* ...............532
  *Morello Cherry* ..........504
  Morus .....................**340**
    alba ...................**468**
    Key to Species .........**340**
    rubra ..................**466**
  *Mossy-cup Oak* ...........436
  Mountain Ash .............488
    *Magnolia* .............470
    Maple ........532, **534,** 540, 552
  Mulberry 322, 324, 325, **340,** 468
    Key to Species .........340
    Red ...................**466,** 468
    *Silkworm* ............468
    White .................466, **468**
  *Necklace Poplar* .........394
  *Negundo:*
    *aceroides* ...........546
    *Negundo* .............546
  *Nettle Tree* .............464
  *Nicker Tree* .............514
  *Northern Cork Elm* .......462
  *Northern Scrub Pine* .....348
  Norway Maple ......540, **542,** 544
    *Pine* .................350
    Spruce ............360, **366**
  Nyssa:
    *multiflora* ..........554
    sylvatica .............**554**
  Oak ...318, 322, 325, **337,** 428, 430
    Bear .................442, **454**
    Black ........318, 446, 450, **452**
    *Black Scrub* .........454
    *Blue* ................438
    *Box White* ..........434
    Bur ..................**436,** 480
    *Chestnut* ...........440
    Chestnut .....440, 442, **444,** 446
    *Chinquapin* .........442
    Chinquapin .......432, **440,** 442
    Dwarf Chinquapin .............
    ............432, 440, **442,** 454
    *Iron* ...............434
    Key to Species ........338
    *Mossy-cup* ..........436
    *Over-cup* ...........436
    Pin ..................**448**
    Post ..............432, **434**
    Red ......430, 444, **446,** 450, 452
    *Rock* ...............444
    *Rock Chestnut* ......444
    Scarlet ....446, 448, **450,** 452
    *Scrub* ..............442
    *Scrub Chestnut* .....442
    *Swamp* ..............448

Oak (Continued)
Swamp White 316, 432, **438**, 442
White ...................319
  **432**, 434, 436, 438, 444, 446
*Yellow* ................440, 452
*Yellow-barked* .............452
Ohio Buckeye ..............**548**
*Oilnut* .......................398
*Old-field Birch* ..............420
Oriental Sycamore ..........**482**
Osage Orange ..............**494**
Osier
 *Golden* ...................384
Ostrya virginiana ..........**410**
*Over-cup Oak* ...............436
*Padus:*
 serotina ..................496
 virginiana ................**498**
Paper Birch 318, 416, 420, **422**, 424
Peach ..................341, **512**
Pear 316, 321, 322, 470, **484**, 486
*Pepperidge* ...................554
Picea ......................**335**
 Abies ....................**366**
 *alba* ......................358
 *brevifolia* .................362
 canadensis ..............**358**
 *excelsa* ...................366
 Key to Species ...........**335**
 mariana .................**362**
  var. semiprostrata ......**362**
 Menziessii ...............**364**
 *nigra* ....................362
  *var. rubra* ..............360
 *Parryana* .................364
 *pungens* ..................364
 *rubens* ...................360
 rubra ...................**360**
*Pie Cherry* ..................504
*Pigeon Cherry* ..............500
Pignut ..................402, **406**
 *Hickory* ...................406
*Pin Cherry* ..................500
 Oak ......................**448**
Pine ..............326, **335**, 382
 Austrian .............350, **352**
 *Black* ....................352
 *Gray* ....................348
 *Hard* ...................346
 Jack ................326, **348**
 Key to Species ...........**335**
 *Northern Scrub* ...........348
 *Norway* ..................350
 Pitch ............344, **346**, 350
 Red ........344, 346, **350**, 352
 Scotch ...............348, **354**
 *Soft* ....................344
 *Spruce* ..................348
 *Weymouth* ................344

Pine (Continued)
 White...**344**, 346, 350, 354, 370
 *Yellow* ...................346
Pinus .....................**335**
 Banksiana ................**348**
 *divaricata* ................348
 Key to Species ...........**335**
 Laricio, var. austriaca ....**352**
 resinosa ..................**350**
 rigida ...................**346**
 Strobus ..................**344**
 sylvestris ...............**354**
Pitch Pine ........344, **346**, 350
*Plane Tree* .................482
Platanus:
 occidentalis ..............**482**
 orientalis ................**482**
Plowrightia morbosa .........498
Plum ..................**341**, 498
 American ...........506, **508**
  var. Gold ..............**508**
 Canada .............**506**, 508
 Cultivated ................**508**
 European ................**508**
  var. Lombard ..........**508**
 *Horse* ...................506
 Japanese .................**508**
  var. Red June .........**508**
 Key to Species ...........341
 *Red* .....................506
 *Wild* .................... .506
*Poison Dogwood* ............528
 *Elder* ....................528
 Ivy ......................**528**
 Sumach .........318, 526, **528**
Poplar 316, 322, 225, **336**, 388, 390
 Balsam .........388, 390, **392**
 *Birch* ....................420
 Carolina ..................
 321, 323, 324, 388, 390, **394**, 396
 Downy Poplar .............**336**
 Key to Species ...........**336**
 Lombardy ....388, 390, 394, **396**
 *Necklace* .................394
 Silver ..........**386**, 388, 390
 *Silver-leaf* ...............386
 *White* ...................386
 *Yellow* ...................474
*Popple* ................388, 390
Populus ...................**336**
 alba .....................**386**
 balsamifera ..............**392**
 *canadensis* ...............**394**
 candicans ................**392**
 deltoides .................**394**
 *dilatata* .................396
 *fastigiata* ................396
 grandidentata ............**390**
 heterophylla .............**336**
 Key to Species ............336

Populus (Continued)
   *monilifera* ..................394
   nigra, var. italica .........**396**
   *pyramidalis* ...............396
   tremuloides ...............**388**
Post Oak ..............432, **434**
*Poverty Birch* ...............420
Prunus ............ 318, **341,** 506
   americana ..................**508**
   *var. nigra* ................506
   avium ....................**502**
   Cerasus ...................**504**
   domestica .................**508**
   Key to Species ............341
   nigra ....................**506**
   pennsylvanica ............**500**
   Persica ..................**512**
   serotina ..................**496**
   triflora ..................**508**
   virginiana ...............**498**
Pseudotsuga:
   *Douglasii* .................368
   *mucronata* ................368
   taxifolia .................**368**
Pyrus:
   americana .................**488**
   Aucuparia ................**488**
   communis .................**484**
   *Cydonia* ..................490
   Malus ....................**486**
   sitchensis ................**488**
*Quaking Aspen* .............**388**
*Quercitron* ..................452
Quercus ....................**337**
   *acuminata* ................440
   alba .....................**432**
   bicolor ...................**438**
   coccinea ..................**450**
   *var. tinctoria* ...........452
   ilicifolia .................**454**
   Key to Species ............**338**
   macrocarpa ...............**436**
   *minor* ...................434
   Muhlenbergii .............**440**
   *nana* ....................454
   *obtusiloba* ...............434
   palustris .................**448**
   *platanoides* ..............438
   prinoides .................**442**
   var rufescens .............**442**
   Prinus ...................**444**
   *pumila* ..................454
   rubra ....................**446**
   stellata ..................**434**
   *tinctoria* ................452
   velutina ..................**452**
Quince .....................**490**
Red Ash ....................**558**
   Birch .................416, **418**

Red Cedar ..........374, 378, **380**
   *Elm* ......................456
   *Fir* ......................368
   *Gum* .....................480
   *Juniper* ..................380
   Maple 323, 324, 325, 536, 538, **540**
   Mulberry ............**466,** 468
   Oak ......430, 444, **446,** 450, 452
   Pine .........344, 346, **350,** 352
   *Plum* .....................506
   Spruce ......358, **360,** 362, 370
Redbud ....................**518**
Rhus .......................**341**
   copallina .................**526**
   glabra ...................**526**
   *hirta* ....................526
   Key to Species ............341
   Toxicodendron ...........**528**
   typhina ..................**526**
   *venenata* ................528
   Vernix ...................**528**
*River Ash* ..................**558**
   *Birch* ....................418
   *Maple* ...................538
Robinia:
   hispida ..................**522**
   Pseudo-Acacia ...........**522**
   viscosa ..................**522**
*Rock Chestnut Oak* .........444
   *Elm* .....................462
   *Maple* ...................536
   *Oak* .....................444
*Rowan Tree* ................488
*Rum Cherry* ................496
*Salisburia adiantifolia* ........382
Salix:
   alba .....................**384**
   var. vitellina ............**384**
   babylonica ...............**384**
   nigra ....................**384**
   *vitellina* ................384
Sassafras ..............318, **476**
   *officinale* ................476
   *Sassafras* ................476
   variifolium ...............**476**
*Savin* ......................380
Scarlet Oak ....446, 448, **450,** 452
*Scotch Fir* .................354
   Pine ..................348, **354**
*Scrub Oak* .................442
   *Chestnut Oak* .............442
*Service Berry* ..............492
   *Tree* ....................488
Shad Bush .................**492**
*Shadblow* ................492
Shag-Bark Hickory ...........
 ......................... 319, **402,** 404, 406
*Shell-bark Hickory* ..........402
*Silkworm Mulberry* ..........468

*Silver Birch* ..................416
   Maple ......325, 536, **538,** 540
   Poplar ..........**386,** 388, 390
   *Spruce* ...................364
*Silver-leaf Poplar* ...........386
*Skunk Spruce* ...............358
Slippery Elm ......**456,** 460, 462
*Small White Birch* ...........420
Small-fruited Hickory ......**406**
Small-toothed Aspen ...........
...........324, 386, **388,** 390, 392
Smooth Alder ..............**426**
   Sumach .............524, **526**
*Soft Maple* .............538, 540
   *Pine* .....................**344**
*Sorbus americana* ...........488
Sour Cherry 316, 496, 498, 502, **504**
   *Gum* .....................554
Speckled Alder .............**426**
Spruce ....**335,** 348, 370, 372, 382
   Black ....................350
        356, 358, 360, **362,** 370, 376
   Blue .............358, 360, **364**
   *Bog* .....................362
   *Cat* .....................358
   *Colorado Blue* ..............364
   *Double* ...................362
   *Douglas* ..................368
   *Hemlock* .................372
   Key to Species .............335
   *Labrador* .................358
   Norway ..............360, **366**
   *Pine* .....................348
   Red ........358, **360,** 362, 370
   *Silver* ...................364
   *Skunk* ...................358
   *Swamp* ..................362
   *Water* ...................362
   White ................**358,** 360
Staghorn Sumach .......524, **526**
Striped Maple ..**532,** 534, 540, 552
*Sugar Berry* ................464
   Maple ......526, **536,** 540, 544
Sumach ...........**341,** 526, 528
   *Chinese* ..................524
   Dwarf ...................**526**
   Key to Species .............341
   Poison ...........318, 526, **528**
   Smooth ............524, **526**
   Staghorn .............524, **526**
   *Swamp* ..................528
*Swamp Ash* ..................560
   *Bay* .....................341
   *Hickory* ..................408
   *Maple* ...................540
   *Oak* .....................448
   *Spruce* ..................362
   *Sumach* ..................528
   White Oak ..316, 432, **438,** 442

Sweet Bay ..........**341,** 470, 472
   *Birch* ...................414
   Buckeye ...................**548**
   Cherry 316, 317, 496, 498, **502,** 504
   Gum .....................**480**
   *Locust* ...................516
Sycamore ..........319, 322, **482**
   Maple ...........540, 542, **544**
   Oriental ..................**482**
*Tacamahac* ..................392
*Tamarack* ...................356
*Thorn* ......................494
   *Apple* ...................494
   Cockspur ..................494
   *Tree* ....................516
   *White* ...................494
*Three-thorned Acacia* ........516
Thuja occidentalis ..........**376**
Tilia americana .............**550**
   Michauxii ................**550**
   vulgaris .................**550**
*Toothache Tree* ..............522
*Tree of Heaven* .............524
Tsuga canadensis ..........**372**
Tulip Tree ............472, **474**
Tupelo ........313, 316, 322, **554**
Ulmus .....................**340**
   alata ....................**462**
   americana ................**460**
   campestris ...............**458**
   fulva ....................**456**
   *glabra* ..................458
   Key to Species .............340
   *pubescens* ................**456**
   racemosa ................**462**
   *Thomasi* .................462
Umbrella Tree .........470, **472**
   *Large-leaved* ..............340
*Viburnum* ..................532
*Virgilia* ....................520
*Walnut* .....................402
   Black ..........398, **400,** 524
   White ...................398
*Water Beech* ................412
   *Elm* ....................460
   *Oak* ....................448
   *Spruce* ..................362
*Western Catalpa* ............562
   Mountain Ash ............**488**
*Weymouth Pine* .............344
*Whistlewood* ................532
White Ash .........319, 322, 327
   328, 406, 474, 542, **556,** 558, 560
   *Birch* ...............420, 422
   *Cedar* ...............374, 376
   Elm ....316, 456, 458, **460,** 462
   *Holly* ...................530
   *Locust* ...................522
   *Maple* ................538, 540

White (Continued.)
Mulberry ...............466, **468**
Oak .......................319
    **432**, 434, 436, 438, 444, 446
Oak Group 319, **338**, 432, 442, 444
Pine ....**344,** 346, 350, 354, 370
*Poplar* ....................386
Spruce ................**358,** 360
*Thorn* ....................494
*Walnut* ...................398
*White-heart Hickory* .........404
*Whitewood* ..............474, 550
Wild Black Cherry ............
...............**496,** 498, 500, 504
*Plum* ......................506
Red Cherry ......498, **500,** 504
Willow ....................... 384

Willow (Continued.)
Black .....................**384**
European Weeping ........**384**
European White ..........**384**
Yellow ...................**384**
Winged Elm .................**462**
Witch Hazel ................**478**
Witches' Brooms ............492
Yellow Birch 318, 414,**410,** 418, 422
*Locust* ...................522
*Oak* ...................440, 452
*Pine* .....................346
*Poplar* ...................474
Willow ...................**384**
Wood ....................**520**
*Yellow-barked Oak* ..........452
Zanthoxylon americanum ....**522**

A CATALOGUE OF SELECTED DOVER BOOKS
IN ALL FIELDS OF INTEREST

# A CATALOGUE OF SELECTED DOVER BOOKS
## IN ALL FIELDS OF INTEREST

AMERICA'S OLD MASTERS, James T. Flexner. Four men emerged unexpectedly from provincial 18th century America to leadership in European art: Benjamin West, J. S. Copley, C. R. Peale, Gilbert Stuart. Brilliant coverage of lives and contributions. Revised, 1967 edition. 69 plates. 365pp. of text.

21806-6 Paperbound $3.00

FIRST FLOWERS OF OUR WILDERNESS: AMERICAN PAINTING, THE COLONIAL PERIOD, James T. Flexner. Painters, and regional painting traditions from earliest Colonial times up to the emergence of Copley, West and Peale Sr., Foster, Gustavus Hesselius, Feke, John Smibert and many anonymous painters in the primitive manner. Engaging presentation, with 162 illustrations. xxii + 368pp.

22180-6 Paperbound $3.50

THE LIGHT OF DISTANT SKIES: AMERICAN PAINTING, 1760-1835, James T. Flexner. The great generation of early American painters goes to Europe to learn and to teach: West, Copley, Gilbert Stuart and others. Allston, Trumbull, Morse; also contemporary American painters—primitives, derivatives, academics—who remained in America. 102 illustrations. xiii + 306pp.

22179-2 Paperbound $3.00

A HISTORY OF THE RISE AND PROGRESS OF THE ARTS OF DESIGN IN THE UNITED STATES, William Dunlap. Much the richest mine of information on early American painters, sculptors, architects, engravers, miniaturists, etc. The only source of information for scores of artists, the major primary source for many others. Unabridged reprint of rare original 1834 edition, with new introduction by James T. Flexner, and 394 new illustrations. Edited by Rita Weiss. 6⅝ x 9⅝.

21695-0, 21696-9, 21697-7 Three volumes, Paperbound $13.50

EPOCHS OF CHINESE AND JAPANESE ART, Ernest F. Fenollosa. From primitive Chinese art to the 20th century, thorough history, explanation of every important art period and form, including Japanese woodcuts; main stress on China and Japan, but Tibet, Korea also included. Still unexcelled for its detailed, rich coverage of cultural background, aesthetic elements, diffusion studies, particularly of the historical period. 2nd, 1913 edition. 242 illustrations. lii + 439pp. of text.

20364-6, 20365-4 Two volumes, Paperbound $6.00

THE GENTLE ART OF MAKING ENEMIES, James A. M. Whistler. Greatest wit of his day deflates Oscar Wilde, Ruskin, Swinburne; strikes back at inane critics, exhibitions, art journalism; aesthetics of impressionist revolution in most striking form. Highly readable classic by great painter. Reproduction of edition designed by Whistler. Introduction by Alfred Werner. xxxvi + 334pp.

21875-9 Paperbound $2.50

VISUAL ILLUSIONS: THEIR CAUSES, CHARACTERISTICS, AND APPLICATIONS, Matthew Luckiesh. Thorough description and discussion of optical illusion, geometric and perspective, particularly; size and shape distortions, illusions of color, of motion; natural illusions; use of illusion in art and magic, industry, etc. Most useful today with op art, also for classical art. Scores of effects illustrated. Introduction by William H. Ittleson. 100 illustrations. xxi + 252pp.

21530-X Paperbound $2.00

A HANDBOOK OF ANATOMY FOR ART STUDENTS, Arthur Thomson. Thorough, virtually exhaustive coverage of skeletal structure, musculature, etc. Full text, supplemented by anatomical diagrams and drawings and by photographs of undraped figures. Unique in its comparison of male and female forms, pointing out differences of contour, texture, form. 211 figures, 40 drawings, 86 photographs. xx + 459pp. 5⅜ x 8⅜.

21163-0 Paperbound $3.50

150 MASTERPIECES OF DRAWING, Selected by Anthony Toney. Full page reproductions of drawings from the early 16th to the end of the 18th century, all beautifully reproduced: Rembrandt, Michelangelo, Dürer, Fragonard, Urs, Graf, Wouwerman, many others. First-rate browsing book, model book for artists. xviii + 150pp. 8⅜ x 11¼.

21032-4 Paperbound $2.50

THE LATER WORK OF AUBREY BEARDSLEY, Aubrey Beardsley. Exotic, erotic, ironic masterpieces in full maturity: Comedy Ballet, Venus and Tannhauser, Pierrot, Lysistrata, Rape of the Lock, Savoy material, Ali Baba, Volpone, etc. This material revolutionized the art world, and is still powerful, fresh, brilliant. With *The Early Work,* all Beardsley's finest work. 174 plates, 2 in color. xiv + 176pp. 8⅛ x 11.

21817-1 Paperbound $3.00

DRAWINGS OF REMBRANDT, Rembrandt van Rijn. Complete reproduction of fabulously rare edition by Lippmann and Hofstede de Groot, completely reedited, updated, improved by Prof. Seymour Slive, Fogg Museum. Portraits, Biblical sketches, landscapes, Oriental types, nudes, episodes from classical mythology—All Rembrandt's fertile genius. Also selection of drawings by his pupils and followers. "Stunning volumes," *Saturday Review.* 550 illustrations. lxxviii + 552pp. 9⅛ x 12¼.

21485-0, 21486-9 Two volumes, Paperbound $10.00

THE DISASTERS OF WAR, Francisco Goya. One of the masterpieces of Western civilization—83 etchings that record Goya's shattering, bitter reaction to the Napoleonic war that swept through Spain after the insurrection of 1808 and to war in general. Reprint of the first edition, with three additional plates from Boston's Museum of Fine Arts. All plates facsimile size. Introduction by Philip Hofer, Fogg Museum. v + 97pp. 9⅜ x 8¼.

21872-4 Paperbound $2.00

GRAPHIC WORKS OF ODILON REDON. Largest collection of Redon's graphic works ever assembled: 172 lithographs, 28 etchings and engravings, 9 drawings. These include some of his most famous works. All the plates from *Odilon Redon: oeuvre graphique complet,* plus additional plates. New introduction and caption translations by Alfred Werner. 209 illustrations. xxvii + 209pp. 9⅛ x 12¼.

21966-8 Paperbound $4.00

DESIGN BY ACCIDENT; A BOOK OF "ACCIDENTAL EFFECTS" FOR ARTISTS AND DESIGNERS, James F. O'Brien. Create your own unique, striking, imaginative effects by "controlled accident" interaction of materials: paints and lacquers, oil and water based paints, splatter, crackling materials, shatter, similar items. Everything you do will be different; first book on this limitless art, so useful to both fine artist and commercial artist. Full instructions. 192 plates showing "accidents," 8 in color. viii + 215pp. 8⅜ x 11¼. 21942-9 Paperbound $3.50

THE BOOK OF SIGNS, Rudolf Koch. Famed German type designer draws 493 beautiful symbols: religious, mystical, alchemical, imperial, property marks, runes, etc. Remarkable fusion of traditional and modern. Good for suggestions of timelessness, smartness, modernity. Text. vi + 104pp. 6⅛ x 9¼. 20162-7 Paperbound $1.25

HISTORY OF INDIAN AND INDONESIAN ART, Ananda K. Coomaraswamy. An unabridged republication of one of the finest books by a great scholar in Eastern art. Rich in descriptive material, history, social backgrounds; Sunga reliefs, Rajput paintings, Gupta temples, Burmese frescoes, textiles, jewelry, sculpture, etc. 400 photos. viii + 423pp. 6⅜ x 9¾. 21436-2 Paperbound $4.00

PRIMITIVE ART, Franz Boas. America's foremost anthropologist surveys textiles, ceramics, woodcarving, basketry, metalwork, etc.; patterns, technology, creation of symbols, style origins. All areas of world, but very full on Northwest Coast Indians. More than 350 illustrations of baskets, boxes, totem poles, weapons, etc. 378 pp. 20025-6 Paperbound $3.00

THE GENTLEMAN AND CABINET MAKER'S DIRECTOR, Thomas Chippendale. Full reprint (third edition, 1762) of most influential furniture book of all time, by master cabinetmaker. 200 plates, illustrating chairs, sofas, mirrors, tables, cabinets, plus 24 photographs of surviving pieces. Biographical introduction by N. Bienenstock. vi + 249pp. 9⅞ x 12¾. 21601-2 Paperbound $4.00

AMERICAN ANTIQUE FURNITURE, Edgar G. Miller, Jr. The basic coverage of all American furniture before 1840. Individual chapters cover type of furniture—clocks, tables, sideboards, etc.—chronologically, with inexhaustible wealth of data. More than 2100 photographs, all identified, commented on. Essential to all early American collectors. Introduction by H. E. Keyes. vi + 1106pp. 7⅞ x 10¾. 21599-7, 21600-4 Two volumes, Paperbound $11.00

PENNSYLVANIA DUTCH AMERICAN FOLK ART, Henry J. Kauffman. 279 photos, 28 drawings of tulipware, Fraktur script, painted tinware, toys, flowered furniture, quilts, samplers, hex signs, house interiors, etc. Full descriptive text. Excellent for tourist, rewarding for designer, collector. Map. 146pp. 7⅞ x 10¾. 21205-X Paperbound $2.50

EARLY NEW ENGLAND GRAVESTONE RUBBINGS, Edmund V. Gillon, Jr. 43 photographs, 226 carefully reproduced rubbings show heavily symbolic, sometimes macabre early gravestones, up to early 19th century. Remarkable early American primitive art, occasionally strikingly beautiful; always powerful. Text. xxvi + 207pp. 8⅜ x 11¼. 21380-3 Paperbound $3.50

ALPHABETS AND ORNAMENTS, Ernst Lehner. Well-known pictorial source for decorative alphabets, script examples, cartouches, frames, decorative title pages, calligraphic initials, borders, similar material. 14th to 19th century, mostly European. Useful in almost any graphic arts designing, varied styles. 750 illustrations. 256pp. 7 x 10. 21905-4 Paperbound $4.00

PAINTING: A CREATIVE APPROACH, Norman Colquhoun. For the beginner simple guide provides an instructive approach to painting: major stumbling blocks for beginner; overcoming them, technical points; paints and pigments; oil painting; watercolor and other media and color. New section on "plastic" paints. Glossary. Formerly Paint Your Own Pictures. 221pp. 22000-1 Paperbound $1.75

THE ENJOYMENT AND USE OF COLOR, Walter Sargent. Explanation of the relations between colors themselves and between colors in nature and art, including hundreds of little-known facts about color values, intensities, effects of high and low illumination, complementary colors. Many practical hints for painters, references to great masters. 7 color plates, 29 illustrations. x + 274pp. 20944-X Paperbound $2.75

THE NOTEBOOKS OF LEONARDO DA VINCI, compiled and edited by Jean Paul Richter. 1566 extracts from original manuscripts reveal the full range of Leonardo's versatile genius: all his writings on painting, sculpture, architecture, anatomy, astronomy, geography, topography, physiology, mining, music, etc., in both Italian and English, with 186 plates of manuscript pages and more than 500 additional drawings. Includes studies for the Last Supper, the lost Sforza monument, and other works. Total of xlvii + 866pp. 7⅞ x 10¾. 22572-0, 22573-9 Two volumes, Paperbound $10.00

MONTGOMERY WARD CATALOGUE OF 1895. Tea gowns, yards of flannel and pillow-case lace, stereoscopes, books of gospel hymns, the New Improved Singer Sewing Machine, side saddles, milk skimmers, straight-edged razors, high-button shoes, spittoons, and on and on . . . listing some 25,000 items, practically all illustrated. Essential to the shoppers of the 1890's, it is our truest record of the spirit of the period. Unaltered reprint of Issue No. 57, Spring and Summer 1895. Introduction by Boris Emmet. Innumerable illustrations. xiii + 624pp. 8½ x 11⅝. 22377-9 Paperbound $6.95

THE CRYSTAL PALACE EXHIBITION ILLUSTRATED CATALOGUE (LONDON, 1851). One of the wonders of the modern world—the Crystal Palace Exhibition in which all the nations of the civilized world exhibited their achievements in the arts and sciences—presented in an equally important illustrated catalogue. More than 1700 items pictured with accompanying text—ceramics, textiles, cast-iron work, carpets, pianos, sleds, razors, wall-papers, billiard tables, beehives, silverware and hundreds of other artifacts—represent the focal point of Victorian culture in the Western World. Probably the largest collection of Victorian decorative art ever assembled—indispensable for antiquarians and designers. Unabridged republication of the Art-Journal Catalogue of the Great Exhibition of 1851, with all terminal essays. New introduction by John Gloag, F.S.A. xxxiv + 426pp. 9 x 12. 22503-8 Paperbound $4.50

A History of Costume, Carl Köhler. Definitive history, based on surviving pieces of clothing primarily, and paintings, statues, etc. secondarily. Highly readable text, supplemented by 594 illustrations of costumes of the ancient Mediterranean peoples, Greece and Rome, the Teutonic prehistoric period; costumes of the Middle Ages, Renaissance, Baroque, 18th and 19th centuries. Clear, measured patterns are provided for many clothing articles. Approach is practical throughout. Enlarged by Emma von Sichart. 464pp.                                    21030-8 Paperbound $3.50

Oriental Rugs, Antique and Modern, Walter A. Hawley. A complete and authoritative treatise on the Oriental rug—where they are made, by whom and how, designs and symbols, characteristics in detail of the six major groups, how to distinguish them and how to buy them. Detailed technical data is provided on periods, weaves, warps, wefts, textures, sides, ends and knots, although no technical background is required for an understanding. 11 color plates, 80 halftones, 4 maps. vi + 320pp. 6⅛ x 9⅛.                                              22366-3 Paperbound $5.00

Ten Books on Architecture, Vitruvius. By any standards the most important book on architecture ever written. Early Roman discussion of aesthetics of building, construction methods, orders, sites, and every other aspect of architecture has inspired, instructed architecture for about 2,000 years. Stands behind Palladio, Michelangelo, Bramante, Wren, countless others. Definitive Morris H. Morgan translation. 68 illustrations. xii + 331pp.                    20645-9 Paperbound $3.50

The Four Books of Architecture, Andrea Palladio. Translated into every major Western European language in the two centuries following its publication in 1570, this has been one of the most influential books in the history of architecture. Complete reprint of the 1738 Isaac Ware edition. New introduction by Adolf Placzek, Columbia Univ. 216 plates. xxii + 110pp. of text. 9½ x 12¾.
21308-0 Clothbound $10.00

Sticks and Stones: A Study of American Architecture and Civilization, Lewis Mumford.One of the great classics of American cultural history. American architecture from the medieval-inspired earliest forms to the early 20th century; evolution of structure and style, and reciprocal influences on environment. 21 photographic illustrations. 238pp.                                    20202-X Paperbound $2.00

The American Builder's Companion, Asher Benjamin. The most widely used early 19th century architectural style and source book, for colonial up into Greek Revival periods. Extensive development of geometry of carpentering, construction of sashes, frames, doors, stairs; plans and elevations of domestic and other buildings. Hundreds of thousands of houses were built according to this book, now invaluable to historians, architects, restorers, etc. 1827 edition. 59 plates. 114pp. 7⅞ x 10¾.
22236-5 Paperbound $3.50

Dutch Houses in the Hudson Valley Before 1776, Helen Wilkinson Reynolds. The standard survey of the Dutch colonial house and outbuildings, with constructional features, decoration, and local history associated with individual homesteads. Introduction by Franklin D. Roosevelt. Map. 150 illustrations. 469pp. 6⅝ x 9¼.                                              21469-9 Paperbound $4.00

THE ARCHITECTURE OF COUNTRY HOUSES, Andrew J. Downing. Together with Vaux's *Villas and Cottages* this is the basic book for Hudson River Gothic architecture of the middle Victorian period. Full, sound discussions of general aspects of housing, architecture, style, decoration, furnishing, together with scores of detailed house plans, illustrations of specific buildings, accompanied by full text. Perhaps the most influential single American architectural book. 1850 edition. Introduction by J. Stewart Johnson. 321 figures, 34 architectural designs. xvi + 560pp.

22003-6 Paperbound $4.00

LOST EXAMPLES OF COLONIAL ARCHITECTURE, John Mead Howells. Full-page photographs of buildings that have disappeared or been so altered as to be denatured, including many designed by major early American architects. 245 plates. xvii + 248pp. 7⅞ x 10¾. 21143-6 Paperbound $3.50

DOMESTIC ARCHITECTURE OF THE AMERICAN COLONIES AND OF THE EARLY REPUBLIC, Fiske Kimball. Foremost architect and restorer of Williamsburg and Monticello covers nearly 200 homes between 1620-1825. Architectural details, construction, style features, special fixtures, floor plans, etc. Generally considered finest work in its area. 219 illustrations of houses, doorways, windows, capital mantels. xx + 314pp. 7⅞ x 10¾. 21743-4 Paperbound $4.00

EARLY AMERICAN ROOMS: 1650-1858, edited by Russell Hawes Kettell. Tour of 12 rooms, each representative of a different era in American history and each furnished, decorated, designed and occupied in the style of the era. 72 plans and elevations, 8-page color section, etc., show fabrics, wall papers, arrangements, etc. Full descriptive text. xvii + 200pp. of text. 8⅜ x 11¼.

21633-0 Paperbound $5.00

THE FITZWILLIAM VIRGINAL BOOK, edited by J. Fuller Maitland and W. B. Squire. Full modern printing of famous early 17th-century ms. volume of 300 works by Morley, Byrd, Bull, Gibbons, etc. For piano or other modern keyboard instrument; easy to read format. xxxvi + 938pp. 8⅜ x 11.

21068-5, 21069-3 Two volumes, Paperbound $10.00

KEYBOARD MUSIC, Johann Sebastian Bach. Bach Gesellschaft edition. A rich selection of Bach's masterpieces for the harpsichord: the six English Suites, six French Suites, the six Partitas (Clavierübung part I), the Goldberg Variations (Clavierübung part IV), the fifteen Two-Part Inventions and the fifteen Three-Part Sinfonias. Clearly reproduced on large sheets with ample margins; eminently playable. vi + 312pp. 8⅛ x 11. 22360-4 Paperbound $5.00

THE MUSIC OF BACH: AN INTRODUCTION, Charles Sanford Terry. A fine, nontechnical introduction to Bach's music, both instrumental and vocal. Covers organ music, chamber music, passion music, other types. Analyzes themes, developments, innovations. x + 114pp. 21075-8 Paperbound $1.25

BEETHOVEN AND HIS NINE SYMPHONIES, Sir George Grove. Noted British musicologist provides best history, analysis, commentary on symphonies. Very thorough, rigorously accurate; necessary to both advanced student and amateur music lover. 436 musical passages. vii + 407 pp. 20334-4 Paperbound $2.75

JOHANN SEBASTIAN BACH, Philipp Spitta. One of the great classics of musicology, this definitive analysis of Bach's music (and life) has never been surpassed. Lucid, nontechnical analyses of hundreds of pieces (30 pages devoted to St. Matthew Passion, 26 to B Minor Mass). Also includes major analysis of 18th-century music. 450 musical examples. 40-page musical supplement. Total of xx + 1799pp.
(EUK) 22278-0, 22279-9 Two volumes, Clothbound $17.50

MOZART AND HIS PIANO CONCERTOS, Cuthbert Girdlestone. The only full-length study of an important area of Mozart's creativity. Provides detailed analyses of all 23 concertos, traces inspirational sources. 417 musical examples. Second edition. 509pp.
(USO) 21271-8 Paperbound $3.50

THE PERFECT WAGNERITE: A COMMENTARY ON THE NIBLUNG'S RING, George Bernard Shaw. Brilliant and still relevant criticism in remarkable essays on Wagner's Ring cycle, Shaw's ideas on political and social ideology behind the plots, role of Leitmotifs, vocal requisites, etc. Prefaces. xxi + 136pp.
21707-8 Paperbound $1.50

DON GIOVANNI, W. A. Mozart. Complete libretto, modern English translation; biographies of composer and librettist; accounts of early performances and critical reaction. Lavishly illustrated. All the material you need to understand and appreciate this great work. Dover Opera Guide and Libretto Series; translated and introduced by Ellen Bleiler. 92 illustrations. 209pp.
21134-7 Paperbound $2.00

HIGH FIDELITY SYSTEMS: A LAYMAN'S GUIDE, Roy F. Allison. All the basic information you need for setting up your own audio system: high fidelity and stereo record players, tape records, F.M. Connections, adjusting tone arm, cartridge, checking needle alignment, positioning speakers, phasing speakers, adjusting hums, trouble-shooting, maintenance, and similar topics. Enlarged 1965 edition. More than 50 charts, diagrams, photos. iv + 91pp.
21514-8 Paperbound $1.25

REPRODUCTION OF SOUND, Edgar Villchur. Thorough coverage for laymen of high fidelity systems, reproducing systems in general, needles, amplifiers, preamps, loudspeakers, feedback, explaining physical background. "A rare talent for making technicalities vividly comprehensible," R. Darrell, *High Fidelity.* 69 figures. iv + 92pp.
21515-6 Paperbound $1.25

HEAR ME TALKIN' TO YA: THE STORY OF JAZZ AS TOLD BY THE MEN WHO MADE IT, Nat Shapiro and Nat Hentoff. Louis Armstrong, Fats Waller, Jo Jones, Clarence Williams, Billy Holiday, Duke Ellington, Jelly Roll Morton and dozens of other jazz greats tell how it was in Chicago's South Side, New Orleans, depression Harlem and the modern West Coast as jazz was born and grew. xvi + 429pp.
21726-4 Paperbound $2.50

FABLES OF AESOP, translated by Sir Roger L'Estrange. A reproduction of the very rare 1931 Paris edition; a selection of the most interesting fables, together with 50 imaginative drawings by Alexander Calder. v + 128pp. 6½x9¼.
21780-9 Paperbound $1.50

AGAINST THE GRAIN (A REBOURS), Joris K. Huysmans. Filled with weird images, evidences of a bizarre imagination, exotic experiments with hallucinatory drugs, rich tastes and smells and the diversions of its sybarite hero Duc Jean des Esseintes, this classic novel pushed 19th-century literary decadence to its limits. Full unabridged edition. Do not confuse this with abridged editions generally sold. Introduction by Havelock Ellis. xlix + 206pp.  22190-3 Paperbound $2.00

VARIORUM SHAKESPEARE: HAMLET. Edited by Horace H. Furness; a landmark of American scholarship. Exhaustive footnotes and appendices treat all doubtful words and phrases, as well as suggested critical emendations throughout the play's history. First volume contains editor's own text, collated with all Quartos and Folios. Second volume contains full first Quarto, translations of Shakespeare's sources (Belleforest, and Saxo Grammaticus), Der Bestrafte Brudermord, and many essays on critical and historical points of interest by major authorities of past and present. Includes details of staging and costuming over the years. By far the best edition available for serious students of Shakespeare. Total of xx + 905pp.
21004-9, 21005-7, 2 volumes, Paperbound $7.00

A LIFE OF WILLIAM SHAKESPEARE, Sir Sidney Lee. This is the standard life of Shakespeare, summarizing everything known about Shakespeare and his plays. Incredibly rich in material, broad in coverage, clear and judicious, it has served thousands as the best introduction to Shakespeare. 1931 edition. 9 plates. xxix + 792pp.  (USO) 21967-4 Paperbound $3.75

MASTERS OF THE DRAMA, John Gassner. Most comprehensive history of the drama in print, covering every tradition from Greeks to modern Europe and America, including India, Far East, etc. Covers more than 800 dramatists, 2000 plays, with biographical material, plot summaries, theatre history, criticism, etc. "Best of its kind in English," New Republic. 77 illustrations. xxii + 890pp.
20100-7 Clothbound $8.50

THE EVOLUTION OF THE ENGLISH LANGUAGE, George McKnight. The growth of English, from the 14th century to the present. Unusual, non-technical account presents basic information in very interesting form: sound shifts, change in grammar and syntax, vocabulary growth, similar topics. Abundantly illustrated with quotations. Formerly Modern English in the Making. xii + 590pp.
21932-1 Paperbound $3.50

AN ETYMOLOGICAL DICTIONARY OF MODERN ENGLISH, Ernest Weekley. Fullest, richest work of its sort, by foremost British lexicographer. Detailed word histories, including many colloquial and archaic words; extensive quotations. Do not confuse this with the Concise Etymological Dictionary, which is much abridged. Total of xxvii + 830pp. 6½ x 9¼.
21873-2, 21874-0 Two volumes, Paperbound $6.00

FLATLAND: A ROMANCE OF MANY DIMENSIONS, E. A. Abbott. Classic of science-fiction explores ramifications of life in a two-dimensional world, and what happens when a three-dimensional being intrudes. Amusing reading, but also useful as introduction to thought about hyperspace. Introduction by Banesh Hoffmann. 16 illustrations. xx + 103pp.  20001-9 Paperbound $1.00

POEMS OF ANNE BRADSTREET, edited with an introduction by Robert Hutchinson. A new selection of poems by America's first poet and perhaps the first significant woman poet in the English language. 48 poems display her development in works of considerable variety—love poems, domestic poems, religious meditations, formal elegies, "quaternions," etc. Notes, bibliography. viii + 222pp.
22160-1 Paperbound $2.00

THREE GOTHIC NOVELS: THE CASTLE OF OTRANTO BY HORACE WALPOLE; VATHEK BY WILLIAM BECKFORD; THE VAMPYRE BY JOHN POLIDORI, WITH FRAGMENT OF A NOVEL BY LORD BYRON, edited by E. F. Bleiler. The first Gothic novel, by Walpole; the finest Oriental tale in English, by Beckford; powerful Romantic supernatural story in versions by Polidori and Byron. All extremely important in history of literature; all still exciting, packed with supernatural thrills, ghosts, haunted castles, magic, etc. xl + 291pp.
21232-7 Paperbound $2.50

THE BEST TALES OF HOFFMANN, E. T. A. Hoffmann. 10 of Hoffmann's most important stories, in modern re-editings of standard translations: Nutcracker and the King of Mice, Signor Formica, Automata, The Sandman, Rath Krespel, The Golden Flowerpot, Master Martin the Cooper, The Mines of Falun, The King's Betrothed, A New Year's Eve Adventure. 7 illustrations by Hoffmann. Edited by E. F. Bleiler. xxxix + 419pp.
21793-0 Paperbound $3.00

GHOST AND HORROR STORIES OF AMBROSE BIERCE, Ambrose Bierce. 23 strikingly modern stories of the horrors latent in the human mind: The Eyes of the Panther, The Damned Thing, An Occurrence at Owl Creek Bridge, An Inhabitant of Carcosa, etc., plus the dream-essay, Visions of the Night. Edited by E. F. Bleiler. xxii + 199pp.
20767-6 Paperbound $1.50

BEST GHOST STORIES OF J. S. LEFANU, J. Sheridan LeFanu. Finest stories by Victorian master often considered greatest supernatural writer of all. Carmilla, Green Tea, The Haunted Baronet, The Familiar, and 12 others. Most never before available in the U. S. A. Edited by E. F. Bleiler. 8 illustrations from Victorian publications. xvii + 467pp.
20415-4 Paperbound $3.00

MATHEMATICAL FOUNDATIONS OF INFORMATION THEORY, A. I. Khinchin. Comprehensive introduction to work of Shannon, McMillan, Feinstein and Khinchin, placing these investigations on a rigorous mathematical basis. Covers entropy concept in probability theory, uniqueness theorem, Shannon's inequality, ergodic sources, the E property, martingale concept, noise, Feinstein's fundamental lemma, Shanon's first and second theorems. Translated by R. A. Silverman and M. D. Friedman. iii + 120pp.
60434-9 Paperbound $1.75

SEVEN SCIENCE FICTION NOVELS, H. G. Wells. The standard collection of the great novels. Complete, unabridged. *First Men in the Moon, Island of Dr. Moreau, War of the Worlds, Food of the Gods, Invisible Man, Time Machine, In the Days of the Comet.* Not only science fiction fans, but every educated person owes it to himself to read these novels. 1015pp.
20264-X Clothbound $5.00

LAST AND FIRST MEN AND STAR MAKER, TWO SCIENCE FICTION NOVELS, Olaf Stapledon. Greatest future histories in science fiction. In the first, human intelligence is the "hero," through strange paths of evolution, interplanetary invasions, incredible technologies, near extinctions and reemergences. Star Maker describes the quest of a band of star rovers for intelligence itself, through time and space: weird inhuman civilizations, crustacean minds, symbiotic worlds, etc. Complete, unabridged. v + 438pp. 21962-3 Paperbound $2.50

THREE PROPHETIC NOVELS, H. G. WELLS. Stages of a consistently planned future for mankind. *When the Sleeper Wakes,* and *A Story of the Days to Come,* anticipate *Brave New World* and *1984,* in the 21st Century; *The Time Machine,* only complete version in print, shows farther future and the end of mankind. All show Wells's greatest gifts as storyteller and novelist. Edited by E. F. Bleiler. x + 335pp. (USO) 20605-X Paperbound $2.50

THE DEVIL'S DICTIONARY, Ambrose Bierce. America's own Oscar Wilde— Ambrose Bierce—offers his barbed iconoclastic wisdom in over 1,000 definitions hailed by H. L. Mencken as "some of the most gorgeous witticisms in the English language." 145pp. 20487-1 Paperbound $1.25

MAX AND MORITZ, Wilhelm Busch. Great children's classic, father of comic strip, of two bad boys, Max and Moritz. Also Ker and Plunk (Plisch und Plumm), Cat and Mouse, Deceitful Henry, Ice-Peter, The Boy and the Pipe, and five other pieces. Original German, with English translation. Edited by H. Arthur Klein; translations by various hands and H. Arthur Klein. vi + 216pp. 20181-3 Paperbound $2.00

PIGS IS PIGS AND OTHER FAVORITES, Ellis Parker Butler. The title story is one of the best humor short stories, as Mike Flannery obfuscates biology and English. Also included, That Pup of Murchison's, The Great American Pie Company, and Perkins of Portland. 14 illustrations. v + 109pp. 21532-6 Paperbound $1.25

THE PETERKIN PAPERS, Lucretia P. Hale. It takes genius to be as stupidly mad as the Peterkins, as they decide to become wise, celebrate the "Fourth," keep a cow, and otherwise strain the resources of the Lady from Philadelphia. Basic book of American humor. 153 illustrations. 219pp. 20794-3 Paperbound $1.50

PERRAULT'S FAIRY TALES, translated by A. E. Johnson and S. R. Littlewood, with 34 full-page illustrations by Gustave Doré. All the original Perrault stories— Cinderella, Sleeping Beauty, Bluebeard, Little Red Riding Hood, Puss in Boots, Tom Thumb, etc.—with their witty verse morals and the magnificent illustrations of Doré. One of the five or six great books of European fairy tales. viii + 117pp. 8⅛ x 11. 22311-6 Paperbound $2.00

OLD HUNGARIAN FAIRY TALES, Baroness Orczy. Favorites translated and adapted by author of the *Scarlet Pimpernel.* Eight fairy tales include "The Suitors of Princess Fire-Fly," "The Twin Hunchbacks," "Mr. Cuttlefish's Love Story," and "The Enchanted Cat." This little volume of magic and adventure will captivate children as it has for generations. 90 drawings by Montagu Barstow. 96pp. (USO) 22293-4 Paperbound $1.95

THE RED FAIRY BOOK, Andrew Lang. Lang's color fairy books have long been children's favorites. This volume includes Rapunzel, Jack and the Bean-stalk and 35 other stories, familiar and unfamiliar. 4 plates, 93 illustrations x + 367pp.
21673-X Paperbound $2.50

THE BLUE FAIRY BOOK, Andrew Lang. Lang's tales come from all countries and all times. Here are 37 tales from Grimm, the Arabian Nights, Greek Mythology, and other fascinating sources. 8 plates, 130 illustrations. xi + 390pp.
21437-0 Paperbound $2.50

HOUSEHOLD STORIES BY THE BROTHERS GRIMM. Classic English-language edition of the well-known tales — Rumpelstiltskin, Snow White, Hansel and Gretel, The Twelve Brothers, Faithful John, Rapunzel, Tom Thumb (52 stories in all). Translated into simple, straightforward English by Lucy Crane. Ornamented with headpieces, vignettes, elaborate decorative initials and a dozen full-page illustrations by Walter Crane. x + 269pp.
21080-4 Paperbound $2.50

THE MERRY ADVENTURES OF ROBIN HOOD, Howard Pyle. The finest modern versions of the traditional ballads and tales about the great English outlaw. Howard Pyle's complete prose version, with every word, every illustration of the first edition. Do not confuse this facsimile of the original (1883) with modern editions that change text or illustrations. 23 plates plus many page decorations. xxii + 296pp.
22043-5 Paperbound $2.50

THE STORY OF KING ARTHUR AND HIS KNIGHTS, Howard Pyle. The finest children's version of the life of King Arthur; brilliantly retold by Pyle, with 48 of his most imaginative illustrations. xviii + 313pp. 6⅛ x 9¼.
21445-1 Paperbound $2.50

THE WONDERFUL WIZARD OF OZ, L. Frank Baum. America's finest children's book in facsimile of first edition with all Denslow illustrations in full color. The edition a child should have. Introduction by Martin Gardner. 23 color plates, scores of drawings. iv + 267pp.
20691-2 Paperbound $2.50

THE MARVELOUS LAND OF OZ, L. Frank Baum. The second Oz book, every bit as imaginative as the Wizard. The hero is a boy named Tip, but the Scarecrow and the Tin Woodman are back, as is the Oz magic. 16 color plates, 120 drawings by John R. Neill. 287pp.
20692-0 Paperbound $2.50

THE MAGICAL MONARCH OF MO, L. Frank Baum. Remarkable adventures in a land even stranger than Oz. The best of Baum's books not in the Oz series. 15 color plates and dozens of drawings by Frank Verbeck. xviii + 237pp.
21892-9 Paperbound $2.25

THE BAD CHILD'S BOOK OF BEASTS, MORE BEASTS FOR WORSE CHILDREN, A MORAL ALPHABET, Hilaire Belloc. Three complete humor classics in one volume. Be kind to the frog, and do not call him names . . . and 28 other whimsical animals. Familiar favorites and some not so well known. Illustrated by Basil Blackwell. 156pp.
(USO) 20749-8 Paperbound $1.50

EAST O' THE SUN AND WEST O' THE MOON, George W. Dasent. Considered the best of all translations of these Norwegian folk tales, this collection has been enjoyed by generations of children (and folklorists too). Includes True and Untrue, Why the Sea is Salt, East O' the Sun and West O' the Moon, Why the Bear is Stumpy-Tailed, Boots and the Troll, The Cock and the Hen, Rich Peter the Pedlar, and 52 more. The only edition with all 59 tales. 77 illustrations by Erik Werenskiold and Theodor Kittelsen. xv + 418pp. 22521-6 Paperbound $3.50

GOOPS AND HOW TO BE THEM, Gelett Burgess. Classic of tongue-in-cheek humor, masquerading as etiquette book. 87 verses, twice as many cartoons, show mischievous Goops as they demonstrate to children virtues of table manners, neatness, courtesy, etc. Favorite for generations. viii + 88pp. 6½ x 9¼.
22233-0 Paperbound $1.25

ALICE'S ADVENTURES UNDER GROUND, Lewis Carroll. The first version, quite different from the final Alice in Wonderland, printed out by Carroll himself with his own illustrations. Complete facsimile of the "million dollar" manuscript Carroll gave to Alice Liddell in 1864. Introduction by Martin Gardner. viii + 96pp. Title and dedication pages in color. 21482-6 Paperbound $1.25

THE BROWNIES, THEIR BOOK, Palmer Cox. Small as mice, cunning as foxes, exuberant and full of mischief, the Brownies go to the zoo, toy shop, seashore, circus, etc., in 24 verse adventures and 266 illustrations. Long a favorite, since their first appearance in St. Nicholas Magazine. xi + 144pp. 6⅝ x 9¼.
21265-3 Paperbound $1.75

SONGS OF CHILDHOOD, Walter De La Mare. Published (under the pseudonym Walter Ramal) when De La Mare was only 29, this charming collection has long been a favorite children's book. A facsimile of the first edition in paper, the 47 poems capture the simplicity of the nursery rhyme and the ballad, including such lyrics as I Met Eve, Tartary, The Silver Penny. vii + 106pp. 21972-0 Paperbound $1.25

THE COMPLETE NONSENSE OF EDWARD LEAR, Edward Lear. The finest 19th-century humorist-cartoonist in full: all nonsense limericks, zany alphabets, Owl and Pussycat, songs, nonsense botany, and more than 500 illustrations by Lear himself. Edited by Holbrook Jackson. xxix + 287pp. (USO) 20167-8 Paperbound $2.00

BILLY WHISKERS: THE AUTOBIOGRAPHY OF A GOAT, Frances Trego Montgomery. A favorite of children since the early 20th century, here are the escapades of that rambunctious, irresistible and mischievous goat—Billy Whiskers. Much in the spirit of Peck's Bad Boy, this is a book that children never tire of reading or hearing. All the original familiar illustrations by W. H. Fry are included: 6 color plates, 18 black and white drawings. 159pp. 22345-0 Paperbound $2.00

MOTHER GOOSE MELODIES. Faithful republication of the fabulously rare Munroe and Francis "copyright 1833" Boston edition—the most important Mother Goose collection, usually referred to as the "original." Familiar rhymes plus many rare ones, with wonderful old woodcut illustrations. Edited by E. F. Bleiler. 128pp. 4½ x 6⅜. 22577-1 Paperbound $1.25

TWO LITTLE SAVAGES; BEING THE ADVENTURES OF TWO BOYS WHO LIVED AS INDIANS AND WHAT THEY LEARNED, Ernest Thompson Seton. Great classic of nature and boyhood provides a vast range of woodlore in most palatable form, a genuinely entertaining story. Two farm boys build a teepee in woods and live in it for a month, working out Indian solutions to living problems, star lore, birds and animals, plants, etc. 293 illustrations. vii + 286pp.

20985-7 Paperbound $2.50

PETER PIPER'S PRACTICAL PRINCIPLES OF PLAIN & PERFECT PRONUNCIATION. Alliterative jingles and tongue-twisters of surprising charm, that made their first appearance in America about 1830. Republished in full with the spirited woodcut illustrations from this earliest American edition. 32pp. 4½ x 6⅜.

22560-7 Paperbound $1.00

SCIENCE EXPERIMENTS AND AMUSEMENTS FOR CHILDREN, Charles Vivian. 73 easy experiments, requiring only materials found at home or easily available, such as candles, coins, steel wool, etc.; illustrate basic phenomena like vacuum, simple chemical reaction, etc. All safe. Modern, well-planned. Formerly *Science Games for Children*. 102 photos, numerous drawings. 96pp. 6⅛ x 9¼.

21856-2 Paperbound $1.25

AN INTRODUCTION TO CHESS MOVES AND TACTICS SIMPLY EXPLAINED, Leonard Barden. Informal intermediate introduction, quite strong in explaining reasons for moves. Covers basic material, tactics, important openings, traps, positional play in middle game, end game. Attempts to isolate patterns and recurrent configurations. Formerly *Chess*. 58 figures. 102pp. (USO) 21210-6 Paperbound $1.25

LASKER'S MANUAL OF CHESS, Dr. Emanuel Lasker. Lasker was not only one of the five great World Champions, he was also one of the ablest expositors, theorists, and analysts. In many ways, his Manual, permeated with his philosophy of battle, filled with keen insights, is one of the greatest works ever written on chess. Filled with analyzed games by the great players. A single-volume library that will profit almost any chess player, beginner or master. 308 diagrams. xli x 349pp.

20640-8 Paperbound $2.75

THE MASTER BOOK OF MATHEMATICAL RECREATIONS, Fred Schuh. In opinion of many the finest work ever prepared on mathematical puzzles, stunts, recreations; exhaustively thorough explanations of mathematics involved, analysis of effects, citation of puzzles and games. Mathematics involved is elementary. Translated by F. Göbel. 194 figures. xxiv + 430pp.

22134-2 Paperbound $3.00

MATHEMATICS, MAGIC AND MYSTERY, Martin Gardner. Puzzle editor for Scientific American explains mathematics behind various mystifying tricks: card tricks, stage "mind reading," coin and match tricks, counting out games, geometric dissections, etc. Probability sets, theory of numbers clearly explained. Also provides more than 400 tricks, guaranteed to work, that you can do. 135 illustrations. xii + 176pp.

20338-2 Paperbound $1.50

MATHEMATICAL PUZZLES FOR BEGINNERS AND ENTHUSIASTS, Geoffrey Mott-Smith. 189 puzzles from easy to difficult—involving arithmetic, logic, algebra, properties of digits, probability, etc.—for enjoyment and mental stimulus. Explanation of mathematical principles behind the puzzles. 135 illustrations. viii + 248pp.

20198-8 Paperbound $1.75

PAPER FOLDING FOR BEGINNERS, William D. Murray and Francis J. Rigney. Easiest book on the market, clearest instructions on making interesting, beautiful origami Sail boats, cups, roosters, frogs that move legs, bonbon boxes, standing birds, etc. 40 projects; more than 275 diagrams and photographs. 94pp.

20713-7 Paperbound $1.00

TRICKS AND GAMES ON THE POOL TABLE, Fred Herrmann. 79 tricks and games— some solitaires, some for two or more players, some competitive games—to entertain you between formal games. Mystifying shots and throws, unusual caroms, tricks involving such props as cork, coins, a hat, etc. Formerly *Fun on the Pool Table*. 77 figures. 95pp.

21814-7 Paperbound $1.00

HAND SHADOWS TO BE THROWN UPON THE WALL: A SERIES OF NOVEL AND AMUSING FIGURES FORMED BY THE HAND, Henry Bursill. Delightful picturebook from great-grandfather's day shows how to make 18 different hand shadows: a bird that flies, duck that quacks, dog that wags his tail, camel, goose, deer, boy, turtle, etc. Only book of its sort. vi + 33pp. 6½ x 9¼. 21779-5 Paperbound $1.00

WHITTLING AND WOODCARVING, E. J. Tangerman. 18th printing of best book on market. "If you can cut a potato you can carve" toys and puzzles, chains, chessmen, caricatures, masks, frames, woodcut blocks, surface patterns, much more. Information on tools, woods, techniques. Also goes into serious wood sculpture from Middle Ages to present, East and West. 464 photos, figures. x + 293pp.

20965-2 Paperbound $2.00

HISTORY OF PHILOSOPHY, Julián Marias. Possibly the clearest, most easily followed, best planned, most useful one-volume history of philosophy on the market; neither skimpy nor overfull. Full details on system of every major philosopher and dozens of less important thinkers from pre-Socratics up to Existentialism and later. Strong on many European figures usually omitted. Has gone through dozens of editions in Europe. 1966 edition, translated by Stanley Appelbaum and Clarence Strowbridge. xviii + 505pp.

21739-6 Paperbound $3.00

YOGA: A SCIENTIFIC EVALUATION, Kovoor T. Behanan. Scientific but non-technical study of physiological results of yoga exercises; done under auspices of Yale U. Relations to Indian thought, to psychoanalysis, etc. 16 photos. xxiii + 270pp.

20505-3 Paperbound $2.50

*Prices subject to change without notice.*
Available at your book dealer or write for free catalogue to Dept. GI, Dover Publications, Inc., 180 Varick St., N. Y., N. Y. 10014. Dover publishes more than 150 books each year on science, elementary and advanced mathematics, biology, music, art, literary history, social sciences and other areas.